SECOND EDITION

Practical Cloud Security
A Guide for Secure Design and Deployment

Chris Dotson

Beijing · Boston · Farnham · Sebastopol · Tokyo    O'REILLY®

Practical Cloud Security

by Chris Dotson

Published by O'Reilly Media, Inc., 1005 Gravenstein Highway North, Sebastopol, CA 95472.

O'Reilly books may be purchased for educational, business, or sales promotional use. Online editions are also available for most titles (*http://oreilly.com*). For more information, contact our corporate/institutional sales department: 800-998-9938 or *corporate@oreilly.com*.

Acquisitions Editor: Megan Laddusaw	**Indexer:** WordCo Indexing Services, Inc.
Development Editor: Rita Fernando	**Interior Designer:** David Futato
Production Editor: Clare Laylock	**Cover Designer:** Karen Montgomery
Copyeditor: Liz Wheeler	**Illustrator:** Kate Dullea
Proofreader: Rachel Head	

March 2019:	First Edition
October 2023:	Second Edition

Revision History for the Second Edition

2023-10-06:   First Release

See *http://oreilly.com/catalog/errata.csp?isbn=9781098148171* for release details.

The O'Reilly logo is a registered trademark of O'Reilly Media, Inc. *Practical Cloud Security*, the cover image, and related trade dress are trademarks of O'Reilly Media, Inc.

978-1-098-14817-1

[LSI]

Table of Contents

Preface. ix

1. Principles and Concepts. 1
    Least Privilege   2
    Defense in Depth   2
    Zero Trust   3
    Threat Actors, Diagrams, and Trust Boundaries   4
    Cloud Service Delivery Models   8
    The Cloud Shared Responsibility Model   8
    Risk Management   12
    Conclusion   13
    Exercises   15

2. Data Asset Management and Protection. 17
    Data Identification and Classification   17
        Example Data Classification Levels   18
        Relevant Industry or Regulatory Requirements   19
    Data Asset Management in the Cloud   21
    Tagging Cloud Resources   22
    Protecting Data in the Cloud   23
        Tokenization   23
        Encryption   24
    Conclusion   31
    Exercises   33

3. Cloud Asset Management and Protection. 35
    Differences from Traditional IT   35
    Types of Cloud Assets   36

Compute Assets   37
Storage Assets   43
Network Assets   48
Asset Management Pipeline   49
Procurement Leaks   50
Processing Leaks   51
Tooling Leaks   52
Findings Leaks   52
Tagging Cloud Assets   52
Conclusion   54
Exercises   56

4. **Identity and Access Management**. **57**
Differences from Traditional IT   59
Life Cycle for Identity and Access   60
Request   62
Approve   62
Create, Delete, Grant, or Revoke   63
Authentication   63
Cloud IAM Identities   63
Business-to-Consumer and Business-to-Employee   64
Multi-Factor Authentication   65
Passwords, Passphrases, and API Keys   68
Shared IDs   70
Federated Identity   71
Single Sign-On   71
Instance Metadata and Identity Documents   73
Secrets Management   75
Authorization   79
Centralized Authorization   80
Roles   81
Revalidate   82
Putting It All Together in the Sample Application   85
Conclusion   87
Exercises   89

5. **Vulnerability Management**. **91**
Differences from Traditional IT   92
Vulnerable Areas   94
Data Access   95
Application   95
Middleware   98

Operating System 99
Network 100
Virtualized Infrastructure 100
Physical Infrastructure 100
Finding and Fixing Vulnerabilities 101
Network Vulnerability Scanners 102
Agentless Scanners and Configuration Management Systems 104
Agent-Based Scanners and Configuration Management Systems 105
Cloud Workload Protection Platforms 107
Container Scanners 107
Dynamic Application Scanners (DAST) 108
Static Application Scanners (SAST) 108
Software Composition Analysis Tools (SCA) 109
Interactive Application Scanners (IAST) 109
Runtime Application Self-Protection Scanners (RASP) 109
Manual Code Reviews 110
Penetration Tests 110
User Reports 112
Example Tools for Vulnerability and Configuration Management 112
Risk Management Processes 115
Vulnerability Management Metrics 115
Tool Coverage 116
Mean Time to Remediate 116
Systems/Applications with Open Vulnerabilities 117
Percentage of False Positives 117
Percentage of False Negatives 117
Vulnerability Recurrence Rate 118
Change Management 118
Putting It All Together in the Sample Application 119
Conclusion 123
Exercises 124

6. Network Security. 125
Differences from Traditional IT 125
Concepts and Definitions 127
Zero Trust Networking 127
Allowlists and Denylists 127
DMZs 129
Proxies 129
Software-Defined Networking 130
Network Functions Virtualization 130
Overlay Networks and Encapsulation 130

Virtual Private Clouds 131
Network Address Translation 132
IPv6 133
Network Defense in Action in the Sample Application 134
Encryption in Motion 135
Firewalls and Network Segmentation 138
Allowing Administrative Access 144
Network Defense Tools 148
Egress Filtering 152
Data Loss Prevention 155
Conclusion 156
Exercises 158

7. Detecting, Responding to, and Recovering from Security Incidents............. 161
Differences from Traditional IT 162
What to Watch 163
Privileged User Access 165
Logs from Defensive Tooling 167
Cloud Service Logs and Metrics 170
Operating System Logs and Metrics 171
Middleware Logs 172
Secrets Server 172
Your Application 172
How to Watch 173
Aggregation and Retention 174
Parsing Logs 175
Searching and Correlation 176
Alerting and Automated Response 176
Security Information and Event Managers 177
Threat Hunting 179
Preparing for an Incident 179
Team 180
Plans 181
Tools 183
Responding to an Incident 185
Cyber Kill Chains and MITRE ATT&CK 185
The OODA Loop 187
Cloud Forensics 188
Blocking Unauthorized Access 189
Stopping Data Exfiltration and Command and Control 189
Recovery 189
Redeploying IT Systems 189

    Notifications   190

    Lessons Learned   190

  Example Metrics   190

  Example Tools for Detection, Response, and Recovery   191

  Detection and Response in a Sample Application   192

    Monitoring the Protective Systems   193

    Monitoring the Application   194

    Monitoring the Administrators   195

    Understanding the Auditing Infrastructure   195

  Conclusion   196

  Exercises   198

Appendix. Exercise Solutions. **199**

Index. **205**

Preface

As the title states, this book is a practical guide to securing your cloud environments. In almost all organizations, security has to fight for time and funding, and it often takes a back seat to implementing features and functions. Focusing on the "best bang for the buck," security-wise, is important.

This book is intended to help you get the most important security controls for your most important assets in place quickly and correctly, whether you're a security professional who is somewhat new to the cloud, or an architect or developer with security responsibilities. From that solid base, you can continue to build and mature your controls.

While many of the security controls and principles are similar in cloud and on-premises environments, there are some important practical differences. For that reason, a few of the recommendations for practical cloud security may be surprising to those with an on-premises security background. While there are certainly legitimate differences of opinion among security professionals in almost any area of information security, the recommendations in this book stem from years of experience in securing cloud environments, and they are informed by some of the latest developments in cloud computing offerings.

This is primarily a book about security, not compliance. That said, if you need to meet specific compliance requirements, such as PCI DSS, HIPAA, or FedRAMP, you will find some limited guidance on designing your security controls so that you will be able to do so.

Who Should Read This Book

This book is designed as an intermediate-level resource and is intended primarily for two types of practitioners:

- Those who have some experience with securing on-premises environments, but little or no experience with cloud environments
- Those who have experience building cloud environments, but little or no experience with securing those cloud environments

The goal of this book is to provide a conceptual-level understanding of the "art of the possible" in cloud security. You won't find a cookbook-style guide on exactly how to implement various controls in specific cloud environments, for a few reasons. One is that such guides tend to become out of date very quickly, because cloud providers are constantly improving their implementations. Another is that the cloud providers generally do a better job of providing explicit how-to guides than I can, because the implementations are specific to the way they've designed their services. A detailed how-to guide by one cloud provider will be more useful than a generic how-to that tries to cover multiple cloud providers.

What I try to provide is the understanding of when you need to find such a guide and use it.

Navigating This Book

The first three chapters deal with understanding your responsibilities in the cloud and how they differ from those in on-premises environments, as well as understanding what assets you have, what the most likely threats to those assets are, and some protections for them.

Chapters 4 through 6 provide practical guidance, in priority order, of the most important security controls that you should consider first:

- Identity and access management
- Vulnerability management
- Network controls

The final chapter deals with how to detect when something's wrong and deal with it. It's a good idea to read this chapter before something actually goes wrong!

What's New in the Second Edition

This new edition has been updated based on developments in the cloud computing and security industries in the years since the release of the first edition. Some examples are:

- More information on zero trust principles as they apply to protecting cloud environments

- Advancements in encryption techniques, such as quantum-resistant encryption algorithms
- Advancements in authentication techniques, such as passwordless technologies and passkeys
- The use of privileged access management tools to protect cloud environments
- Verification of workload identities in addition to human identities
- The importance of protecting software supply chains, including build and deployment environments in the cloud, with transparency through a Software Bill of Materials (SBOM)
- Updates based on changes to offerings by major cloud providers since the previous publication
- Updated examples of the different types of defensive tools and technologies available today

In addition, you can now check your newfound understanding of cloud security concepts as you read. I have added some questions and exercises to the end of each chapter, and the answers are in the Appendix.

Conventions Used in This Book

The following typographical conventions are used in this book:

Italic
Indicates new terms, URLs, email addresses, filenames, and file extensions.

`Constant width`
Used for program listings, as well as within paragraphs to refer to program elements such as variable or function names, databases, data types, environment variables, statements, and keywords.

`Constant width bold`
Shows commands or other text that should be typed literally by the user.

`Constant width italic`
Shows text that should be replaced with user-supplied values or by values determined by context.

This element signifies a tip or suggestion.

This element signifies a general note.

 This element indicates a warning or caution.

O'Reilly Online Learning Platform

 For almost 40 years, *O'Reilly Media* has provided technology and business training, knowledge, and insight to help companies succeed.

Our unique network of experts and innovators share their knowledge and expertise through books, articles, conferences, and our online learning platform. O'Reilly's online learning platform gives you on-demand access to live training courses, in-depth learning paths, interactive coding environments, and a vast collection of text and video from O'Reilly and 200+ other publishers. For more information, please visit *http://oreilly.com*.

How to Contact Us

Please address comments and questions concerning this book to the publisher:

O'Reilly Media, Inc.
1005 Gravenstein Highway North
Sebastopol, CA 95472
800-889-8969 (in the United States or Canada)
707-829-7019 (international or local)
707-829-0104 (fax)
support@oreilly.com
https://www.oreilly.com/about/contact.html

We have a web page for this book, where we list errata, examples, and any additional information. You can access this page at *https://oreil.ly/PracticalCloudSecurity2e*.

For news and information about our books and courses, visit *https://oreilly.com*.

Find us on LinkedIn: *https://linkedin.com/company/oreilly-media*.

Follow us on Twitter: *https://twitter.com/oreillymedia*.

Watch us on YouTube: *https://youtube.com/oreillymedia*.

Acknowledgments

This book would not have happened without the encouragement and support of my wonderful wife, Tabitha Dotson, who told me that I couldn't pass up this opportunity and juggled schedules and obligations for over a year to make it happen. I'd also like to thank my children, Samantha (for her extensive knowledge of Greek mythology) and Molly (for constantly challenging assumptions and thinking outside the box).

It takes many people besides the author to bring a book to publication, and I didn't fully appreciate this before writing one. I'd like to thank my first edition editors, Andy Oram and Courtney Allen; my second edition editors, Rita Fernando and Megan Laddusaw; my first edition reviewers, Hans Donker, Darren Day, and Edgar Ter Danielyan; my second edition reviewers, Lee Atchison, Karan Dwivedi, and Akhil Behl; and the rest of the wonderful team at O'Reilly who have guided and supported me through this.

Finally, I'd like to thank all of my friends, family, colleagues, and mentors over the years who have answered questions, bounced around ideas, listened to bad puns, laughed at my mistakes, and actually taught me most of the content in this book.

CHAPTER 1

Principles and Concepts

Yes, this is a practical guide, but we do need to cover a few cloud-relevant security principles and concepts at a high level before we dive into the practical bits. If you're a seasoned security professional, but new to the cloud, you may want to skim down to "The Cloud Shared Responsibility Model" on page 8.

The reason for covering these principles and concepts first is because they are used implicitly throughout the rest of the book when I discuss designing and implementing security controls to stop attackers. Conceptual gaps and misunderstandings in security can cause lots of issues. For example:

- If you're not familiar with least privilege, you may understand authorization for cloud services well, but still grant too much access to people or automation in your cloud account or on a cloud database with sensitive information.

- If you're not familiar with defense in depth, then having multiple layers of authentication, network access control, or encryption may not seem useful.

- If you don't know a little about threat modeling—the likely motivations of attackers, and the trust boundaries of the system that you're designing—you may be spending time and effort protecting the wrong things.

- If you don't understand the cloud service delivery models and the shared responsibility model, you may spend time worrying about risks that are your cloud provider's responsibility and miss risks that are your responsibility to address.

- If you don't know a little about risk management, you may spend too much time and effort on low risks rather than managing your higher risks.

I'll cover this foundational information quickly so that we can get to cloud security controls.

Least Privilege

The principle of *least privilege* simply states that people or automated tools should be able to access only what they need to do their jobs, and no more. It's easy to forget the automation part of this; for example, a component accessing a database should not use credentials that allow write access to the database if write access isn't needed.

A practical application of least privilege often means that your access policies are *deny by default*. That is, users are granted no (or very few) privileges by default, and they need to go through the request and approval process for any privileges they require.

For cloud environments, some of your administrators will need to have access to the cloud console—a web page that allows you to create, modify, and destroy cloud assets such as virtual machines. With many providers, anyone with access to your cloud console will have godlike privileges by default for everything managed by that cloud provider. This might include the ability to read, modify, or destroy data from any part of the cloud environment, regardless of what controls are in place on the operating systems of the provisioned systems. For this reason, you need to tightly control access to and privileges on the cloud console, much as you tightly control physical data center access in on-premises environments, and record what these users are doing.

Defense in Depth

Many of the controls in this book, if implemented perfectly, would negate the need for other controls. *Defense in depth* is an acknowledgment that almost any security control can fail, either because an attacker is sufficiently determined and skilled or because of a problem with the way that security control is implemented. With defense in depth, you create multiple layers of overlapping security controls so that if one fails, the one behind it can still catch the attackers.

You can certainly go to silly extremes with defense in depth, which is why it's important to understand the threats you're likely to face. However, as a general rule, you should be able to point to any single security control you have and say, "What if this fails?" If the answer is unacceptable, you probably have insufficient defense in depth. You may also have insufficient defense in depth if a single failure can make several of your security controls ineffective, such as an inventory issue that causes multiple tools to miss a problem.

Zero Trust

Many products and services today claim to be zero trust, or to support zero trust principles. The name is confusing, because zero trust does not mean a complete lack of trust in anything, and the confusion is worse because it's used for so many different marketing purposes. There are many different definitions and different ideas about what is meant by zero trust.

We are probably stuck with the term at this point, but "zero trust" should really be called something else, such as "zero implicit trust" or "zero assumed trust without a good reason."[1] The core principle is that trust from a user or another system should be earned, rather than given simply because the user is able to reach you on the network, or has a company-owned device, or some other criterion that's not well controlled.

The implementation of zero trust will differ widely depending on whether you're talking about trusting devices, network connections, or something else. One commonly used implementation of zero trust is requiring encryption and authentication for all connections, even ones that originate and terminate in supposedly trusted networks. This was always a good idea, but it's even more important in cloud environments where the perimeter is less strictly designed and internet connectivity is easy.

Another common implementation of zero trust principles is limiting users' network access to only the applications that they need, challenging the implicit trust that all users should be able to connect to all applications, even if they cannot log in. If you think this sounds a lot like least privilege and defense in depth, you're right. There is considerable overlap between zero trust principles and some of the other principles in this chapter.

A third example of zero trust is the use of multi-factor authentication of users, with reauthentication required either periodically or when higher-risk transactions are requested. In this case, we're challenging the implicit trust that whoever has the password for an account, or controls a particular session for an application, is the intended user.

When following zero trust principles, you should only trust an interaction if you have strong evidence that the trust is warranted, such as by proof of strong authentication, or authorization, or correct configuration. That evidence should either be from something you directly control (such as your own authentication system or device management system), or from some third party that you have explicitly evaluated as competent to make trust decisions for you. Like other principles in this chapter, it can be disruptive to the user experience if taken to extremes.

---

1 If you're expecting tips on how to pick catchy marketing names, you're probably reading the wrong book!

Threat Actors, Diagrams, and Trust Boundaries

There are different ways to think about your risks, but I typically favor an asset-oriented approach. This means that you concentrate first on what you need to protect, which is why I dig into data assets first, in Chapter 2.

It's also a good idea to keep in mind who is most likely to cause you problems. In cybersecurity parlance, these are your potential "threat actors." For example, you may not need to guard against a well-funded state actor, but you might be in a business where a cyber-criminal can make money by stealing your data, or where a "hacktivist" might want to deface your website for political or social reasons. Keep these people in mind when designing all of your defenses.

While there is plenty of information and discussion available on the subject of threat actors, motivations, and methods,[2] in this book we'll consider four main types of threat actors that you may need to worry about:

- Organized crime or independent criminals, interested primarily in making money
- Hacktivists, interested primarily in discrediting you by releasing stolen data, committing acts of vandalism, or disrupting your business
- Inside attackers, usually interested in discrediting you or making money
- State actors, who may be interested in stealing secrets or disrupting your business to advance a foreign government's political mission or cause

To borrow a technique from the world of user experience design, you may want to imagine a member of each applicable group, give them a name, jot down a little about that "persona" on a card, and keep the cards visible when designing your defenses.

The second thing you have to do is figure out what needs to talk to what in your application, and the easiest way to do that is to draw a picture and figure out where your weak spots are likely to be. There are entire books on how to do this,[3] but you don't need to be an expert to draw something useful enough to help you make decisions. However, if you are in a high-risk environment, you should probably create formal diagrams with a suitable tool rather than draw stick figures.

---

2 The Verizon Data Breach Investigations Report (*https://oreil.ly/ydkVz*) is an excellent free resource for understanding different types of successful attacks, organized by industry and methods, and the executive summary is very readable.

3 I recommend *Threat Modeling: Designing for Security*, by Adam Shostack (Wiley, 2014).

Although there are many different application architectures, for the sample application used for illustration here, I will show a simple three-tier design. Here is what I recommend for a very simple application component diagram:

1. Draw a stick figure and label it "user." Draw another stick figure and label it "administrator" (Figure 1-1). You may find later that you have multiple types of users and administrators, or other roles, but this is a good start.

Figure 1-1. User and administrator roles

2. Draw a box for the first component the user talks to (for example, the web servers), draw a line from the user to that first component, and label the line with how the user talks to that component (Figure 1-2). Note that at this point, the component may be a serverless function, a container, a virtual machine, or something else. This will let anyone talk to it, so it will probably be the first thing attacked. We really don't want the other components trusting this one more than necessary.

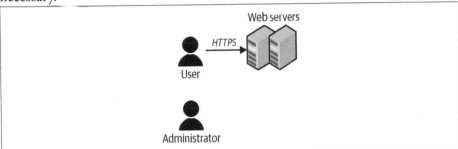

Figure 1-2. First component

3. Draw other boxes behind the first for all of the other components that first system has to talk to, and draw lines going to those (Figure 1-3). Whenever you get to a system that actually stores data, draw a little symbol (I use a cylinder) next to it and jot down what data is there. Keep going until you can't think of any more boxes to draw for your application.

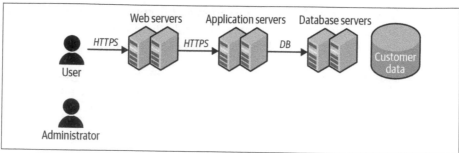

Figure 1-3. Additional components

4. Now draw how the administrator (and any other roles you've defined) accesses the application. Note that the administrator may have several different ways of talking to this application; for example, via the cloud provider's portal or APIs, or through the operating system, or in a manner similar to how a user accesses it (Figure 1-4).

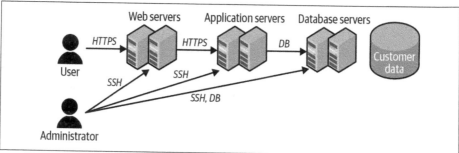

Figure 1-4. Administrator access

5. Draw some trust boundaries as dotted lines around the boxes (Figure 1-5). A trust boundary means that anything inside that boundary can be at least somewhat confident of the motives of anything else inside that boundary, but requires verification before trusting anything outside of the boundary. The idea is that if an attacker gets into one part of the trust boundary, it's reasonable to assume they'll eventually have complete control over everything in it, so getting through each trust boundary should take some effort. Note that I drew multiple web servers inside the same trust boundary; that means it's okay for these web servers to trust each other, and if someone has access to one, they effectively have access to all. Or, to put it another way, if someone compromises one of these web servers, no further damage will be done by having them all compromised.

In this context, zero trust principles lead us to reduce these trust boundaries to the smallest reasonable size—for example, a single component, which here might be an individual server or a cluster of servers with the same data and purpose.

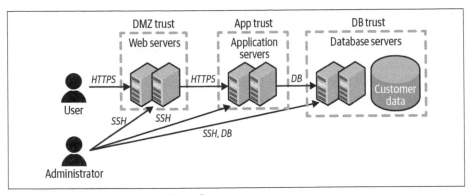

Figure 1-5. Component trust boundaries

6. To some extent, we trust our entire system more than the rest of the world, so draw a dotted line around all of the boxes, including the admin, but not the user (Figure 1-6). Note that if you have multiple admins, like a web server admin and a database admin, they might be in different trust boundaries. The fact that there are trust boundaries inside of trust boundaries shows the different levels of trust. For example, the servers here may be willing to accept network connections from servers in other trust boundaries inside the application, but still verify their identities. On the other hand, they may not be willing to accept connections from systems outside of the whole application trust boundary.

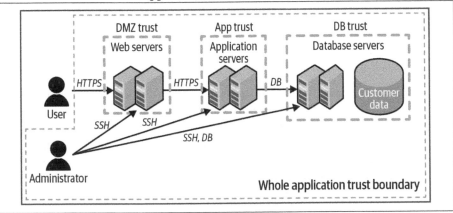

Figure 1-6. Whole application trust boundary

We'll use this diagram of an example application throughout the book when discussing the shared responsibility model, asset inventory, controls, and monitoring. Right now, there are no cloud-specific controls shown in the diagram, but that will change as we progress through the chapters. Look at any place a line crosses a trust boundary. These are the places we need to focus on securing first!

Cloud Service Delivery Models

There is an unwritten law that no book on cloud computing is complete without an overview of Infrastructure as a Service (IaaS), Platform as a Service (PaaS), and Software as a Service (SaaS). Rather than give the standard overview, I'd like to quickly say that IaaS services typically allow you to create virtual computers, storage, and networks; PaaS services are typically higher-level services, such as databases, that enable you to build applications; and SaaS services are applications used by end users. You can find many expanded definitions and subdivisions of these categories, but these are the core definitions.

These service models are useful only for a general understanding of concepts; in particular, the line between IaaS and PaaS is becoming increasingly blurred. Is a content delivery network service that caches information for you around the internet to keep it close to users a PaaS or an IaaS? It doesn't really matter. What's important is that you understand what is (and isn't!) provided by the service, not whether it fits neatly into any particular category.

The Cloud Shared Responsibility Model

The most basic security question you must answer is, "What aspects of security am I responsible for?" This is often answered implicitly in an on-premises environment. The development organization is responsible for code errors, and the operations organization (IT) is responsible for everything else. Many organizations now run a DevOps model where those responsibilities are shared, and team boundaries between development and operations are blurred or nonexistent. Regardless of how it's organized, almost all security responsibility is inside the company.

Perhaps one of the most jarring changes when moving from an on-premises environment to a cloud environment is a more complicated shared responsibility model for security. In an on-premises environment, you may have had some sort of internal document of understanding or contract with IT or some other department that ran servers for you. However, in many cases business users of IT were used to handing the requirements or code to an internal provider and having everything else done for them, particularly in the realm of security.

Even if you've been operating in a cloud environment for a while, you may not have stopped to think about where the cloud provider's responsibility ends and where yours begins. This line of demarcation is different depending on the types of cloud services you're purchasing. Almost all cloud providers address this in some way in their documentation and training materials, but the best way to explain it is to use the analogy of eating pizza.

With Pizza as a Service,[4] let's say you're hungry for pizza. There are a lot of choices! You could just make a pizza at home, although you'd need to have quite a few ingredients and it would take a while. You could run to the grocery store and grab a take and bake; that only requires you to have an oven and a place to eat it. You could call your favorite pizza delivery place. Or, you could just go sit down at a restaurant and order a pizza. If we draw a diagram of the various components and who's responsible for them, we get something like Figure 1-7.

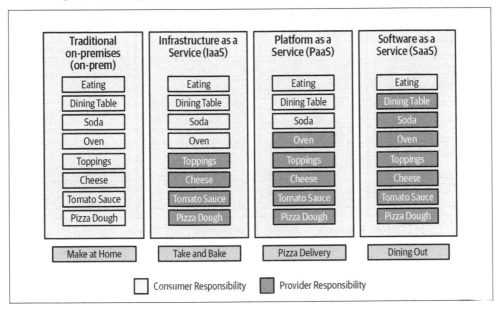

Figure 1-7. Pizza as a Service

The traditional on-premises world is like making a pizza at home. You have to buy a lot of different components and put them together yourself, but you get complete flexibility. Anchovies and cinnamon on wheat crust? If you can stomach it, you can make it.

When you use Infrastructure as a Service, though, the base layer is already done for you. You can bake it to taste and add a salad and drinks, and you're responsible for those things. When you move up to Platform as a Service, even more decisions are already made for you, including how your pizza is baked. (As mentioned in the previous section, sometimes it can be difficult to categorize a service as IaaS or PaaS, and they're growing together in many cases. The exact classification isn't important; what's important is that you understand what the service provides and what your responsibilities are.)

---

4 Original concept from Albert Barron's 2014 LinkedIn article, "Pizza as a Service" (*https://oreil.ly/l_RCH*).

When you get to Software as a Service (compared to dining out in Figure 1-7), it seems like everything is done for you. It's not, though. You still have a responsibility to eat safely, and the restaurant is not responsible if you choke on your food. In the SaaS world, this largely comes down to managing access control properly.

If we draw the diagram but focus on technology instead of pizza, it looks more like Figure 1-8.

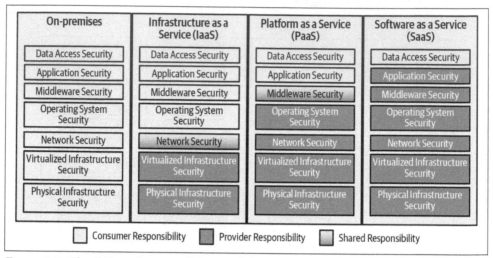

Figure 1-8. Cloud shared responsibility model

The reality of cloud computing is unfortunately a little more complicated than eating pizza, so there are some gray areas. At the bottom of the diagram, things are concrete (often literally). The cloud provider has complete responsibility for physical infrastructure security—which often involves controls beyond what many companies can reasonably do on-premises, such as biometric access with anti-tailgating measures, security guards, slab-to-slab barriers, and similar controls to keep unauthorized personnel out of the physical facilities.

Likewise, if the provider offers virtualized environments, the virtualized infrastructure security controls keeping your virtual environment separate from other virtual environments are the provider's responsibility. When the Spectre and Meltdown vulnerabilities came to light in early 2018, one of the potential effects was that users in one virtual machine could read the memory of another virtual machine on the same physical computer. For IaaS customers, fixing that part of the vulnerability was the responsibility of the cloud provider—Amazon, Microsoft, Google, and IBM all had to make updates to their hypervisors, for example—but fixing the vulnerabilities within the operating system was the customer's responsibility.

Network security is shown as a shared responsibility in the IaaS section of Figure 1-8. Why? It's hard to show on a diagram, but there are several layers of networking, and the responsibility for each lies with a different party. The cloud provider has its own network that is its responsibility, but there is usually a virtual network on top (for example, some cloud providers offer a virtual private cloud), and it's the customer's responsibility to carve this into reasonable security zones and put in the proper rules for access between them. Many implementations also use overlay networks, firewalls, and transport encryption that are the customer's responsibility. This will be discussed in depth in Chapter 6.

Operating system security is usually straightforward: it's your responsibility if you're using IaaS, and it's the provider's responsibility if you're purchasing platform or software services. In general, if you're purchasing those services, you have no access to the underlying operating system. (As a general rule of thumb, if you have the ability to break it, you usually have the responsibility for securing it!)

Middleware, in this context, is a generic name for software such as databases, application servers, or queuing systems. They're in the middle between the operating system and the application—not used directly by end users, but used to develop solutions for end users. If you're using a PaaS, middleware security is often a shared responsibility; the provider might keep the software up to date (or make updates easily available to you), but you retain the responsibility for security-relevant settings such as encryption.

The application layer is what the end user actually uses. If you're using SaaS, vulnerabilities at this layer (such as cross-site scripting or SQL injection) are the provider's responsibility, but if you're reading this book you're probably not just using someone else's SaaS. Even if all of the other layers have bulletproof security, a vulnerability at the application security layer can easily expose all of your information.

Finally, data access security is almost always your responsibility as a customer. If you incorrectly tell your cloud provider to allow access to specific data, such as granting incorrect object storage permissions, middleware permissions, or SaaS permissions, there's really not much the provider can do other than try to detect the problem and warn you.

The root cause of many security incidents is an assumption that the cloud provider is handling something, when it turns out *nobody* was handling it. Many real-world examples of security incidents stemming from poor understanding of the shared responsibility model come from open Amazon Simple Storage Service (Amazon S3) buckets. Sure, S3 storage is secure and encrypted, but none of that helps if you don't set your access controls properly. This misunderstanding has caused the loss of:

- Data on 198 million US voters
- Auto-tracking company records
- Wireless customer records
- Over 3 million demographic survey records
- Over 50,000 Indian citizens' credit reports
- Over 100,000 students' grades and personal info
- Thousands of hours of audio and video recordings that contain private conversations

There are many more examples. Although there has been considerable progress, the shared responsibility model is often still misunderstood. Many IT decision makers still believe that public cloud providers are responsible for securing not just the cloud services they offer, but also customer applications and data in the cloud. If you read your agreement with your cloud provider, you'll find this just isn't true!

Risk Management

Risk management is a deep subject, with entire books written about it. If you're really interested in a deep dive, I recommend reading *The Failure of Risk Management: Why It's Broken and How to Fix It*, by Douglas W. Hubbard (Wiley, 2020), and NIST Special Publication 800-30 Rev 1 (*https://oreil.ly/fj5Fh*). In a nutshell, humans are really bad at assessing risk and figuring out what to do about it. This section is intended to give you just the barest essentials for managing the risk of security incidents and data breaches.

At the risk of stating the obvious, a risk is something bad that could happen. In most risk management systems, the level of risk is based on a combination of how probable it is that the bad thing will happen (likelihood), and how bad the result will be if it does happen (impact). For example, something that's very likely to happen (such as someone guessing your password of "1234") and will be very bad if it does happen (such as you losing all of your customers' files and paying large fines) would be a high risk. Something that's very unlikely to happen (such as an asteroid wiping out two different regional data centers at once) but that would be very bad if it does happen (going out of business) might only be a low risk, depending on the system you use for deciding the level of risk.[5]

---

[5] Risks can also interact, or aggregate. There may be two risks that each have relatively low likelihood and limited impacts, but they may be likely to occur together, and the impacts can combine to be more severe. For example, the impact of either power line in a redundant pair going out may be negligible, but the impact of both going out may be really bad. This is often difficult to anticipate; the Atlanta airport power outage in 2017 (*https://oreil.ly/8VXtI*) is a good example.

In this book, I'll talk about unknown risks (where we don't have enough information to know what the likelihoods and impacts are) and known risks (where we at least know what we're up against). Once you have an idea of the known risks, you can do one of four things with them:

1. Avoid the risk. In information security, this typically means you turn off the system—no more risk, but also none of the benefits you had from running the system in the first place.

2. Mitigate the risk. It's still there, but you do additional things to lower either the likelihood that the bad thing will happen or the impact if it does happen. For example, you may choose to store less sensitive data so that if there is a breach, the impact won't be as bad.

3. Transfer the risk. You pay someone else to manage things so that the risk is their problem. This is done a lot with the cloud, where you transfer many of the risks of managing the lower levels of the system to the cloud provider.

4. Accept the risk. After looking at the overall risk level and the benefits of continuing the activity, you may decide to write down that the risk exists, get all of your stakeholders to agree that it's a risk, and then move on.

Any of these actions may be reasonable. However, what's not acceptable is to either have no idea what your risks are, or to have an idea of what the risks are and accept them without weighing the consequences or getting buy-in from your stakeholders. At a minimum, you should have a list somewhere in a spreadsheet or document that details the risks you know about, the actions taken, and any approvals needed.

Conclusion

Even though there are often no perfect answers in the real world, understanding some foundational concepts will help you make better choices in securing your cloud environments.

Least privilege is basically just recognizing that giving privileged access to anything or anyone is a risk, and you don't want to take more risks than necessary. It's an art, of course, because there are sometimes trade-offs between risk and productivity, but the general principle is good—only give the minimum amount of privilege necessary. This is often overlooked for automation, but is arguably even more important there because many real-world attacks hinge upon fooling a system or automation into taking unexpected actions.

Defense in depth is recognizing that we're not perfect, and the systems we design will not be perfect. It's also a nod to the basic laws of probability—if you have two independent things that both have to fail for a bad thing to happen, it's a lot less likely to happen. If you have to flip a coin and get tails twice in a row, your chances of that are only 25%, compared to the 50% chance of getting tails on one coin flip. We aspire to have security controls that are much more effective than a coin toss, but the principle is the same. If you have two overlapping, independent controls that are 95% effective, then the combination of the two will be 99.75% effective! There are diminishing returns with this approach, however, so five or six layers in the same area is probably not a good use of resources.

Threat modeling is the process of understanding who is likely to attack your system and why, and understanding the components of your system and how they work together. With those two pieces of information, you can look at your system through the eyes of potential attackers, and try to spot areas where the attackers may be able to do something undesirable. Then, for each of those areas, you can put obstacles (or, more formally, "controls" and "mitigations") in place to thwart the attackers. In general, the most effective places to put mitigations are on trust boundaries, which are the places where one part of your system needs to trust another part.

Understanding cloud delivery models can help you focus on the parts of the overall system that you're responsible for, so that you don't waste time trying to do your cloud provider's job, and so that you don't assume that your cloud provider is taking care of something that's really your responsibility. While there are standardized terms for different cloud delivery models, such as IaaS, PaaS, and SaaS, some services don't fit neatly into those buckets. They're conceptually useful, though, and the most important thing is to understand where your provider's responsibility ends and yours begins in the cloud shared responsibility model. In an on-premises world, the security of the entire system will often be the responsibility of a single organization within a company, whereas in cloud deployments, it's almost always split among at least two different companies!

Finally, while humans are pretty good at assessing risk in "is this predator going to eat me?" types of situations, we're not naturally very good at it in more abstract situations. Risk management is a discipline that makes us better at assessing risk and figuring out what to do about it. The easiest form of risk management is estimating the likelihood that something bad will happen and the impact of how bad it will be if it does happen, and then making decisions based on the combination of likelihood and impact. Risk management can lower our overall risk by letting us focus on the biggest risks first.

Now that we have these concepts and principles in our tool kit, let's put them to use in protecting the data and other assets in our cloud environments.

Exercises

1. Which of these are good examples of the principle of least privilege in action? Select all that apply.

   a. Having different levels of access within an application, with users only able to access the functions that they require for their work

   b. Requiring both a password and a second factor in order to log in

   c. Giving an inventory tool read-only access rather than read/write access

   d. Use of a tool such as *sudo* to allow a user to only execute certain commands

2. Which of these are good examples of the principle of defense in depth? Select all that apply.

   a. Encrypting valuable data, and also keeping people from reading the encrypted data unless they need to see it

   b. Having very strict firewall controls

   c. Ensuring that your trust boundaries are well defined

   d. Having multi-factor authentication

3. What are some common motivations for threat actors? Select all that apply.

   a. Stealing money

   b. Stealing secrets

   c. Disrupting your business

   d. Embarrassing you

4. Which of these items is always the cloud provider's responsibility?

   a. Physical infrastructure security

   b. Network security

   c. Operating system security

   d. Data access security

5. What are the most important factors in assessing how severe a risk is? Select the two that apply.

   a. The chances, or likelihood, that an event will happen

   b. How bad the impact will be if an event happens

   c. Whether or not you can transfer the risk to someone else

   d. Whether the actions causing the risk are legal or illegal

CHAPTER 2

Data Asset Management and Protection

Now that Chapter 1 has given you some idea of where your cloud provider's responsibility ends and yours begins, your first step to securing your cloud environment is to figure out where your data is—or is going to be—and how you're going to protect it. There is often a lot of confusion about the term "asset management." What exactly are our assets, and what do we need to do to manage them? The obvious (and unhelpful) answer is that assets are anything valuable that you have. Let's start to home in on the details.

In this book, I've broken up asset management into two parts: data asset management and cloud asset management. *Data assets* are the important information you have, such as customer names and addresses, credit card information, bank account information, or credentials to access such data. *Cloud assets* are the things you have that store and process your data—compute resources such as servers or containers, storage such as object stores or block storage, and platform instances such as databases or queues. Managing these assets is covered in the next chapter. While you can start with either data assets or cloud assets, and may need to go back and forth a bit to get a full picture, I find it easier to start with data assets.

The theory of managing data assets in the cloud is no different than on-premises, but in practice there are some cloud technologies that can help.

Data Identification and Classification

If you've created at least a "back-of-the-napkin" diagram and threat model as described in the previous chapter, you'll have some idea of what your important data is, as well as the threat actors you have to worry about and what they might be after. Let's look at different ways threat actors might attack your data.

One of the more popular information security models is the *CIA triad*: confidentiality, integrity, and availability. A threat actor trying to breach your data confidentiality wants to steal it, usually to sell it for money or embarrass you. A threat actor trying to breach your data integrity wants to change your data, such as by altering a bank balance. (Note that this can be effective even if the attacker cannot *read* the bank balances; I'd be happy to have my bank balance be a copy of Bill Gates's, even if I don't know what that value is.) A threat actor trying to breach your data availability wants to take you offline for fun or profit, or use ransomware to encrypt your files.[1]

Most of us have limited resources and must prioritize our efforts.[2] A data classification system can assist with this, but resist the urge to make it more complicated than absolutely necessary.

Example Data Classification Levels

Every organization is different, but the following rules provide a good, simple starting point for assessing the value of your data, and therefore the risk of having it breached:

Low or public
> While the information in this category may or may not be intended for public release, if it were released publicly the impact to the organization would be very low or negligible. Here are some examples:
>
> - Your servers' public IP addresses
>
> - Application log data without any personal data, secrets, or value to attackers
>
> - Software installation materials without any secrets or other items of value to attackers

Moderate or private
> This information should not be disclosed outside of the organization without the proper nondisclosure agreements. In many cases (especially in larger organizations) this type of data should be disclosed only on a need-to-know basis within the organization. In most organizations, the majority of information will fall into this category. Here are some examples:
>
> - Detailed information on how your information systems are designed, which may be useful to an attacker
>
> - Information on your personnel, which could provide information to attackers for phishing or pretexting attacks

---

1 Ransomware is both an availability and an integrity breach, because it uses unauthorized modifications of your data in order to make it unavailable.

2 If you have unlimited resources, please contact me!

- Routine financial information, such as purchase orders or travel reimbursements, which might be used, for example, to infer that an acquisition is likely

High or confidential

This information is vital to the organization, and disclosure could cause significant harm. Access to this data should be very tightly controlled, with multiple safeguards. In some organizations, this type of data is called the "crown jewels." Here are some examples:

- Information about future strategy, or financial information that would provide a significant advantage to competitors
- Trade secrets, such as the recipe for your popular soft drink or fried chicken
- Secrets that provide the "keys to the kingdom," such as full access credentials to your cloud infrastructure
- Sensitive information placed into your hands for safekeeping, such as your customers' financial data
- Any other information where a breach might be newsworthy

Note that laws and industry rules may effectively dictate how you classify some information. For example, the European Union's General Data Protection Regulation (GDPR) has many different requirements for handling personal data, so with this system you might choose to classify all personal data as "moderate" risk and protect it accordingly. Payment Card Industry Data Security Standard (PCI DSS) requirements would probably dictate that you classify cardholder data as "high" risk if you have it in your environment.

Also, note that there are cloud services that can help with data classification and protection. As examples, Amazon Macie (*https://oreil.ly/znsxp*) can help you find sensitive data in Amazon S3 buckets, Google Cloud Sensitive Data Prevention (*https://oreil.ly/MSzAr*) can help you classify or mask certain types of sensitive data, and Microsoft Purview (*https://oreil.ly/av897*) can classify data on Azure cloud services.

Whatever data classification system you use, write down a definition of each classification level and some examples of each, and make sure that everyone generating, collecting, or protecting data understands the classification system.

Relevant Industry or Regulatory Requirements

As mentioned in the preface, this is a book on security, not compliance. As a gross overgeneralization, compliance is about proving your security to a third party—and that's much easier to accomplish if you have actually secured your systems and data. The information in this book will help you with being secure, but there will be additional compliance work and documentation to complete after you've secured your systems.

That said, some compliance requirements may inform your security design. So, even at this early stage, it's important to make note of a few industry or regulatory requirements:

EU GDPR

This regulation may apply to the personal data of any European Union or European Economic Area citizen, regardless of where in the world the data is. The GDPR requires you to catalog, protect, and audit access to "any information relating to an identifiable person who can be directly or indirectly identified in particular by reference to an identifier." The techniques in this chapter may help you meet some GDPR requirements, but you must make sure that you include relevant personal data as part of the data you're protecting.

US FISMA or FedRAMP

The Federal Information Security Management Act is applied per agency, whereas Federal Risk and Authorization Management Program certification may be used with multiple agencies, but both require you to classify your data and systems in accordance with FIPS 199 (*http://bit.ly/2BQRBJc*) and other US government standards. If you're in an area where you may need one of these certifications, you should use the FIPS 199 classification levels.

US ITAR

If you are subject to International Traffic in Arms Regulations, in addition to your own controls, you will need to choose cloud services that support ITAR. Such services are available from some cloud providers and are managed only by US personnel.

Global PCI DSS

If you're handling credit card information, the Payment Card Industry Data Security Standard dictates that there are specific controls that you have to put in place, and there are certain types of data you're not allowed to store.

US HIPAA

If you're in the US and dealing with any protected health information (PHI), the Health Insurance Portability and Accountability Act mandates that you include that information in your list and protect it, which often involves encryption.

There are many other regulatory and industry requirements around the world, such as MTCS (Singapore), G-Cloud (UK), and IRAP (Australia). If you think you may be subject to any of these, review the types of data they are designed to protect so that you can ensure that you catalog and protect that data accordingly.

Data Asset Management in the Cloud

Most of the preceding information is good general practice and not specific to cloud environments. However, cloud providers are in a unique situation to help you identify and classify your data. For starters, they will be able to tell you everywhere you are storing data, because they want to charge you for the storage!

In addition, use of cloud services brings some level of standardization by design. In many cases, your persistent data in the cloud will be in one of the cloud services that store data, such as object storage, file storage, block storage, a cloud database, or a cloud message queue, rather than being spread across thousands of different disks attached to many different physical servers.

Your cloud provider gives you the tools to inventory these storage locations, as well as to access them (in a carefully controlled manner) to determine what types of data are stored there. There are also cloud services that will look at all of your storage locations and automatically attempt to classify where your important data is. You can then use this information to tag your cloud assets that store data.

 When you're identifying your important data, don't forget about passwords, API keys, and other secrets that can be used to read or modify that data! We'll talk about the best way to secure secrets in Chapter 4, but first you need to know exactly where they are.

If we look at our sample application that we diagrammed in Chapter 1, there's obviously customer data in the database. However, where else do you have important assets? Here are some things to consider:

- The web servers have log data that may be used to identify your customers.
- Your web server has a private key for a Transport Layer Security (TLS) certificate; with that and a little Domain Name System (DNS) or Border Gateway Protocol (BGP) hijacking, anyone could pretend to be your site and steal your customers' passwords (and some types of second factors) as they try to log in.
- Do you keep a list of password hashes to verify your customers? Hopefully you're using some sort of federated ID system, as described in Chapter 4, but if not, the password hashes are a nice target for attackers.[3]

---

3 Remember LinkedIn's 6.5 million password hashes that were stolen, cracked offline, and then used to compromise other accounts where users reused their LinkedIn password? This has happened many times, and sites like have i been pwned (*https://haveibeenpwned.com*) can tell you about all of the breaches that may contain your email or password data.

- Your application server needs a password or API key to access the database. With this password, an attacker could read or modify everything in the database that the application can.

Even in this really simple application, there are a lot of nonobvious things you need to protect. Figure 2-1 repeats Figure 1-6 from the previous chapter, adding the data assets in the boxes.

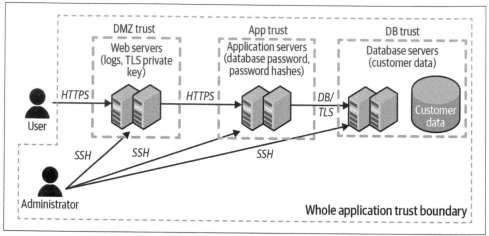

Figure 2-1. Sample application diagram with data assets

Tagging Cloud Resources

Most cloud providers, as well as container management systems such as Kubernetes, have the concept of tags. A *tag* is usually a combination of a name (or "key") and a value. These tags can be used for lots of purposes, from categorizing resources in an inventory, to making access decisions, to choosing what to alert on. For example, you might have a key of PII-data and a value of yes for anything that contains personally identifiable information, or you might use a key of datatype and a value of PII.

The problem is clear: if everyone in your organization uses different tags, they won't be very useful! Have a policy to use tags. To support this policy, create a tag standard with a list of tags and explanations for when they must be used, use these same tags across multiple cloud providers, and require them to be applied by any automated tools that create cloud resources.

In smaller organizations, a simple tag standard will probably suffice. In larger organizations, this tag standard should probably be treated as a versioned, backward-compatible standard with an assigned owner and periodic reviews. Some tags will likely be organization-wide and some specific to subsections of the organization. Even if one of your cloud providers doesn't explicitly support the use of tags, there are often other description fields that may be used to hold tags in easy-to-parse formats such as JSON. Tags rarely cause any harm, so use them liberally; if you don't need them, they're easily ignored.

Tags are free to use, so there's rarely any technical concern with creating a lot of them, but you should be careful not to make the tag standard so complicated that it confuses the humans who have to write rules for applying and consuming tag data. In addition, cloud providers do impose some limits on how many tags a particular resource can have (usually between 15 and 64 tags per resource).

Some cloud providers even offer automation to check whether tags are properly applied to resources, so that you can catch untagged or mistagged resources early and correct them. For example, if you have a rule that every asset must be tagged with the maximum data classification allowed on that asset, then you can run automated scans to find any resources where the tag is missing or where the value isn't one of the classification levels you have decided upon.

Table 2-1 shows the different names given to tagging by different cloud providers. Kubernetes, which may run on-premises or on any IaaS provider, uses the term "labels."

Table 2-1. Tagging features

Infrastructure	Feature name
Amazon Web Services	Tags
Microsoft Azure	Tags
Google Compute Platform	Labels and network tags
IBM Cloud	Tags

We will talk more about tagging resources in Chapter 3, but for now, jot down some data-related tags that may apply to your different cloud resources, such as `dataclass:low`, `dataclass:moderate`, `dataclass:high`, or `regulatory:gdpr`.

Protecting Data in the Cloud

Several of the data protection techniques discussed in this section may also be applied on-premises, but many cloud providers give you easy, standardized, and less expensive ways to protect your data.

Tokenization

Why store the data when you can store something that functions similarly to the data, but is useless to an attacker? *Tokenization*, which is most often used with credit card numbers, replaces a piece of sensitive data with a token (usually randomly generated).

It has the benefit that the token generally has the same characteristics (such as being 16 digits long) as the original data, so underlying systems that are built to take that data don't need to be modified. Only one place (a "token service") knows the actual sensitive data. Tokenization can be used on its own or in conjunction with encryption, discussed next.

Examples include cloud services that work with your browser to tokenize sensitive data before sending it, and cloud services that sit in between the browser and the application to tokenize sensitive data before it reaches the application.

Encryption

Encryption is the silver bullet of the data protection world; we want to "encrypt all the things." Unfortunately, it's a little more complicated than that. There are three types of data you might need to encrypt:

- Data in motion (being transmitted across a network)
- Confidential computing, or data in use (currently being processed in a computer's CPU or held in RAM)
- Data at rest (on persistent storage, such as a disk)

Encryption of data in motion is discussed in detail in Chapter 6. In this section, we'll discuss the other two uses of encryption.

 More bits are not always necessary or useful once you get to a certain point; encryption is often broken due to a flaw in the implementation rather than brute force. In addition, there's often a performance trade-off with using a cipher algorithm with more bits, particularly if you use something without hardware acceleration. If you don't want to make a deep study of it, it's usually safe to adopt the same cipher requirements as large private and governmental organizations that have studied the subject extensively.

Confidential computing

Encryption of data in use is now available from several cloud providers, and is typically marketed to organizations with very sensitive data under the name *confidential computing*. Because it changes the way the processor accesses memory, it requires support in the hardware platform, and then the feature must be exposed by the cloud provider.

The most common cloud implementation is to encrypt process or virtual machine memory so that even a privileged user (or an attacker or malware impersonating a privileged user) cannot read it, and the processor can read it only when executing code for a specific process or virtual machine.[4] If you are in a very high-security environment and your threat model includes protecting data in memory from a privileged user, or you want additional isolation between you and another tenant in the cloud, you should seek out a platform that supports memory encryption. This often goes by hardware-specific brand names such as Intel SGX/TGX, AMD SEV, and IBM Z Pervasive Encryption.

Encryption of data at rest

Encryption of data at rest can be the most complicated to implement correctly. The problem is not in encrypting the data; there are many libraries to do this. The problem is that once you've encrypted the data, you now have an encryption key that can be used to access it. Where do many people put this? In the clear, right next to the data! Imagine locking a door and then hanging the key on a hook next to it helpfully labeled "key." To have real security (instead of just ticking a checkbox indicating that you've encrypted data), you must have proper key management. Fortunately, there are cloud services to help.

 Encrypted data can't be effectively compressed or deduplicated. If you want to make use of compression or deduplication, do that before encrypting it.

In traditional on-premises environments with high security requirements, you would purchase a hardware security module (HSM) to hold your encryption keys, usually in the form of an expansion card or a module accessed over the network. An HSM has significant logical and physical protections against unauthorized access. With most systems, anyone with physical access can try to tamper with it, but an HSM has sensors to wipe out the data as soon as someone tries to take it apart, scan it with X-rays, fiddle with its power source, or look threateningly in its general direction.

HSMs are expensive, and so are not feasible for most on-premises deployments. However, in cloud environments, advanced technologies such as HSMs and encryption key management systems are now within reach of projects with modest budgets.

Some cloud providers have an option to rent a dedicated HSM for your environment. While this may be required for the highest-security environments, a dedicated HSM is still expensive in a cloud environment, and is often harder to spin up automatically. Another good option is a key management service (KMS), which is run by the cloud provider and usually uses an HSM on the backend to keep keys safe. A KMS is

---

4 Note that in-memory encryption protects data only from attacks from outside the process; if you manage to trick the process itself into doing something it shouldn't, it can read the memory and divulge the data.

usually a multitenant service, which is a slightly larger attack surface, and you do have to trust both the HSM and the KMS (instead of just the HSM), which adds a little additional risk. However, compared to performing your own key management—often incorrectly—a KMS provides excellent security at a very low cost. You can have the benefits of proper key management in projects with more modest security budgets.

Table 2-2 lists the key management options offered by the major cloud providers, as of this writing.

Table 2-2. Key management options

Provider	Dedicated HSM option	Key management service
Amazon Web Services	Cloud HSM	Amazon KMS
Microsoft Azure	Azure Dedicated HSM	Key Vault
Google Compute Platform	Cloud HSM	Cloud KMS
IBM Cloud	Cloud HSM	Key Protect

So, how do you actually use a KMS correctly? This is where things get a little complicated.

Key management. The simplest approach to key management is to generate a key, encrypt the data with that key, stuff the key into the KMS, and then write the encrypted data to disk along with a note indicating which key was used to encrypt it. There are two main problems with this approach:

1. It puts a lot of load on the KMS. There are good reasons for wanting a different key for every file, so a KMS with a lot of customers would have to store billions or trillions of keys with near instantaneous retrieval.

2. If you want to securely erase the data, you have to trust the KMS to irrevocably erase the key when you're done with it, and not leave any backup copies lying around. Alternatively, you have to overwrite all of the encrypted data,[5] which can take a while.

You may not want to wait hours or days for your data to be overwritten. It's better if you have the option to quickly and securely erase data objects in two ways: either by deleting a key at the KMS, which may effectively erase a lot of different objects at

---

[5] Despite the findings of a well-known USENIX paper (*https://oreil.ly/FSbkW*) from 1996 by Peter Gutmann exploring the ability to recover data on a hard disk that's been overwritten, it's not practical today. Recovering overwritten data from solid state drives (SSDs) is slightly more practical due to the way writes happen, but most SSDs have a "secure erase" feature to sanitize the entire drive; see Michael Wei et al.'s 2011 USENIX paper (*https://oreil.ly/ec5Hp*) for more details.

once; or by deleting a key where the data is actually stored, to delete a single data object. For these reasons, you typically have two levels of keys: a *key encryption key* (KEK) and a *data encryption key* (DEK). As the names suggest, the key encryption key is used to encrypt (or "wrap") data encryption keys, and the wrapped keys are stored right next to the data. The key encryption key usually stays in the KMS and never comes out, for safety. The wrapped data encryption keys are sent to the HSM for unwrapping when needed, and then the unwrapped keys are used to encrypt or decrypt the data. You never write down the unwrapped keys. When you're done with the current encryption or decryption operation, you forget about them.[6]

The use of keys is easier to understand with a real-world analogy. Imagine you are selling your house (which contains all of your data), and you provide a key to your realtor to unlock your door. This house key is like a data encryption key; it can be used to directly access your house (data). The realtor will place this key into a key box on your door, and protect it with a code provided by the realtor service. This code is like the key encryption key, and the realtor service that hands out codes is like the key management service. In this mildly strained analogy, you actually take the key box to the KMS, and it gives you a copy of the key inside with the agreement that you won't make a copy of it (write it to disk) and you'll melt (forget) that copy when finished with it. You never actually see the code that opens the box.

The end result is that when you walk up to the house (data), you know the data key's right there, but it can't be opened without another key or password. Of course, in the real world, a hammer and a little time would get the key out of the box, or would allow you to break a window and not need the key. The cryptographic equivalent of the hammer is guessing the key or password used to protect the data key. This is usually done by trying all of the possibilities (brute force) or, for keys based on passwords, trying many common passwords (a dictionary attack). If the encryption algorithm and the implementation of that algorithm are correct, the expected time for the "hammer" to get into the box is considerably longer than the expected lifetime of the universe.

Server-side and client-side encryption. The great news is that you usually don't have to do most of this key management yourself! For most cloud providers, if you're using their storage and their KMS, and you turn on KMS encryption for your storage instances, the storage service will automatically create data encryption keys, wrap them using a key encryption key that you can manage in the KMS, and store the wrapped keys along with the data. You can still manage the keys in the KMS, but you don't have to ask the KMS to wrap or unwrap them, and you don't have to perform

---

6 This is an extremely simplified explanation. For a really deep discussion of all things cryptographic, see Bruce Schneier's book *Applied Cryptography*, 2nd ed. (Wiley, 1996).

the encryption or decryption operations yourself. Some providers call this *server-side encryption*.

Because the multitenant storage service does have the ability to decrypt your data, an error in that storage service could potentially allow an unauthorized user to ask the storage service to decrypt your data. For this reason, having the storage service perform the encryption/decryption is not *quite* as secure as doing the decryption in your own instance—if you implement it correctly, using well-known libraries and processes. Doing the encryption and decryption in your own application is often called *client-side encryption*. However, unless you have a very low risk tolerance (and a budget to match that low risk tolerance), I recommend that you use well-tested cloud services and allow them to handle the encryption/decryption for you.

Note that when using client-side encryption, the server does not have the ability to read the encrypted data because it doesn't have the keys. This means no server-side searches, calculation, indexing, malware scans, or other high-value tasks can be performed. Homomorphic encryption may make it feasible for operations such as addition to be performed correctly on encrypted data without decrypting the data, but as of this writing it's too slow to be practical.

 Unless you have devoted most of your distinguished career to cryptography, do not attempt to create or implement your own crypto systems. Even when performing the encryption/decryption in your own application, use only well-tested and supported library implementations of secure algorithms.

If your organization doesn't have a list of approved cryptographic algorithms, a good source for recommended algorithms is NIST SP 800-131A (*https://oreil.ly/AbAjn*).

Cryptographic erasure. It's actually difficult to reliably destroy large amounts of data.[7] It takes a long time to overwrite the data completely, and even then there may be other copies sitting around. We can solve this through *cryptographic erasure*. With this approach, rather than storing clear-text data on the disk, we store only an encrypted version. Then, when we want to make data unrecoverable, we can wipe or revoke access to the key encryption key in the KMS, which will make all of the data encryption keys "wrapped" with that key encryption key useless, wherever they are in the world. We can also wipe a specific piece of data by wiping out just its wrapped data encryption key, so a multiterabyte file can be effectively made unrecoverable by overwriting a 256-bit key.

---

7 Although paradoxically, it's often easy to do by accident!

How encryption foils different types of attacks

As we've discussed, encryption of data at rest can protect data from attackers by limiting their choices; the data is available in the clear only in a few places, depending on where in the system the encryption is being performed. Let's look at a simple example application using a database to see how our encryption choices protect us. The relevant layers of this application are:

1. The storage system that the disks go in, which may encrypt data before sending it to the disks

2. The Database-as-a-Service platform offering, which may encrypt data before sending it to the storage system

3. The application, which may encrypt data before sending it to the database

Let's explore the benefits, drawbacks, and residual risk of encryption at each of these layers.

Disk-level encryption. Attackers might successfully steal disks from the data center or the dumpster, or steal tapes in transit. If the storage subsystem is encrypting data before storing it on disk, these attackers can't make use of the data even with physical access to the disks or tapes. The attackers only have access to an unintelligible "bag of bits," and the keys to decrypt the data are safely stored elsewhere, on the storage subsystem!

There used to be performance trade-offs for encrypting data sent to disk, but with hardware cryptographic acceleration this is largely no longer an issue; cloud providers routinely encrypt almost all data stored to disk, except in some bare-metal cases where you manage the disks directly. So, there are very few drawbacks to disk-level encryption in a cloud environment, and it's probably done for you.

This is great news, but stolen or lost media typically isn't a large risk in cloud environments, given the physical controls and equipment disposal controls most cloud providers implement. (Disk-level encryption is far more important for portable devices such as smartphones and laptops, where devices get lost or stolen regularly and decommissioning processes may not be as mature.)

Encryption performed only to "check the encryption box" will often only help to mitigate this threat of physical theft—and sometimes not even this threat, because this protection also fails if you store unwrapped keys on the same media as the data.

However, what if the attackers are able to impersonate an administrator of the storage system that the disks can go in? Since the storage subsystem performs the decryption, attackers at that layer (or above) will be able to see the unencrypted data.

Platform-level encryption.   What if you have the database (or other service) encrypt the data before sending it to the storage subsystem? In that case, anyone with access to the storage subsystem under the database will only have a bag of bits; they can destroy the data or make it temporarily unavailable, but should not be able to read or tamper with it.

The trade-off for encrypting at this layer is often a little worse; because the database is encrypting the data prior to sending it to storage, that means it can't be compressed or deduplicated by the storage subsystem, which in turn means that storage costs may be higher. Depending on the database engine, there may also be some performance trade-offs.

While database-level encryption protects you from things that go wrong at the layers underneath it, there's still some risk. The database has users who are allowed to see the data in the database, and the database service has administrators who may be able to access any database. Cloud providers often have several layers of controls to prevent their administrators from reading or tampering with customer data, so that's a relatively low risk. However, the larger risk is that if an attacker gets access to the API key that your application uses to talk to the database, the attacker will be able to read and write everything in the database that the application can!

Application-level encryption.   Now we're at the top of the stack. If your application encrypts data prior to sending it to the database, then anyone at the database level is left holding a bag of bits unless they can get into the application, or can steal the application's encryption key.

Whereas you may lose some performance or cost-effectiveness when encrypting at the database layer, there's a more significant trade-off here, with application-level encryption. Because the database cannot see the unencrypted data, it cannot search for specific data items, sort the data, report on it, or perform similar functions. The application has to do these things (or live without them), which can have significant performance or functionality impacts. I generally recommend implementing application-level encryption only for the most sensitive data your application processes, and letting the lower layers handle encryption for everything else.

If an attacker gains unauthorized access to the application, all bets are off from an encryption standpoint, because the application must be able to read the data in order to function. However, defense in depth techniques can help. For example, using separate data stores protected by access control lists (ACLs) and separate encryption keys for different applications can lower the impact of such a breach, by keeping the attacker from being able to read anything other than what the compromised application has access to.

Quantum-Safe Cryptography

Quantum computers are expected to be much better at some tasks than classical computers, and some of those tasks have security implications for encryption. A well-known example is that if you can factor large numbers quickly, then you can break an important cryptographic algorithm.

Although quantum computers cannot enable these attacks yet, one of the risks is that attackers will harvest encrypted data now so that they can decrypt it later. For this reason, there is an industry-wide push to move to quantum-safe algorithms long before these attacks become feasible in the real world.

Algorithms used for encryption of data in motion are most at risk, and future versions of TLS are expected to use quantum-safe algorithms. While encryption of data at rest via AES-256 is expected to be safe for the foreseeable future, it's worth noting that many schemes use a non-quantum-safe algorithm to encrypt the AES symmetric key. This is done so that you can make the key available to many different individuals without encrypting multiple copies of the data with different AES keys, but any products that do this will need to update to reencrypt the AES keys using a quantum-safe algorithm, or the data at rest may also be compromised.

For an in-depth look at quantum-safe cryptography, one good reference currently in development is NIST SP 1800-38 (*https://oreil.ly/z3KTj*).

This is another example of where designing for defense in depth can help. Design the system so that if you make encrypted versions of your data publicly available without the keys, in theory nobody can read them. In addition, protect the encrypted data wherever possible so that if that assumption fails, your data is still safe.

Conclusion

When planning your cloud strategy, you need to figure out what data you have—both the obvious and non-obvious parts. Classify each type of data by the impact to you if it's read, modified, or deleted by an attacker. Get organizational-wide agreement on which tags to use in a "tag standard," and use the tagging features offered by your cloud provider to tag resources that contain data.

If possible, you should decide on an encryption strategy before you create cloud resources that store data, because it can be difficult to change later. In most cases, you should use your cloud provider's key management system to manage the encryption keys, and you should use built-in encryption in the database and storage services. If you have really sensitive information, consider encrypting it yourself in your application prior to storing it, and use only well-tested implementations of secure algorithms.

Carefully control the users and systems that have access to the keys, and set up alerts to let you know when the keys are being accessed in any unusual fashion. Use of a key management system will provide another layer of protection in addition to the access controls on the storage instances, and can also provide you with an easy way to cryptographically erase the information when you're done with it.

One of the concerns with encryption is that it can reduce performance, due to the extra processing time required to encrypt and decrypt the data. Fortunately, this is no longer as big a concern as it once was; hardware is cheap, and all of the major chip makers have some form of hardware acceleration built into their CPUs. Performance concerns are rarely a good excuse for not encrypting data, but there are some trade-offs, and you can be certain only by testing with real-world loads.

A more important concern around encryption is the availability of your data. If you cannot access the encryption keys, you cannot access your data. Ensure that you have some sort of "break the glass" process for getting access to the encryption keys, and make sure that it's "noisy" and cannot be used without detection and alerting.

Finally, if the "bottom" of the stack is the physical hardware and the "top" of the stack is the application, you get protection against more types of breaches by having the encryption happen as close to the top of the stack as possible. The trade-offs are getting less functionality, performance, and cost-effectiveness from the lower layers, and having to do more work yourself.

In a cloud environment, your data assets are stored and processed by different types of cloud assets. In the next chapter, we'll see what the different types are and how to track and protect them.

Exercises

1. What is a reasonable number of data classification levels for most organizations?

    a. 3

    b. 30

    c. 300

2. What are some good examples of data assets you may need to protect in the cloud? Select all that apply.

    a. Password hashes

    b. API keys

    c. Documents and images you store for your customers

    d. IP addresses of your end users

3. In what states can data be encrypted and decrypted? Select all that apply.

    a. When data is at rest, and written to some persistent storage

    b. When data is in use in memory

    c. When data is in motion, and transmitted from one place to another

    d. When data is deleted, and removed from use

4. Which of the following statements about key management is true?

    a. A hardware security module is required for proper key management.

    b. You should never write encryption keys alongside the data, even if the keys themselves are encrypted using a different key that's not stored with the data.

    c. Cloud providers have services to do some of the key management for you.

5. If you have the disk controller encrypt data as it's written to the physical disk, what types of attackers will be blocked by this encryption?

    a. Attackers who gain unauthorized access to an application that uses the disk

    b. Attackers who gain unauthorized access to a database used by the application

    c. Attackers who gain access to the physical disk

CHAPTER 3

Cloud Asset Management and Protection

At this point, you should have a good idea of what data you have, where it's stored, and how you plan to protect it at rest. Now it's time to look at other cloud assets and how to inventory and protect them.

As mentioned in Chapter 2, cloud providers maintain a list of which assets you have provisioned, because they want to be able to bill you. They also provide APIs to view this list, and sometimes they have specialized applications to help you with inventory and asset management.

 In general, your cloud provider will know only about assets you provision via its portal or APIs. For example, if you provision a virtual machine and then manually create containers on it, the cloud provider will have no way of knowing about the containers.

Cloud infrastructure and services are often inexpensive and easy to provision, which can quickly lead to having a huge number of assets strewn all over the world and forgotten. Each of these forgotten assets is like a ticking time bomb, waiting to explode into a security incident.

Differences from Traditional IT

One important difference with cloud asset management and protection is that you generally don't have to worry about physical assets or protection at all for your cloud environments. You can gleefully outsource physical asset tags, anti-tailgating, slab-to-slab barriers, placement of data center windows, cameras, and other physical security and physical asset tracking controls.

Another important difference lies in the IT group's participation in the process of provisioning cloud assets. In a traditional IT environment, creating an asset such as a server is often difficult and time-consuming. It usually requires going to a centralized IT group, which will follow a detailed provisioning process and maintain a list of assets in a database or a spreadsheet. There is a natural barrier to creating shadow IT (IT resources that are hidden or not officially approved for use), because IT typically requires capital assets. In most organizations, large capital expenditures are carefully controlled.

One important benefit of cloud computing is replacing these large capital expenditures with monthly expenses, and offloading the capacity planning to an IaaS provider. This is great, but it also means that it's more difficult for the IT and finance areas of the business to be effective gatekeepers for IT resources. Anyone in any area of the business can easily provision a huge number of IT resources with only a credit card (and sometimes not even that). This can quickly lead to asset management problems.

Prior to the cloud, most organizations had some amount of shadow IT. In the cloud era, this problem is often far worse—and the assets aren't just servers.

Types of Cloud Assets

Before we can effectively manage cloud assets, we need to understand what they are and their security-relevant characteristics. I find that creating clearly defined categories of assets helps to organize my thinking. For this reason, I have categorized cloud assets as compute, storage, and network assets, but you could choose different categories.

More types of cloud assets are created every day, and it's likely that you will not have all of these types of assets. You also don't need to track all of these assets in a single place. The important thing is to know about all assets that are relevant to your security.

If you are coming into an environment with a large number of existing cloud assets, keep in mind that you don't have to have a completely comprehensive solution for asset management immediately. Concentrate on the assets that are the most security-relevant to get immediate value, and then add additional types of assets to your inventory incrementally. For many organizations, the most security-relevant assets will be a few types of data storage and compute assets.

As you read through the types of cloud assets, it may help to jot down notes about the types of assets that you know you have, and put stars next to the ones that are most relevant for security. Although this chapter is primarily about asset management, some of the security properties of these assets may inform the current or future designs of your cloud environment. In the second part of this chapter, I'll share some ideas on how to inventory the cloud asset types you've identified here.

 Many cloud assets are ephemeral, in that they are created and deleted fairly often. This can make asset management more difficult, and it may also make some popular methods of asset tracking, such as tracking by IP address, ineffective.

Compute Assets

Compute assets typically take data, process it, and do something with the results. For example, a very simple compute resource might take data from a database and send it to a web browser on request, or send it to a business partner, or combine it with data in another database.

These cloud asset categories are not completely distinct. Compute resources may also store data, particularly temporary data. With some types of regulated data, it may be necessary to ensure that you're tracking every place that data could be, so don't forget about temporary data storage.

Virtual machines

Virtual machines (VMs) are the most familiar cloud asset type. VMs run operating systems and processes that perform business functions. VMs in cloud environments behave very similarly to their on-premises equivalents in many cases.

Virtual Machine Attacks

VMs in the cloud differ fundamentally from on-premises VMs in one important way: in a cloud environment, you may be sharing the same *physical* system with other cloud customers. These other customers might simply be inconsiderate and cause "noisy neighbor" problems by using up all of the processor time, network bandwidth, or storage bandwidth so that your VM cannot get its work done efficiently. However, they might also be deliberately malicious and attempt to exploit the fact that you're on the same physical hardware to attack the confidentiality, integrity, and availability of your system. These are additional risks to the standard "front-channel" risks for servers, such as the use of stolen credentials or the exploitation of software vulnerabilities on the server.

In general, there are two primary ways that other customers (or even attackers who have gained access to your own VMs) might attack you. The first is via a "hypervisor breakout" or "VM escape," where an attacker on one VM is able to breach the hypervisor and take full control over the physical system. Fortunately, this isn't easy, because hypervisors are designed to accept very little input from the virtual machines. In general, a VM that wants to take over the hypervisor needs to find a vulnerability

---

in either the paravirtualized storage or network interfaces, which is not a large attack surface. If physical systems are like separate buildings, virtual machines are like separate apartments that can contact the superintendent only via two mail slots labeled "network" and "storage." I call these *back-channel* attacks, because they attack the infrastructure behind the VM.

The other way that attackers may gain information is through *side-channel* attacks, which are based on unintended side effects of running code on a physical system. When running on the same hardware, attackers may be able to deduce important information about your VM, such as passwords or encryption keys, by carefully watching the timing of processor instructions or cache accesses. This is essentially how the famous Spectre and Meltdown vulnerabilities work.

This doesn't mean you shouldn't use VMs; the risks of these types of side-channel and back-channel attacks are acceptable to most organizations, and you should probably worry about other things first. However, it's important to know that sharing physical hardware creates some potential vulnerabilities. The good news is that, like physical security, mitigating these types of attacks is almost always the responsibility of your cloud provider (although in some cases you may also need to install operating system fixes on your VMs).

VMs always have an operating system, which includes a kernel as well as other "user-space" programs shipped with the kernel by the operating system vendor. Some servers can perform all of their functions using only the software shipped as part of the OS. However, most VMs have additional software installed, such as platform/middleware software and custom application code that your organization has written.

Because so many different components can be mixed together to make up a VM, we need to be careful about vulnerability management, access management, and configuration management for each of the different layers of a server. Successful attackers may get access to any data the VM has access to. Attackers may also use that compromised VM to attack the rest of your infrastructure, or other organizations (which can be a reputational hit for you).

Here are some example inventory items to track for VMs:

- The operating system name and version. Operating system vendors support versions with security fixes for only a limited amount of time, so it's important to stay reasonably up to date and run a supported version of your OS.
- The names and versions of any platform or middleware software. This may be software such as web servers, database servers, or queue managers. It's important to track this software for vulnerability management purposes (in case security advisories are released) as well as for license management.
- Any custom application code on the VM that your organization maintains.

- The IP addresses of the VM and what virtual private cloud network it's in, if applicable.
- The users allowed access to the operating system, and to the platform/middleware/application software if different.

Most of these are the same as with on-premises VMs. However, cloud VMs generally only take a minute or two to create (although initialization may take longer), which means that they can be created and deleted as needed. This is great for scaling up and down quickly to meet demand, but can make asset management more difficult. For this reason, you will probably need to use agents installed on your VMs or an inventory system from your cloud provider to collect all of the relevant information automatically.

In addition to tracking the VMs themselves (often called "instances"), you also need to track the "images" or templates that are copied to create new VMs. You don't want new servers to come online with critical vulnerabilities, even if they are patched quickly after starting.

Some cloud providers provide "bare-metal" systems in addition to VMs.[1] These have the same security needs as VMs, but may also have firmware that occasionally needs to be updated.

Many cloud providers also provide "dedicated" VMs. These are created in the same way as regular VMs, except that the provider promises to not schedule any other customer's VMs on the same physical systems with yours, which can prevent noisy neighbor problems and side-channel attacks.

Bare-metal machines and dedicated VMs are not subject to the risks described in "Virtual Machine Attacks" on page 37, but typically cost more. As with all security decisions, you must weigh the costs and benefits. In general, I do not require bare-metal machines or dedicated VMs for additional security until the more common problems, such as vulnerability management and access management, are well under control.

Note that many of the following asset types can be seen as a deconstruction of a VM into smaller components provided "as a service."

---

1 There are people who claim that bare metal is not cloud. By the most commonly accepted definition, NIST SP 800-145 (*https://oreil.ly/hzQjr*), the essential characteristics of cloud computing are on-demand self-service, broad network access, resource pooling, rapid elasticity, and managed service. None of these essential characteristics require virtualization technology, although there can be arguments over the definition of "rapid."

Containers

Like VMs, containers run processes that perform business functions, such as web servers or custom application code. However, unlike VMs, they do not contain a full operating system. Containers use the kernel of the VM they are hosted on, and might not have any of the other software that comes with the operating system.

Containers can start up in under a second, which means that in many environments they are created and deleted almost constantly.

Container Attacks

Whereas the hypervisors that run VMs have a very small attack surface, the shared kernel used by all of the containers has a much larger attack surface. For example, the Linux kernel contains over 300 system calls, many of which may be used by containers. A vulnerability in any of these system calls may allow code running in one container to gain access to the entire system.

This doesn't mean that containers are inherently insecure, but you should be careful not to use containers as your only trust boundary between components with wildly different security requirements. For example, having containers that allow internet users to run their own code on the same server as containers that process your most sensitive data is probably asking for trouble.

Container isolation will continue to mature over time. Containers may be limited to fewer system calls using technologies like *seccomp*, reducing the likelihood that a vulnerability in one of these system calls can be exploited. The kernel may also perform additional checks as another layer of protection against containerized processes "escaping." Hybrid solutions that combine the greater isolation of VMs with the ease of deployment offered by containers, such as Firecracker (*https://oreil.ly/4ixDY*), are also an option.

If your containers do contain a full copy of the operating system and allow administrators to log in, they are basically miniature VMs. Although containers can be used in this "mini-VM" model, this isn't the best way to use them. Your asset management strategy for containers will depend partly upon how you are using them. We will look at two models, the native container model and the mini-VM model, and a way of managing containers.

Native container model.   In a pure native container model:

- Containers should hold the bare minimum operating system components needed to perform their function.

- Each container should perform only a single function (or "concern" in some documentation).
- Containers are immutable, meaning that they don't change over time. A container may make changes in some other component, such as writing data to a storage service, but that storage is maintained separately from the container itself. This means containers have a perfect copy of the code in the image during their lifetimes—they don't update their own code, and nobody logs in to change it.
- Rather than updating running containers, old containers are destroyed and new containers are created with updated code.

Native, immutable containers should not need to have administrators logging in to them for routine maintenance, although you probably need some provision for obtaining emergency access occasionally for troubleshooting. If container logins are not allowed in general, access management to the containers becomes less of a risk than with servers. Vulnerability and configuration management are still important risks, but the scope for a given container is much narrower than the scope for a server that might perform many different functions.

Native containers are generally created and destroyed much more often than VMs. That means it makes more sense to inventory the container images than the containers themselves, and just keep track of which image a container is copied from to make sure you don't have any out-of-date containers. A container image needs to be inventoried primarily in order to track the software and configurations in the image, so that the image may be updated with security fixes and new configurations as vulnerabilities are discovered.

Mini-VM container model.   In a model where you treat containers like miniature VMs:

- Containers will usually run a full copy of the user-mode components of the operating system.
- Containers perform multiple functions or concerns, such as running two different types of services in the same container.
- Containers allow administrative logins and change over time.

If you're using containers like mini-VMs, you should inventory and protect them just like VMs. This usually means installing inventory agents, even if such agents are normally considered too "heavyweight" for containers in a native container model. It also means tracking users, software, and all the other items mentioned in the preceding section on VMs.

In both models, you should inventory and update the images, because you don't want new containers to be brought up with vulnerabilities.

Container orchestration systems. Containers are great, but what's even better is to have something that takes care of bundling containers together to perform higher-level functions, starting up multiple copies of these bundles, performing load balancing with those copies, and providing other features such as easy ways for the components to talk to one another. This type of system is called a *container orchestration system*. This functionality is very useful, which also makes it appealing to attackers.

The most popular implementation of container orchestration as of this writing is Kubernetes, along with variants of Kubernetes like OpenShift and K3s. In a Kubernetes deployment, the primary assets are clusters, which hold pods, which hold containers, which are created from images. In a Kubernetes environment, consider inventorying the following components:

- Kubernetes clusters, so that access to them can be controlled and the Kubernetes software may be kept up to date. Vulnerabilities in the Kubernetes software, configuration, or access controls could compromise all of the pods running on it, and Kubernetes has been actively targeted by attackers.[2]

- Kubernetes pods, which may contain one or more containers. The Kubernetes command line or API may be used to track the pods currently in existence and which containers make up those pods.

- Container images, so that you can keep them up to date and not start vulnerable containers in your cluster.

Application Platform as a Service

Application-Platform-as-a-Service (aPaaS) offerings, such as AWS Elastic Beanstalk, Azure Pipelines, Google App Engine, and IBM Cloud Code Engine allow you to deploy your code without provisioning VMs yourself. These offerings also provide many resources, such as databases, as part of the platform. So, for example, a deployment may consist of the code you've written plus a database provisioned by the aPaaS. The deployment starts running when you create it and stops running when you destroy it, but you never have to actually create a VM or container to hold it; that's done for you by your cloud provider.

Security of an aPaaS is very specific to the aPaaS and to the provider's implementation of that aPaaS. It's important to understand the isolation model that keeps your compute, network, and storage assets separate from those of other cloud customers. For example, with many deployments, you will be running on the same VMs as other customers, which provides limited compute isolation. You will often not be able to

---

2 You can find some procedure examples of attacks on Kubernetes on the MITRE ATT&CK website (*https:// oreil.ly/OjOWb*).

contact other containers on the network, so you may have good network isolation. Storage isolation will depend upon what level, if any, of encryption is performed by the persistent storage services available from your provider, and may vary from one storage service to another.

When you create an aPaaS deployment, you need to track both the deployment itself and its dependencies (such as build packs or other subcomponents) for the purposes of vulnerability and configuration management. However, you don't need to inventory anything about the underlying compute resources or storage resources, because these are outside of your control.

Serverless functions

Serverless functions are a way to have your code running only when needed; some examples are AWS Lambda, Azure Functions, Google Cloud Functions, and IBM Cloud Functions.

Serverless offerings differ from aPaaS offers because nothing runs until its service has been requested; there's nothing specific to you that sits around waiting for incoming requests. This means you don't have to track both an image and the instances that are created from that image, because there are no long-running instances. It's only serverless from your perspective as a consumer, because the provider hides the servers behind a layer of abstraction.

For serverless assets, you don't need to inventory any operating system or platform components. You only need to inventory the serverless deployments you have so that you can manage vulnerabilities in your code and control access to the function.

Storage Assets

Storage assets typically persist data, and as such tend to be more permanent than the other types of assets mentioned here. Sometimes data is described as "sticky" or as having "gravity," because moving large amounts of data around can be difficult and time-consuming. You identified your most important data and storage assets in Chapter 2, but there may be other storage assets that you haven't considered. We'll look at some of the possibilities here.

Because I recommend an asset-oriented approach to risk assessment for most organizations, this book places particular emphasis on storage assets. Access management is the most important security consideration for all of the cloud storage assets listed in this section.

Block storage

Block storage is just the cloud version of a hard drive; data is made available in small blocks (say, 16 KB) to a server in the same manner as a disk controller. Some examples are AWS Elastic Block Storage, Azure Disk Storage, Google Persistent Disk, and IBM Cloud Block Storage.

The primary security concern with block storage is access management, because an attacker who gets direct access to the block storage bypasses any operating system–level controls you may have on the server using that storage.

File storage

File storage is the cloud version of a filesystem, organizing data into directories and files. Some examples are AWS Elastic File System, Azure Files, Google Cloud Storage FUSE, and IBM Cloud File Storage. As with block storage, the primary concern is access management. Although the filesystem itself often provides access control lists for the files, these are enforced by the operating system, not by the file storage. An attacker with access to the file storage can read all files stored there.

Object storage

In storage terms, an *object* is very similar to a flat file, in that it is a stream of bytes with metadata about the object. The primary differences are:

- Files are stored in folders that may be inside other folders. Objects are all thrown together into a "bucket," without any further levels of organization inside the bucket.[3]

- Objects may have custom metadata associated with them. Files are limited to the types of metadata that a filesystem provides, such as creator, creation time, and permissions.

- Objects cannot be changed after creation. To make updates, you replace the object with a new object, although there are ways to copy parts of existing objects. With files, you may update only part of a file, or add additional data to it.

- Object storage offers per-object access control that is enforced by the object storage system. File storage typically enforces access control to the whole filesystem, but then depends upon the operating system using the filesystem to enforce per-file controls.

---

3 You can simulate a folder hierarchy in object storage by using object names with slashes in them. However, if you want to display the objects in a "folder" named *A*, the object storage system is really just searching for all object names that begin with *A/*.

Most object storage offers different layers of access control, such as high-level policies for a bucket and individual ACLs for specific objects. There have been many notable data breaches when object storage bucket policies were set for open access, so it's very important to keep track of your object storage assets and the access control policies for each one.

Some examples of object storage services are Amazon S3, Azure Blob Storage, Google Cloud Storage, and IBM Cloud Object Storage.

Images

Images are chunks of code—including all the underlying system components, such as the operating system—that you use to run VMs, containers, or aPaaS deployments in a cloud environment. You make a copy of an image and start that copy running. The new copy, or instance, may begin to diverge from the image at that point. VMs, bare-metal systems, containers, and aPaaS environments all copy images to create running systems. In many organizations, there is a hierarchy of images, where you start with a "Golden Image" that has specific patches and hardening and then create additional images from that "Golden Image."

While images are stored on some type of cloud storage, such as block storage or object storage, access to images is often controlled separately from the underlying storage.

Different types of cloud assets and providers manage images in different ways, but often there are many people in the organization who can get access to the contents of the images and create instances from them. For this reason, images shouldn't contain every bit of information needed for an instance to run. For example, images should not contain sensitive information such as passwords or API keys, because not everyone who has access to create or view the image should know these secrets. An image should be configured so that when a copy (instance) of that image is started, the instance gets the secrets from a secure location that very few people have access to. This is discussed further in "Secrets Management" on page 75. Depending on how you build images, you may be able to perform some checks to ensure secrets aren't included in the image.

If your images do need to contain sensitive information, it's important to control access to them so that an attacker can't look into an image, pull out the credentials, and use them. In addition, all images must be tracked so that they can be kept up to date with security patches for the operating system, middleware/platform, or custom application software. Otherwise, you'll create cloud assets that are vulnerable as soon as they are created. This is discussed further in Chapter 5.

Cloud databases

Entire treatises have been written about the different types of databases, such as relational, document, time series, graph, key-value, and columnar databases. Choosing the correct database type for your application is important for both functionality and performance reasons.

Database choices can also have significant impacts on the security of the overall application. For example, some in-memory databases used for fast performance do not offer encryption by default either over the network or on disk, which may be a security and/or compliance risk depending on the types of data stored.

All cloud databases can provide access control to the whole database, and some database types can also provide more fine-grained access control to data in the database. At a minimum, you need to inventory your databases and what types of data are stored in each of them. You also need to manage access to each database as a whole, and potentially to different areas in the database, such as schemas.

Message queues

Message queues allow components to send small amounts of data (typically less than 256 KB) to one another, usually through a publisher/subscriber model. Although this can be convenient, even these small chunks may contain sensitive data such as personally identifiable information, so it's important to protect access to your message queues. In addition, if some of your components take instructions from messages, an attacker with write access to the message queue might be able to make something undesirable happen.

Secrets, such as encryption keys or passwords, should not be sent across a message queue in general, but should use a storage service specifically designed for this type of data, as described in the following subsection and in Chapter 4.

Configuration storage

In many cases, a cloud deployment brings together code and configuration. The same code is usually shared between different instances of the application, and instances are deployed to different areas or regions using different configurations. *Configuration storage* allows you keep this configuration information separate from the code. Some examples are etcd, HashiCorp Consul, and AWS Systems Manager Parameter Store.

Secrets configuration storage

Secrets configuration storage is a type of configuration storage specifically designed to hold secret data that may be used to access other systems. Just as it's a good practice to separate your code and configurations, it's also a good idea to separate access to your secrets from other configuration data. Many people may need to be able to view your code and your configurations, but very few people should be able to view the secrets! Therefore, it's important to identify any assets that store secrets, make sure they're built to protect those secrets, and carefully control access.

This is discussed in more detail in Chapter 4. Some examples of secret storage solutions are HashiCorp Vault, Keywhiz, Kubernetes Secrets, AWS Secrets Manager, Azure Key Vault, Google Secret Manager, and IBM Cloud Secrets Manager. Because of the concentrated risk in having all of your secrets in one location, you do need to be very careful when using a secrets manager. I recommend using one provided by a cloud provider "as a service" in most cases.

Encryption key storage

Encryption keys are a specific type of secret that are used for encrypting and decrypting data. As with secrets configuration, there are many benefits to using a special-purpose service for this type of data, such as being able to perform wrap and unwrap operations without exposing the master key. You need to identify any assets that store encryption keys and carefully control access to these, in addition to controlling access to the encrypted data.

These types of systems were discussed in detail in Chapter 2. The main types of encryption key storage are dedicated hardware security modules and multitenant key management systems.

Certificate storage

Another specialization of secret storage, *certificate storage* systems can safely store your X.509 private keys, which are used to cryptographically prove that you own the certificates. In addition, these systems can alert you when one of your certificates is due to expire, if you're not using automation (such as tools implementing the ACME protocol) to renew them.

Source code repositories and deployment pipelines

Many organizations carefully track other types of assets, but allow their source code to be distributed all over the place and built using many different pipelines.

In many cases, source code doesn't need to be kept secret if good practices such as separating out configuration and secrets are followed. However, ensuring that an attacker doesn't modify your source code or any artifacts during the deployment path is very important,[4] so these assets need to be tracked to protect their integrity.

In addition, you need to have a good inventory of your source code repositories in order to effectively check for vulnerabilities. There are tools available to check for bugs in code you've written as well as known vulnerabilities in code you have incorporated from other sources. These tools cannot operate on code that they are not aware of! This will be covered in more depth in Chapter 5.

Network Assets

Network assets are the cloud equivalent of on-premises switches, routers, virtual local area networks (VLANs), subnets, load balancer appliances, and similar assets. They enable communication between other assets and the outside world, and they often perform some security functions.

Virtual private clouds and subnets

Virtual private clouds (VPCs) and *subnets* are high-level ways to draw boundaries around what's allowed to talk to what. It's important to have a good inventory of these; as mentioned earlier, many other controls, such as network scanners, depend on having good inputs for what to scan to be effective. Subnets and VPCs are discussed further in Chapter 6.

Content delivery networks

Content delivery networks (CDNs) can distribute content globally for low-latency access. While the information in a CDN may not be sensitive in most cases, an attacker with access to the CDN can poison the content with malware, Bitcoin miners, or distributed denial-of-service (DDoS) code.

DNS records

You need to track your DNS domains and the registrars you use to register them. Although TLS connections offer protection against spoofing, some browsers do not default to TLS, and users often ignore the warnings. Spoofing DNS records can lead someone to go to an attacker's site instead of yours, and then the attacker can steal their credentials, read all of the data going through to your site, and even change data in transit.

---

4 A famous "supply chain" attack like this was executed against SolarWinds in December 2020; it compromised the build system to insert malware into the build.

In addition to security concerns, if you don't track one of your DNS domains and forget to renew it, you'll have a service outage!

TLS certificates

TLS certificates—often still called SSL certificates, and more properly X.509 certificates—rely on cryptographic principles. They are the best line of defense against an attacker spoofing your website. You need to track your TLS certificates for the following reasons:

- There are cases where an entire class of certificates needs to be reissued, such as when a particular cryptographic algorithm is found to be weak or when a certificate authority has a security issue.

- Just as with DNS domains, if you forget to renew a certificate, you will often have a service outage because connections will fail when a certificate has expired.

- You must track who has access to the private keys, because these individuals have the ability to impersonate your site. It's worth noting that automated certificate renewals, combined with alerting on any access to the private keys, can actually prevent *any* humans from accessing the private keys except in emergency "break-glass" situations. This both improves security and reduces the risk of outages from expired certificates.

If you have a large number of certificates, consider using a certificate storage service, discussed earlier, to track them.

Load balancers, reverse proxies, and web application firewalls

DNS records usually point to load balancers, reverse proxies, or web application firewalls for processing and traffic direction. It's important to have a good inventory of these assets for proper access control, because they can usually see and modify all of the network traffic to your applications. These are covered in more detail in Chapter 6.

Asset Management Pipeline

So, now that you know what types of assets to look for, what can you do to track them? In most organizations, there are natural control points on the way to provision services and infrastructure. These will vary between organizations, but you must find the control points and tighten them up to ensure you know about all of your cloud assets and manage the risks appropriately.

I like to explain this using a plumbing analogy. Imagine you have a pipeline containing your various cloud assets, flowing from your cloud providers and leading to your different security systems. You must try to prevent all of the asset management "leaks" that could allow assets to get left out of important security efforts. This is true whether you're running your entire company's IT, or whether you're only responsible for a single application. Conceptually, this looks like Figure 3-1. Now we'll look at the different kinds of leaks that can occur.

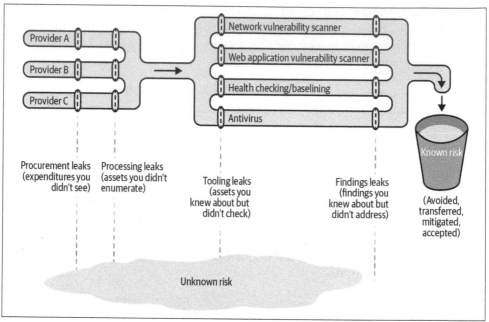

Figure 3-1. Sample asset management pipeline

Procurement Leaks

At the source, you have multiple ways for assets to be created. You may have several cloud providers with different delivery models (IaaS, PaaS, SaaS) provisioning many different types of assets. In most cases, you'll be charged for these assets. That often means that a good first step is looking at the procurement process.

 Some cloud providers have built-in asset management systems that already integrate with the other services they provide, and may even have ways to bring in assets from your on-premises environments or other cloud providers. This is a growing field, so look into what your providers offer before building a custom solution.

This isn't foolproof—some cloud resources can be provisioned without spending any money, and in larger organizations people may be able to categorize their cloud expenses in different ways. However, it's a good start.

Look through your IT charges. For each cloud expense, you need to go to the individual responsible for incurring the charges and get some limited auditing credentials.[5] This will allow you to automatically pull inventory information. A "leak" here usually means that you've missed an entire cloud provider, either because you didn't see the expense or because it's a free service.[6]

Processing Leaks

The second step is to use those audit credentials to find out exactly what the cloud providers are doing for you. That means you need to use their portals, APIs, or inventory systems to pull a list of assets. Note that you may have assets inside of other assets. For example, you may have a web server inside a container inside a VM.

Every cloud provider has a portal, API, or set of command-line utilities that can be used to retrieve information about assets. Almost always, automation using the API or command-line tools is preferable because manual inventories are difficult to keep up to date. However, a manual inventory is better than nothing, and might even be sufficient for a few types of assets if changes are very infrequent.

In addition to portals and APIs, some cloud providers and third parties have inventory or security tracking systems. Some systems allow you to track down to the level of what's installed on different virtual machines, feed directly into other available security services (such as scanners), and import assets from other providers or on-premises infrastructure. Table 3-1 lists some current services as of this writing.

Table 3-1. Options for auditing cloud activity

Infrastructure	Ways to audit usage
Amazon Web Services	API, portal, command line, AWS Systems Manager Inventory
Microsoft Azure	API, portal, command line, Azure Automation Inventory
Google Cloud Platform	API, portal, command line, Cloud Security Command Center Asset Inventory
IBM Cloud	API, portal, command line, IBM Cloud Security Advisor

Make sure you delve into each asset type to find additional assets that could be important from a security perspective. A "leak" here means that you queried the cloud provider for assets, but you didn't inventory some cloud assets for that provider. For example, you may have inventoried all of the virtual machines, but missed the object storage buckets that your team provisioned. If you don't inventory those

---

5 Make sure to follow the least privilege principle, and ensure that credentials for inventory automation don't provide more power to your inventory system than absolutely necessary! An inventory system should not need to read anything but metadata or modify anything other than tags.

6 Note that free services are often not entirely "free"; the provider may get to use your data or get certain rights to your data, so you should inspect the terms of service!

object storage buckets, your downstream tools and processes cannot check the buckets to make sure that access to them is controlled properly, or that they've been assigned the proper tags.

Tooling Leaks

The third step is to ensure that each tool that helps check the security of your assets is tied into this asset inventory and can obtain the information it needs to do its job. Here are some examples:

- Your network vulnerability scanner should be able to obtain the IP addresses in use from the VM information or VPC subnet information.

- Your web application vulnerability scanner should be able to obtain the URLs of each of your web applications.

- Your health checking or baselining system needs to know about the different VMs so that it can check the configurations of each.

- If your organization uses Windows systems, your antivirus solution will need a list of all those systems in order to effectively track alerts and ensure antivirus signatures are up to date.

A "leak" in this area means that you knew about some assets but didn't have your tools or processes check those assets for security issues. More information on these tools and protective measures will be given in Chapter 5, but there's really no way for the tools to find security issues in assets that they don't know about.

Findings Leaks

The final step is to ensure you're actually addressing any findings from your tooling systems. This may seem obvious, but in practice these findings are often ignored, particularly with "noisy" scanning systems that create a lot of false positives.

It's perfectly acceptable to decide to accept a finding (risk) without fixing it, but ignoring the findings without any sort of review is a "leak."

Tagging Cloud Assets

It makes sense to categorize and organize your assets when creating them, so that you know what they contain and what they are used for. Tags can make automation and access control much easier. Just as you tagged your data assets with the types of data on them in Chapter 2, you also need to tag other types of assets to indicate both the types of data processed by them and why the assets are needed.

It's important to use the same data tags from Chapter 2 to indicate the types of data processed on compute assets, so that you have a consistent view of where your data is stored and processed. However, while it's relatively simple to come up with a set of data classification levels or a list of compliance requirements, there are almost endless possibilities for other operational tags.

Here are some examples of the types of tags that may be useful:

- Function of the asset
- Environment type for the asset, such as development, test, or production
- Application or project that the asset is used for
- Department that is responsible for the asset
- Version number
- Automation tags, which can indicate whether the asset should be selected for action by scripts, scanners, or other automation

 With many cloud providers, tags are case sensitive, so *ApplicationA* and *applicationA* won't match.

Looking at our sample application from Chapter 1, we can add some tags to the servers, as seen in Figure 3-2.

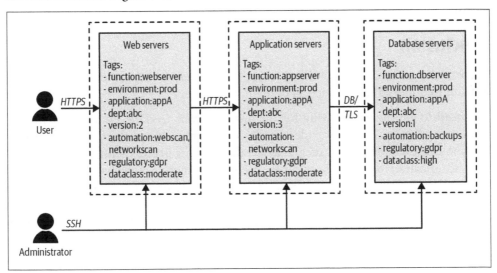

Figure 3-2. Sample application diagram with tags

Proper tagging can enable automated security checks. For example, perhaps you have a very sensible policy that sensitive data must not be stored or accessed on development and test systems. To help enforce this policy, you could:

1. Have automation that searches VMs and tags them with `dataclass:sensitive-data` if the automation detects either certain types of data (such as credit card numbers) or credentials to access sensitive data (such as the production database).

2. Have automation in your build processes to automatically tag VMs as `environment:development`, `environment:test`, or `environment:production` as they're created.

3. Create a report of any assets that have a `dataclass:sensitive-data` tag along with either an `environment:development` or an `environment:test` tag.

For tags to be effective, you must maintain a consistent set of tag names and allowed values, which means having a tagging standard and sticking to it. In most smaller organizations, the tagging standard should be organization-wide. A larger organization will need to agree on some organization-wide tags as well as allowing tags specific to business units. In either case, there should be a clear owner of the tagging standard who adds additional tags to the official list as needed.

You may want to develop automation to collect all of the tags currently in use and report on any that are not specified in the tagging standard for your organization or business unit.

Conclusion

There are so many different cloud as-a-service offerings available today that it can be difficult to understand and track all of them.

You need to get the biggest bang for the buck for your tracking efforts. This means prioritizing the tracking of providers and assets where losing track of an asset is most likely to cause a large impact, such as assets that store or process sensitive data or that have administrative control over other assets. For example, you may choose not to worry about tracking all of your virtual machine images until you have tight tracking of all of your databases where customer data is stored, your existing virtual machines that have access to those databases, and your source code (and dependent libraries) that processes customer data.

Use a pipeline approach that tracks cloud providers, assets created by those providers, what your security tooling does with those assets, and what you do with the findings from those security tools. If you have on-premises resources, treat those the same way as resources at a third-party cloud provider, although you may not have tagging or an API for automation.

Asset management can also have important benefits besides security. For example, you may discover that you have assets that are no longer needed, and deleting these can cut costs in addition to reducing security risks. If you're having difficulty getting support for an asset management solution based solely on security requirements, try also pitching it as a cost-control measure.

Now that you understand the different types of cloud assets available and some good ways to keep track of them, let's look at how to protect these assets and the data in them from one of the most common causes of breaches—issues with identity and access management.

Exercises

1. What are some reasons why manual tracking of cloud assets is error-prone? Select all that apply.

   a. There are too many cloud assets.

   b. Cloud assets are created and destroyed often.

   c. There is often a single team that deploys cloud assets.

   d. APIs make tracking cloud assets more difficult.

2. What are some types of cloud infrastructure assets? Select all that apply.

   a. Compute assets

   b. Storage assets

   c. Network assets

   d. Encrypted assets

3. True or false: Containers are inherently insecure and should not be used when security is important.

4. Which of these are common leaks in an asset management pipeline? Select all that apply.

   a. Missing a cloud provider

   b. Missing assets from a cloud provider

   c. Not feeding the correct assets into your security tooling

   d. Having known risks

5. What are some reasonable tags for cloud assets? Select all that apply.

   a. The asset owner

   b. The types of data on the asset

   c. The type of environment the asset is part of, such as development, test, or production

   d. The function of the asset in your application, such as web server or application server

CHAPTER 4

Identity and Access Management

Identity and access management (IAM) is perhaps the most important set of security controls. In breaches involving web applications, lost or stolen credentials have been attackers' most-used tool for several years running.[1] If attackers have valid credentials to log in to your system, all of the patches and firewalls in the world won't keep them out!

Identity and access management are often discussed together, but it's important to understand that they are distinct concepts:

- An *identity* is how a person (or automation) is represented in the system.[2] The process of verifying that the entity making a request is really the owner of the identity is called *authentication* (often abbreviated as "authn").

- *Access management* is about allowing identities to perform the tasks they need to perform (and, in a least privilege environment, *only* the tasks they need to perform). The process of checking what privileges an identity should have is called *authorization* (often abbreviated as "authz").

Authentication is proving that you are who you say you are. In the physical world, this might take the form of presenting an ID card, which was issued by a trusted authority and has your picture on it. Anyone can inspect that credential, look at you, and decide whether to believe that you are who you say you are. As an example, if you drive up to a military base and present your driver's license, you're attempting to

---

1 See, for example, the Verizon Data Breach Investigations Report (*https://oreil.ly/Ealmn*).

2 There is also the process of verifying that a person is who they say they are before giving them an identity, generally called *identity proofing*. That's usually performed by corporate onboarding processes and help desk password recovery processes, and is not normally the responsibility of users of cloud services.

authenticate yourself with the guard. The guard may choose to believe you, or may decide you've provided someone else's driver's license or that it's been forged, or may tell you that the base only accepts military IDs and not driver's licenses.

Authorization refers to the ability to perform a certain action, and generally depends first on authentication (knowing who someone is). For example, the guard at the base may say, "Yes, I believe you are who you say you are, but you're not allowed to enter this base." Or you may be allowed in, but not allowed access to most buildings once inside.

In IT security, we often muddle these two concepts. For example, we may create an identity for someone (with associated credentials such as a password) and then implicitly allow anyone with a valid identity to access all data on the system. Or we may revoke someone's access by deleting the person's identity—that works, but it's like tearing up their driver's license instead of just denying them access. Although these solutions may be appropriate in some cases, it's important to understand the distinction. Is it really appropriate to authorize every user for full access to the system? What if you have to give someone outside the organization an identity in order to allow them to access some other area of the system—will that user also automatically gain access to internal resources?

Note that the concepts (and analogies) can get complicated very quickly. For example, imagine a system where instead of showing your license everywhere, you check out an access badge that you show to others, and a refresh badge that you need to show only to the badge issuer. The access badge authenticates you to everyone, but works for only one day, after which you have to go to the badge office and show the refresh badge to get a new access badge. Each site where you present your access badge verifies the signature on it to make sure it's valid, and then calls a central authority to ask whether you're on the list for access to that resource. This is similar to the way some IT access systems work, although fortunately your browser and the systems providing service to you take care of these details for you!

An important principle with identity and access management, as well as in other areas of security, is to minimize the number of organizations and people whom you have to trust. For example, except for cases where zero-knowledge encryption will work,[3] you're going to have to trust your cloud provider's authentication and authorization processes to keep your data from being seen by unauthorized people. You have to accept the risk that if your provider is completely compromised, your data is compromised. However, since you've already decided to trust the cloud provider, you want to avoid trusting any other people or organizations if you can instead leverage

---

3 Zero-knowledge encryption means that your provider has no technical way of decrypting the data, usually because you only send encrypted data without the keys. This sharply limits what the provider can do, and is most suitable for backup services where the provider just needs to hold a lot of data without any processing.

that existing trust without incurring additional risk.[4] Think of it like paying an admission fee; once you've paid the "fee" of trusting a particular organization, you should use it for all it's worth to avoid introducing additional risk into the system.

Differences from Traditional IT

In traditional IT environments, access management is often performed in part by physical access controls (who can enter the building) or network access controls (who can connect to the network remotely). As an example, you may be able to count on a perimeter firewall as a second layer of protection if you fire an admin and forget to revoke their access to one of the servers.

It's important to note that even in a non-cloud environment, this is often a very weak level of security—are you confident that the access controls for all of your Ethernet ports, wireless access points, and VPN endpoints will stand up to even casual attack? In most organizations, someone could ask to use the bathroom and plug a $5 remote access device into an Ethernet port on the way there, or steal wireless or VPN credentials to get in without even stepping foot on the premises. The chance of any given individual having their credentials stolen might be small, but the overall odds of having unauthorized people on the network increase quickly as you add more and more people to the environment.[5] This is doubly true in cloud environments, where all access is remote access and the odds are even higher that you will have unauthorized people on a supposedly secure network.

In traditional environments, access control is sometimes performed simply by revoking a user's entire identity, so that they can no longer log in at all. But when using cloud environments, this often won't take care of the entire problem. For convenience, many services provide long-lived authentication tokens that will continue to work even without the ability to log in on a new session. Unless you're careful to have an "offboarding" feed that notifies applications when someone leaves so that the application can revoke all access, people may retain access to things you didn't intend. As an example, if you use a webmail service, when was the last time you typed in your webmail password? Changing your password or preventing you from using the login page wouldn't do any good if webmail providers didn't also revoke the access tokens stored in your browser cookies during a password change operation.

---

4 I like to jokingly refer to this as the "principle of already screwed." It's good to have a way to monitor your provider's actions, though, to detect a potential compromise.

5 If you are 99.9% sure that any given user's credentials won't be stolen in a year, and you have 1,000 users, then you're only 36.7% sure that *none* of your users' credentials will be stolen in a year. Probabilities are fun!

There are many examples of data breaches caused by leaving Amazon S3 buckets open to public access. If these were file shares left open to anyone in the company behind a corporate firewall, they might not have been found by an attacker or researcher on the internet. (In any organization of a reasonable size, there are almost certainly bad actors on the internal network who could have stolen that information, perhaps without detection, but the likelihood of attack is higher when it's internet-facing.)

The point behind these examples is that many organizations find that they've lived with lax IAM controls on-premises, and need to improve them significantly for the cloud. Fortunately, there are services available to make this easier.

Life Cycle for Identity and Access

Many people make the mistake of thinking of IAM as only authentication and authorization. Although those are both very important, IAM also includes other parts of the identity life cycle. In the earlier example about attempting to enter a military base, we assumed that you, the requester, already had an identity (your driver's license)—but how did you get that? And who put your name on the list of people who were allowed on the base?

Many organizations handle this poorly. Requesting an identity might be done by calling or messaging an administrator, who approves and creates the identity without keeping any record of it. This might work fine for really small organizations or low-risk environments, but many times you need a system to record when someone requests access, how the requester was authenticated, and who approved the new identity or the access.

Even more important is the backend of the life cycle. You need a system that will automatically check every so often if a user's identity and access are still needed. Perhaps the person has left the company, or moved to a different department, and should no longer have access. (Or worse, imagine having the unpleasant task of firing someone, and realizing a month later that due to human error the person still has access to an important system!)

There are many different versions of IAM life cycle diagrams, with varying amounts of detail in the steps. The one in Figure 4-1 shows the minimum number of steps, and addresses both creation and deletion of identities along with creation and deletion of access rules for those identities. Identity and access may be handled by different systems or the same system, but the steps are similar.

Note that you don't necessarily need a fancy automated system to implement every one of these steps. In an environment with few requesters and few approvers, a mostly manual process can work fine as long as it's consistently implemented and there are checks to prevent a single human error from causing problems. As of this writing, most automated systems to manage the entire life cycle (often called identity governance systems) are geared toward larger enterprises; they are usually expensive and difficult to implement. However, there is a growing trend to provide these governance solutions in the cloud like other services. These are often included as part of other identity and access services, so even smaller organizations will be able to benefit from them.

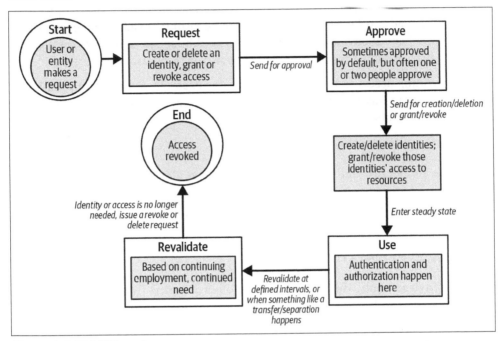

Figure 4-1. IAM life cycle

Also note that the processes and services used might differ considerably, depending on who the entities are. The types of identity and access management used to give your employees access to your cloud provider and your internal applications differ considerably from those used to grant your customers end-user access to your applications. I'll distinguish between these two general cases in the following discussion.

 Don't forget about identities for non-human things in the system, such as applications. These need to be managed too, just like human identities. Many teams do a great job of controlling access for people, but have very lax controls on what automation is authorized to do.

Let's go through each of these steps. The process starts when someone or something puts in a request. This might be the manager of a newly hired employee, or some automation such as your HR system.

Request

The life cycle begins when an entity makes an identity or access management request. This entity should usually be authenticated in some fashion. Inside your organization, you don't want any anonymous requests for access, although in some cases the authentication may be as simple as someone visually or aurally recognizing the person.

When providing access to the general public—for example, for a web application— you often want to link to some other identity, such as an existing email address or a mobile phone number.

The common requests are:

- Create an identity (and often implicitly grant that identity at least a base level of access).
- Delete an identity, if the entity no longer needs to authenticate anywhere.
- Grant access to an existing identity—for example, to a new system.
- Revoke access from an existing identity.

In cloud environments, the request process often happens "out of band," using a request process inside your organization that doesn't involve the cloud IAM system yet.

Approve

In some cases, it's acceptable to implicitly approve access. For example, when granting access to a publicly available web application, anyone who requests access is often approved automatically, provided that they meet certain requirements. These requirements might be anti-fraud in nature, such as providing a valid mobile number or email address, providing a valid credit card number, completing a CAPTCHA or "I am not a robot" form, or not originating from an anonymizing location such as an end-user VPN provider or a known Tor exit node.

However, inside an organization, most access requests should be explicitly approved. In many cases, two approvals are reasonable—for example, by the user's immediate supervisor, as well as the owner of the system to which access is being requested. The important thing is that the approver or approvers are in a position to know whether the requested access is reasonable and necessary. This is also an internal process for your team that usually happens with no interaction with your cloud providers.

Create, Delete, Grant, or Revoke

After approval, the actual action to create an identity, delete an identity, grant access, or revoke access may happen automatically. For example, the request/approve system may use cloud provider APIs to create the identity or grant the access.

In other cases, this may generate a ticket, email, or other notification requiring a person to take manual action. For example, an admin may need to log in to the cloud portal to create the new identity and grant it a certain level of access. Automation is preferable, particularly for frequently requested items, to reduce the possibility of human error.

Authentication

So far, much of what has been discussed is not really different from access management in on-premises environments—before an identity exists, you have to request it and have a process to create it. However, authentication is where cloud environments begin to differ because of the many identity services available.

It's important to distinguish between the identity *store*, which is the database that holds all of the identities, and the *protocol* used to authenticate users and verify their identities, which can be OpenID, SAML, LDAP, or others.

There are different cloud services available to help, depending on who is being authenticated:

- Authenticating your organization's employees with your cloud providers falls under business-to-business (B2B) authentication, and the cloud service is often called something like "Cloud IAM."
- Authenticating your organization's customers with your own applications running in the cloud is often called business-to-consumer (B2C) authentication, and the cloud service is often called something like "Customer IAM" or "CIAM."
- Authenticating your organization's employees with your own applications is often called business-to-employee (B2E) authentication; it may use the same services as B2C authentication or may be called something like "Workforce Identity."

Cloud IAM Identities

Most cloud providers offer IAM services that must be used when accessing their cloud services. These are usually available for no additional charge. They allow you to have one central location to manage the identities of cloud administrators in your organization, along with the access that you have granted those identities to all of the services that cloud provider offers.

This can be a big help. If you are using dozens or hundreds of services from a cloud provider, it can be difficult to get a good picture of what level of access a given person has if you have to go separately to every service. It can also be difficult to make sure you've revoked all of their access when that person leaves your organization. Removing access is especially important, given that many of these services may be used directly from the internet!

Table 4-1 lists some examples of identity services to authenticate your cloud administrators with cloud provider services.

Table 4-1. Cloud provider identity services

Provider	Cloud identity service
Amazon Web Services	AWS IAM
Microsoft Azure	Azure Active Directory
Google Cloud Platform	Cloud IAM
IBM Cloud	Cloud IAM

Business-to-Consumer and Business-to-Employee

In addition to the identities your organization uses for accessing cloud provider services, you may also need to manage identities for your end users, whether they are external customers or your own employees.

Although you can do customer identity management yourself by simply creating rows in a database with passwords, this is often not an ideal experience for your end users, who will have to juggle yet another login and password. In addition, there are significant security pitfalls to avoid when verifying passwords, as described in "Passwords, Passphrases, and API Keys" on page 68. There are two better options:

- Use an existing identity service. This may be an internal identity service for your employees or your customers' employees. For end users, it may also be an external service such as Facebook, Google, or LinkedIn. This requires you to trust that identity service to properly authenticate users for you. It also makes your association with the identity service obvious to your end users when they log in, which may not always be desirable.

- Use customer identities specific to your application, and use a cloud service to manage these customer identities. Users still have another credential to deal with, but at least you don't have to verify the credential.

The names of these Identity-as-a-Service (IDaaS) offerings do not always make it clear what they do. Table 4-2 lists some examples from major cloud infrastructure providers as well as third-party providers. There are many third-party providers in this space and they change often, so this isn't an endorsement of any particular providers. For business-to-employee cases, most of these IDaaS services can also use your employee information store, such as your internal directory.

Table 4-2. ID management systems

Provider	Customer and workforce identity management cloud services
Amazon Web Services	Amazon Cognito
Microsoft Azure	Azure Active Directory B2C
Google Cloud Platform	Identity Platform
IBM Cloud	App ID
Okta	Customer Identity Cloud, Workforce Identity Cloud
Ping	PingOne for Customers, PingOne for Workforce

 Note that whether you're creating identities yourself or using a cloud service, any personally identifiable information you collect or process may be subject to regulatory requirements such as the EU GDPR.

Multi-Factor Authentication

Multi-factor authentication is one of the best ways to guard against weak or stolen credentials, and if implemented properly will only place a small additional burden on users. Most of the identity services shown in Table 4-2 support multi-factor authentication.

As background, the different authentication factors are commonly defined as:

1. Something you know. Passwords are the best-known examples, but personal identification numbers (PINs)—which, unlike a password, can only be used in conjunction with a specific device you have—are becoming more popular.

2. Something you have. For example, an access badge, a mobile phone, or a piece of data that is impractical to memorize, such as a randomly generated private key.

3. Something you are. For example, your fingerprint, face, or retinal pattern.

As the name implies, multi-factor authentication involves using more than one of these factors for authentication. Using two of the same factor, like two different passwords, doesn't help much because the same attack could be used to get both passwords! The most common implementation is *two-factor authentication* (2FA), which uses something you know (like a password) and something you have (like your mobile phone).

2FA does not require one of the factors to be a password. *Password-less* logins that have two factors (such as a physical device you have and your fingerprint to unlock the device) can be considerably more secure and convenient than password authentication.

2FA should be the default for most access; if implemented correctly, it requires very little extra effort for most users. You should absolutely use 2FA any place where the impact of lost or stolen credentials would be high, such as for any privileged access, access to read or modify sensitive data, or access to systems such as email that can be leveraged to reset other passwords. For example, if you're running a banking site, you may decide that the impact is low if someone is able to read a user's bank balance, but high (with 2FA required) if someone is attempting to transfer money. Requiring additional authentication for higher-risk activities is called *step-up authentication*.

If you're managing a cloud environment, unauthorized administrative access to the cloud portal or APIs is a very high risk to you, because an attacker with that access can usually leverage it to compromise all of your data. You should turn on two-factor authentication for this type of access; most cloud providers natively support this. Alternatively, if you're using single sign-on (SSO), discussed in "Single Sign-On" on page 71, your SSO provider may already perform 2FA for you.

Many services offer multiple authentication methods. The most common methods are:

Passwords and passphrases (something you know)
A password is not tied to a particular device, and will work from anywhere. The problems with passwords are plentiful and well known: many people choose passwords that are commonly used and subject to dictionary attacks, or are simple and short enough to be cracked with brute-force attacks, or are reused across multiple services so that compromising one service gives an attacker the password for another (which can be discovered through credential stuffing attacks). It's really past time to stop using them, but change is hard.

PINs (something you know)
On the surface, PINs may seem like they're worse than passwords, because they're usually simpler, but the important thing about PINs is that *they are only useful when paired with a specific physical device.* Someone who guesses your PIN without having the associated device (usually a mobile phone, laptop, or hardware security key) cannot gain access to it, which makes a successful attack much harder.

SMS text messages to a mobile device (something you have)
This method has fallen out of favor because of the ease of stealing someone's phone number (via SIM cloning or number porting) or intercepting the message,

so new implementations should not use it, and existing implementations should move to another method. This does require cellular network access to receive the text messages.

Time-based one-time passcodes, or TOTPs (something you have)
This method requires providing a mobile device with an initial "secret" (usually transferred by a 2D barcode). The secret is a formula for computing a one-time password every minute or so. The one-time password needs to be kept safe for only a minute or two, but the initial secret can allow any device to generate valid passwords and so should be destroyed or put in a physically safe place after use. After the initial secret is transferred, network access is not required for the mobile device, only a synchronized clock. The main drawback is that TOTPs are less convenient for users and are "phishable," meaning that an attacker who fools you into entering both the password and the passcode into a fake site can gain access.

Hash-based one-time passcodes, or HOTPs (something you have)
These are similar to TOTPs in both advantages and disadvantages, but use a counter instead of the time, so don't require a synchronized clock. However, they can get out of sync if too many codes are generated and not used.

Push notifications to a mobile device (something you have)
With this method, an already authenticated client application on a mobile device makes a connection to a server, which "pushes" back a one-time-use code or asks for permission. This is secure as long as the authentication for the already authenticated client application is secure, but does require network access for the mobile device. The primary drawback is that an attacker may be able to fool the user into saying yes either with a clever forgery site or by fatiguing the user with lots of requests.

Fingerprint readers, face readers, and retina readers (something you are)
While these biometric methods are often foolable with enough effort (creating replica fingers or faces or eyes), the implementations continue to improve and they are good enough as a single factor to meet most security requirements.

A hardware device, such as one complying with the FIDO Universal 2nd Factor (U2F) or FIDO2 standards (something you have)
FIDO U2F is only a second authentication factor, generally used with a password, while FIDO2 can function as a combined multi-factor device to allow password-less authentication. FIDO2 devices are also called *passkeys* (*https://oreil.ly/vo9ed*). This is by far the best option, because the passkey knows what application it's talking to and can't be fooled by fake sites. Initially, these were only available as standalone hardware security keys, but the technology is now built into most laptops and mobile devices. Use of this type of authentication is likely to become

ubiquitous in the near future, integrated with smartphones and wearable technologies such as watches and rings. A FIDO2 device can be unlocked with a PIN or a biometric factor, which combines two factors into one device for very strong, phishing-resistant, passwordless authentication.

 Note that many of these methods to verify "something you have" are vulnerable to social attacks, such as calling the user under false pretenses and asking for the one-time passcode! Even the strongest forms of authentication, such as FIDO2, can be subject to downgrade attacks if the user goes to a fake site that says, "That didn't work, please try a different (weaker) method." In addition to rolling out multi-factor authentication, you must provide some minimal training to users to help them recognize common attacks.

All major cloud providers offer ways to implement multi-factor authentication, although Google uses the friendlier term "2-Step Verification."

Passwords, Passphrases, and API Keys

If you're using multi-factor authentication, passwords or passphrases are no longer your only line of defense. That said, unless you've gone to a full passwordless model, it's still important to choose good passwords. This is often even more true in cloud environments, because in many cases an attacker can guess passwords directly over the internet from anywhere in the world.

"Passphrase" is just a term for a longer, more secure password, so I'll use the more generic term "password" here. While there is lots of advice and debate about good passwords, my recommendations for choosing passwords are simple:

1. Never reuse passwords unless you genuinely don't care about an unauthorized user getting access to the resources protected by that password. For example, you might use the same password on a dozen forum systems because you don't really care if someone posts as you on any or all of those forums. (Even then, though, there is still some risk that the user can somehow leverage that access to reset other passwords, so it's best not to reuse passwords at all.) When you type a password into a site, you should assume that the site's administrators are malicious and will use the password you have provided to break into other sites.

2. Not reusing passwords means you'll end up with a lot of passwords, so use a reputable password wallet to keep track of them. Store copies of any master passwords or recovery keys in a physically secured location, such as a good safe or a bank safe deposit box.

3. For passwords that you do not need to remember (for example, that you can copy and paste from your password wallet), use a secure random generator.

Twenty characters is a good target, although you may find some systems that won't accept that many characters; for those, use as varied a character set as possible.[6]

4. For passwords you do need to remember, such as the password for your password wallet, create a six-word Diceware (*https://oreil.ly/GvcDi*) password[7] and put the same non-alphabetic character, such as a dollar sign, equals sign, or comma, between each word. Feel free to regenerate the password a few times until you find one that you can construct some sort of silly story about to help you remember it. This will be easy to memorize quickly and nearly impossible for an attacker to guess. The only drawback is that it takes a while to type, so you don't want to have to type it constantly!

API keys are very similar to passwords but are designed for use by automation, not people. For that reason, you cannot use multi-factor authentication with API keys, and they should be long random strings, as noted in item 3 in the preceding list. Unlike most user identities where you have a public user ID and a private password, you usually have only a private API key that tells the system who you are and also authenticates you.

Verifying Passwords

You may also be tasked with verifying users' passwords, which can be much more complicated than it seems. Avoid this task if possible!

The simplest way to verify passwords is to store a list of the users and passwords and then check to see whether the password entered matches what's on the list. This is a very bad idea, however, because if someone gets access to your list, they have everything they need to impersonate every user on the list!

A much better method is to not store the passwords themselves, but to store something that can be used to verify the passwords. This is implemented using a *one-way hash*, which is something you can derive with a function if you have the password, but which cannot be used to go backward to get the password. However, the devil is in the details—if you use the wrong function or the wrong parameters for the function, the passwords can be easily obtained ("cracked") through a brute-force attack,

---

6 Password strength is usually measured in "bits of entropy." A *very* oversimplified explanation is that if you give an attacker all of the information you can about how a password is constructed but not the actual password, such as "it's 20 uppercase alphabetic characters," the number of bits of entropy is about $\log_2(number\ of\ possible\ passwords)$.

7 Diceware is based on the idea that it's far easier for humans to remember phrases than characters, and that almost everyone can find some six-sided dice. You can download the Diceware word list, then roll dice to randomly pick five or six words off the list. There are also web pages that generate a passphrase locally for you. The result is an extremely secure password that's easy to remember.

by guessing a lot of possible passwords. Perfectly good hash algorithms such as SHA-256 are terrible for password hashes because they're fast to compute, by design.

As of this writing, password hashes should be stored using scrypt, bcrypt, PBKDF2, or Argon2 functions with reasonable parameters. The recommendations for functions and parameters change over time as cracking hardware gets more sophisticated and weaknesses are found in hashing algorithms, so you must reevaluate your choices at least annually. When you change algorithms or parameters, all new passwords will use the new methods, but by design there's no way to convert the old hashes to new hashes. If there's an urgent need to change (such as evidence of a breach that might have gained access to password hashes), you must reset all user passwords immediately.

Even if you store hashes securely, you should have a testing mechanism in place to prevent users from using really easy-to-guess passwords like *abc123* or *Fall2018*. Attackers are increasingly using techniques such as "password spraying," where they try an easy password on hundreds or thousands of IDs at once. This often doesn't trigger any alarms because it shows up as only a single failed login for each ID. You should also monitor for a lot of failures coming from one location, which is often indicative of credential stuffing attacks, where an attacker gets a list of passwords from one site and tries them on other sites.

For cloud services and applications, use a federated identity from another provider or a consumer/employee IAM cloud service where possible. For system-level access, use key-based authentication or centralized authentication with password strength testing. Don't store and verify password hashes yourself unless there is no good alternative.

Shared IDs

Shared IDs are identities for which more than one person has the password or other credentials, such as the built-in *root* or *Administrator* account on a system. These can be difficult to handle well in cloud environments, just as they are on-premises.

Where possible, every user or tool should have its own ID that's not used by anyone or anything else. Many systems allow users to assume a privileged role or separate higher-privileged ID for some activities, such as by using *sudo* on Unix-like systems. When you do need to use shared IDs, you need to be able to tell exactly which individual (or automated tooling) was using the ID for any access.

If you do have to share an ID, such as *root*, the system you're using the shared ID on has no way of distinguishing who was using it. That means you need to have a separate process and tooling to check out the shared credentials and then change them when they're checked back in. This tooling is usually called a *privileged access management* (PAM) or *privileged identity management* (PIM) system, and it can also perform other functions, such as recording the session or prohibiting the use of some commands.

Federated Identity

Federated identity is a concept, not a specific technology. It means that you may have identities on two different systems, and the administrators of those systems can both agree to use technologies that link those identities together so that you don't have to manually create separate accounts on each system. From your perspective as a user, you have only a single identity.

In practice what this usually means is that Company A and Company B both use your corporate email address, such as *user@company-a.com*, as your identity, and Company B defers to Company A to actually authenticate you. Company A will then pass an assertion or token back with its seal of approval: "Yes, this is indeed *user@company-a.com*; I have verified them, here is my signature to prove that it's me, and you've already agreed that you'll trust me to authenticate users with identifiers that end in *@company-a.com.*"

Single Sign-On

Single sign-on (SSO) is a set of technology implementations that rely upon the concept of federated identity.

In the bad old days, every website had a separate login and password. That's a lot of passwords for users to keep track of! The predictable result is that users often reuse the same password across multiple sites, meaning that the user's password is only as well protected as the weakest site.

Enter SSO. The idea is that instead of a website asking for a user's ID and password, the website instead redirects the user to a centralized identity provider (IdP) that it trusts. (Note that the identity provider may not even be part of the same organization—the only requirement is that the website trusts it.) The IdP will do the work of authenticating the user, via means such as a username and password, and hopefully an additional authorization factor. It will then send the user back to the original website with proof that it has verified the user. In some cases, the IdP will also send information (such as group membership) that the website can use to make authorization decisions, such as whether the user should be allowed in as a regular user, as an administrator, or not at all.

For the most part, SSO works only for websites and mobile applications, although this is beginning to change. You may need a different protocol (such as LDAP, Kerberos, TACACS+, or RADIUS) for performing centralized authentication to non-web assets like network devices or operating systems.

Rarely do you find something that's both easier for users *and* provides better security! Users only have to remember one set of credentials, and because these credentials are only ever seen by the identity provider (and not any of the individual sites), a compromise of those sites won't compromise the user's credentials. In addition, your SSO provider can implement controls that follow other zero trust principles, such as checking whether an unmanaged or out-of-date device is being used, or if the user's credentials are being used from two different countries at the same time. These types of controls are very difficult to implement individually on each application.

The only drawback to SSO is that it is slightly more difficult for a website to implement than poor authentication mechanisms, such as comparing against a plain-text password or an insecurely hashed password in a database.

SAML and OIDC

As of this writing, Security Assertion Markup Language (SAML—the abbreviation rhymes with "camel") and OpenID Connect (OIDC) are the most common SSO technologies. While the end results are similar, the mechanisms they use are somewhat different.

The current SAML version is 2.0, and it has been around since 2005. This is one of the most common SSO technologies, particularly for large enterprise applications. While there are many in-depth explanations of how SAML works, here is a very simplified version:

1. You point your web browser at a web page you want to access (called a *service provider*, or SP).

2. The SP web page says, "Hey, you don't have a SAML cookie, so I don't know who you are. Go over here to this identity provider web page and get one," and redirects you.

3. You go to the IdP and log in using your username, password, and hopefully a second factor, or a passwordless method.

4. When the IdP is satisfied it's really you, it gives your browser a cookie with a cryptographically signed XML "assertion" that says, "I'm the identity provider, and this user is authenticated," and then redirects you back.

5. Your web browser hands that cookie back to the first web page (SP). The SP verifies the cryptographic signature and says, "You managed to convince the IdP of your identity, so that's good enough for me. Come on in."

After you've logged in once, this all happens automatically for a while until those assertion documents expire, at which point you have to log in to the IdP again.

One important thing to note is that there was never any direct communication between the initial web page and the identity provider—your browser did all of the hard work to get the information from one place to another. That can be important in some cases where network communications are restricted.

Also note that SAML provides only identity information, by design. Whether or not you're authorized to log in or take other actions is a different question, although some SAML implementations pass additional information along with the assertion (such as group membership) that can be used by the application to make authorization decisions.

OpenID Connect is a much newer authentication layer, finalized in 2014, on top of OAuth 2.0. It uses JSON Web Tokens (JWTs, sometimes pronounced "jots") instead of XML, and uses somewhat different terminology ("relying party" is usually used in OIDC versus "service provider" in SAML, for example).

OIDC offers both *Authorization Code Flows* (for traditional web applications) and *Implicit Flows* (for applications implemented using JavaScript on the client side). While there are numerous differences from SAML, the end results are similar in that the application you're authenticating with never sees your actual password, and you don't have to reauthenticate for every application.

Some services can take requests from OIDC-enabled applications and "translate" these to requests to a SAML IdP. In larger organizations, it's very common to have both standards in use, and most IdPs support both.

SSO with legacy applications

What if you want to provide single sign-on to a legacy application that doesn't support it? One option is to put something in front of the application that handles the SSO requests and then tells the legacy application who the users are.

The legacy application will trust this frontend service (often a reverse proxy) to perform authentication, but it's very important that it not accept connections from anything else. Techniques like this are sometimes needed when moving an existing application to the cloud, until the application can be reworked to allow SSO natively. Many of the Identity-as-a-Service providers listed earlier also offer ways to SSO-enable legacy applications.

Instance Metadata and Identity Documents

As mentioned earlier in this chapter, we often assume that automation, such as a program running on a system, has already been assigned an identity and a way to prove that identity. For example, if I start up a new system, I can create a username and password for that system to use and supply that username and password to the system as part of the process of creating it. However, in many cloud environments, there are easier ways.

A process running on a particular system can contact a well-known endpoint that will tell it all about the system it's running on, and the process will also provide a cryptographically signed way to prove that system's identity. The exact details differ from provider to provider, but conceptually it looks like Figure 4-2.

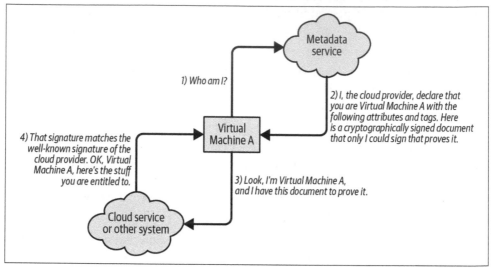

Figure 4-2. Using identity documents

This is not foolproof, however, in that any process on the system can request this metadata, regardless of its privilege level on the system. This means you either need to put only processes of the same trust level on the system, or take actions to block lower-privileged processes from assuming the identity of the entire system. This can be a particular concern in container environments, where any container on a host system could request the identity document and then pretend to be that host system. In cases like this, you need to block the containers from reaching the metadata service.

This system also requires the cloud service to recognize the particular type of document and signature that the metadata service is using. If only there were a standard format for these documents and signatures, so that the cloud service could choose to trust containers created in a particular cluster or virtual machines created in a specific cloud account! Enter SPIFFE (*https://spiffe.io*), which is a standard method for allowing a *workload* (which may be a container, a virtual machine, a multi-node application, etc.) to authenticate with something else. SPIRE is a reference implementation of the SPIFFE specification. As of this writing, SPIFFE is not widely used, but eventually it or a similar specification is likely to eliminate the widespread use of static API keys for authentication. Instead of configuring the system to trust anyone who gets the API key, you'll configure it to only trust those workloads that can both show you a valid ID and are on your list of things to trust.

If you can use identity documents, then you don't need to do as much secrets management. As a workload, I can make a simple request and be given the secrets that I need to access other resources, and then forget the secrets and ask again if I need them later. However, given that identity documents are not yet in widespread use, and that many types of resources don't accept them yet, you'll need some tools and techniques for managing secrets. We'll look at those next.

Secrets Management

I talked about passwords earlier primarily in the context of a person authenticating with a system. Administrative users and end users have had secrets management techniques for as long as there have been secrets, ranging from good (password wallets and physical safes) to really bad (the ubiquitous Post-it note on the monitor or under the keyboard). While the term *secrets management* generally applies any time you have a secret to remember, it's usually used more specifically to refer to secrets used by one system to talk to another.

For example, let's look at the case where an application server needs to talk to a database server. Clearly, multi-factor authentication can't be used here; the application server doesn't have a hardware security key or a fingerprint![8] This means you need to be very careful with the authentication credentials for system-to-system connections, because they may be your only line of authentication defense.

System-to-system authentication credentials may involve a password, API key, cryptographic token, or public/private key pair. All of these solutions have something that needs to be kept secret. We refer to all of these things simply as *secrets*, and secrets management is about making them available to the entity that needs them—and nobody else. (In addition, you may have items unrelated to authentication that need to be kept secret, such as encryption keys; while these are also technically secrets, they're usually covered more specifically under *encryption key management*.)

Secrets are dangerous things that should be handled carefully. Here are some principles for managing secrets:

- Secrets should be easy to change at regular intervals and whenever there's any reason to think they may have leaked out. If changing the secret means that you have to take the application down and manually change it in many places, that's a problem.

---

8 Some applications can remember a TOTP secret and use it to log in along with a password, but this is usually only done in cases where a testing tool is pretending to be a user logging in. If an attacker gets into that application, they'll find both the password and the TOTP secret in the same place, so in this situation the second factor doesn't really help from a security perspective.

- Secrets should always be encrypted at rest and in motion, and they should be distributed to systems only after proper authentication and authorization.

- If possible, no human should know the secrets—not the developers who write the code, not the operators who can look at the running system, nobody. This often is not possible, but we should at least strive to minimize number of people who know secrets!

- The system storing and handing out the secrets should be well protected. If you put all the secrets in a vault and then hand out keys to the vault to dozens of people, that's a problem.

- Secrets should be as useless to an attacker as possible while allowing the system to function. This is again an instance of least privilege; try not to keep secrets around that offer the keys to the kingdom, such as providing *root* access to all systems, but instead have limited secrets, such as a secret that allows read-only access to a specific database.

- All accesses and changes to secrets should be logged.

Even organizations that do a great job with authentication and authorization often overlook secrets management. For example, you may do a great job keeping track of which people have personal IDs with access to a database, but how many people know the password that the application server uses to talk to the database? Does it get changed regularly, and immediately if someone leaves the team? In the worst case, this password is in the application server code and checked into some public repository, such as GitHub.[9]

There have been many breaches resulting from accidentally storing secrets, such as AWS API keys, in source code. The code needs the credentials to function when it's deployed, but putting secrets directly into source code (or into the source code repository as part of a configuration file) is a really bad idea, for two reasons:

- The source code repository likely was not designed primarily for keeping information secret. Its primary function is protecting the *integrity* of the source code—preventing unauthorized modification to insert a backdoor, for example. In many cases, it may show the source code to everyone by default as part of a social coding initiative.

- Even if the source code repository is perfectly safe, it's very unlikely that everyone who has access to the source code should also be authorized to see the secrets used in the production environment.

---

9 There is actually a common term for secrets found in public GitHub repositories: "GitHub dorks." This has been such a widespread issue that GitHub now has ways to block code pushes that contain secrets.

The most obvious solution is to take the secrets out of the source code and place them somewhere else, such as in a safe place in your deployment tooling or on a dedicated secrets server.

In most cases, a deployment of an application will consist of three pieces that come together:

- The application code
- The configuration for this particular deployment
- The secrets needed for this particular deployment

Storing all three of these things together is a really bad idea, as previously discussed. Having configuration and secrets together is also often a bad idea, because systems designed to hold configuration data may not be properly designed for keeping that data secret.

Let's take a look at four reasonable approaches to secrets management, ranging from minimally secure to highly secure.

The first approach is to use existing configuration management systems and deployment systems for storing secrets. Many popular systems today have some ability to hold secrets in addition to normal configuration data—for example, Ansible Vault and Chef encrypted data bags. This can be a reasonable approach if the deployment tooling is careful with the secrets, and more importantly if access to the deployment system and encryption keys is tightly controlled. However, there are often too many people who can read the secrets. In addition, changing secrets usually requires redeploying the system, which may be more difficult in some environments.

The second approach is to use a secrets server. With a separate secrets server, you need only a reference to the secret in the configuration data and the ability to talk to the secrets server. At that point, either the deployment software or the application can get the secret by authenticating with the secrets server using a secrets server password…but you see the problem, right? Now you have another secret (the password to the secrets server) to worry about.

Although imperfect, there's still considerable value to this approach to secrets management:

- The secrets server requests can be logged, so you may be able to detect and prevent an unauthorized user or deployment from accessing the secrets. This is discussed more in Chapter 7.
- The secrets server may use other ways to determine that the request is legitimate than just the password, such as the IP address range requesting the secret. As discussed in Chapter 6, IP allowlisting usually isn't sufficient by itself, but it is a useful secondary control.

- You can easily update the secrets later, and all of your systems that retrieve the secrets will get the new ones automatically.

The third approach has all of the benefits of a secrets server, but uses a secure introduction method to reduce the likelihood that an attacker can get the credentials to access the secrets server:

1. Your deployment tooling communicates with the secrets server to get a one-time-use secret, which it passes along to the application.

2. The application then trades that in for the real secret to the secrets server, and it uses that to obtain all the other secrets it needs and hold them in memory. If someone has already used the one-time secret, this step will fail, and the application can send an alert that something is wrong.

Your deployment tooling still needs one set of static credentials to your secrets server, but this allows it only to obtain one-time keys and not to view secrets directly. (If your deployment tooling is completely compromised, then an attacker could deploy a fake copy of an application to read secrets, but that's more difficult than reading the secrets directly and is more likely to be detected.)

Operations personnel cannot view the secrets, or the credentials to the secrets server, without more complicated memory-scraping techniques. For example, instead of simply reading the secret out of a configuration file, a rogue operator would have to dump the system memory out and search through it for the secret, or attach a debugger to a process to find the secret.

The fourth approach, if available, is to leverage some offerings built into your cloud platform by its provider to avoid the "turtles all the way down" problem:

1. Some cloud providers offer instance metadata or identity documents to systems provisioned in the cloud. Your application can retrieve this identity document, which will say something like, "I am server ABC. The cloud provider cryptographically signed this document for me, which proves my identity."

2. The secrets server then knows the identity of the server, as well as metadata such as tags attached to the server. It can use this information to authenticate and authorize an application running on the server and provide it the rest of the secrets it needs to function. In the future, you may be able to use the identity document directly with most cloud services, and not need the secrets server at all!

Let's summarize the four reasonable approaches to secrets management:

- The first approach stores secrets only in the deployment system, using features designed to hold secrets, and tightly controls access to the deployment system. Nobody sees the secrets by default, and only authorized individuals have the technical ability to view or change them in the deployment system.

- The second approach is to use a secrets server to hold secrets. Either the deployment server or the deployed application contacts the secrets server to get the necessary secrets and use them. In many cases the secrets are still visible in the configuration files or environment variables of the running application after deployment, so operations personnel may be able to easily view the secrets or the credentials to the secrets server.

- The third approach has the deployment server only able to get a one-time token and pass it to the application, which then retrieves the secrets and holds them in memory. This protects you from having the credentials to the secrets server or the secrets themselves intercepted.

- The fourth approach leverages the deployment platform itself as the root of trust. For example, an IaaS provider hands out signed identity documents to virtual machines that the secrets server can use to decide which secrets to provide to that virtual machine.

Several products and services are available to help you manage secrets. HashiCorp Vault and Keywhiz are standalone products that may be implemented on-premises or in the cloud, and AWS Secrets Manager is available through an as-a-service model.

Authorization

Once you've completed the authentication phase and you know who your users are, it's time to make sure they are limited to performing only the actions they are supposed to perform. Some examples of authorization include granting permission to access an application at all, to access an application with write access, to access a portion of the network, or to access the cloud console.

End-user applications often handle authorization themselves. For example, there may be a database row or document for each user listing the access level that user has. This makes some sense, because each application may have specific functions to authorize, but it means that you have to visit every application to see all of the access a user has.

The most important concepts to remember for authorization are *least privilege* and *separation of duties*. As a reminder, least privilege means that your users, systems, or tools should be able to access only what they need to do their jobs, and no more. In practice, this usually means that you have a "deny by default" policy in place, so that unless you specifically authorize something, it's not allowed.

Separation (or segregation) of duties actually comes from the world of financial controls, where two signatures may be needed for checks over a certain amount. In the world of cloud security, this usually translates more generally into making sure that no one person can completely undermine the security of the entire environment. For example, someone with the ability to make changes on systems should not also have the ability to alter the logs from those systems, or the responsibility for reviewing the logs from those systems.

For cloud services and internal applications, *centralized authorization* is becoming more popular.

Centralized Authorization

The problems with the old, ad hoc practice of scattering identities all over the place have been solved through federated identities and single sign-on. However, you may still have authorization records scattered all over the place—every application may be keeping its own record of who's allowed to do what in that application.

You can deauthorize someone completely by deleting their identity (assuming persistent access tokens don't keep them authorized for a while), but what about revoking only some access? The ability to remove someone's identity is important, but it's a pretty heavy-handed way to perform access management. You often need more fine-grained ways to manage access. Centralized authorization can let you see and control what your users have access to in a single place.

In a traditional application, all of the authorization work was performed internally in the application. In the world of centralized authorization, the responsibilities typically get divided up between the application and the centralized authorization system. There are more details in some systems, but here are the basic components:

Policy Enforcement Point (PEP)
> This point is implemented in the application, where the application controls access. If you don't have the specified access in the policy, the service or application won't let you perform that function. The application checks for access by asking the Policy Decision Point for a decision.

Policy Decision Point (PDP)
> This point is implemented in the centralized authorization system. The PDP takes the information provided by the application (such as identity and requested function), consults its policy, and gives the application its decision on whether access is granted for that particular function.

Policy Administration Point (PAP)
> This point is also implemented in the centralized authorization system. This is usually a web user interface and associated API where you can tell the centralized authorization system who's allowed to do what.

Most cloud providers have a centralized access management solution that their services will consult for access decisions, rather than making the decisions on their own. You should use these mechanisms where available, so that you can see all of the access granted to a particular administrator in one place.

Roles

Many cloud providers offer *roles* or *trusted profiles*, which are similar to shared IDs in that you assume a role, perform actions that role allows, and drop the role. This is slightly different from the traditional definition of a role, which is a set of permissions or entitlements granted to a user or group.

The primary difference between shared IDs and cloud provider roles is that a shared ID is a standalone identity with fixed credentials. A cloud provider role is not a full identity; it is a special status taken on by another identity that is authorized to access a role, and is then assigned temporary credentials to access that role.

Role-based access can add an additional layer of security by requiring users or services to explicitly assume a separate role for more privileged operations, following the principle of least privilege. Most of the time the user can't perform those privileged activities unless they explicitly put on the role "hat" and take it off when they're done. The system can also log each request to take on a role, so administrators can later determine who had that role at a particular time and compare that information to actions on the system that have security consequences.

People aren't the only entities who can assume roles. Some components (such as virtual machines) can assume a role when created and perform actions using the privileges assigned to that role.

Revalidate

At this point, your users and automation should have identities and be authorized to do only what they need to do. You need to make sure that this withstands the test of time.

As previously mentioned, the revalidation step is very important in both traditional and cloud environments, but in cloud environments you may not have any additional controls (such as physical building access or network controls) to save you if you forget to revoke access. You need to periodically check each authorization to ensure that it still needs to be there.

The first type of revalidation is automated revalidation based on certain parameters. For example, you should have a system that automatically puts in a request to revoke all access when someone leaves the organization. Note that simply deleting the user's identity may not be sufficient, because the user may have cached credentials such as access tokens that can be used even without the ability to log in. In situations like this, you need an *offboarding feed*, which is a list of entities whose access should be revoked. Any system that hands out longer-lived credentials such as access tokens must process this offboarding feed at least daily and immediately revoke those entities' access.

The second type of revalidation requires human judgment to determine whether a particular entity still needs access. There are generally two types of judgment-based revalidation:

Positive confirmation
> This is stronger—it means that access is lost unless someone explicitly says, "This access is still needed."

Negative confirmation
> This is weaker—it means that access is retained unless someone says, "This access is no longer needed."

Negative confirmation is appropriate for lower-impact authorization levels, but for types of access with high impact to the business, you should use positive confirmation. The drawbacks to positive confirmation are that it's more work, and access may be accidentally revoked if the request isn't processed in time (which may cause operational issues).

The largest risk addressed by revalidation is that someone who has left the organization (perhaps under contentious circumstances) retains access to systems. In addition to this, though, access tends to accumulate over time, like junk in the kitchen junk drawer (you know the one). Revalidation clears out this junk.

However, note that if it's difficult to get access, your users will often claim they still need access, even if they no longer do. Your revalidation efforts will be much more effective at pruning unnecessary access if you also have a fast, easy process for granting access when needed. If that's not possible, then it may be more effective to automatically revoke access if not used for a certain period of time instead of asking if it's still needed. This also has risks, because you may find nobody available has access when needed!

Cloud Identity-as-a-Service offerings are increasingly offering management of the entire identity life cycle in addition to authentication and authorization services. In other words, providers are recognizing the importance of the relationship's ending as well as the relationship's beginning, and they are helping to streamline and formalize endings.

What Are All These Tools?

The names of the various tools to help with secrets and identity management can be confusing. There is some disagreement on naming, and many products perform more than one function, but here's a cheat sheet with some of the most common names and functions:

- A *password wallet* is something individuals use to securely store passwords and automatically fill them in. Some password wallet programs also have the ability to share passwords with other users.

- A *credential vault, privileged access management system,* or *privileged identity management system* is a system that allows individuals (and sometimes automation) to store credentials, check them out, and use them. A main point is to ensure individual accountability, so that you know which entity is using a credential at any given time. The system may also perform other functions, such as discovering existing privileged accounts, recording sessions, or controlling what commands can be issued.

- A *directory service* keeps a list of users and groups, and usually has a way to authenticate them. Directory services are now often a component of other products.

- An *identity access management* system or *identity provider* is a system that can perform many of the types of authentication covered earlier, and that implements federation protocols such as SAML and OIDC.

- An *identity governance* system is a system that handles the request, approval, and revalidation parts of the life cycle; it may also have other functionality, such as helping you find separation of duties issues or simplify roles.

- A *secrets management* system is mostly geared toward securely storing credentials for automation to use, although individuals may also use it. It's often part of a deployment pipeline that allows the new deployment to get the secrets it needs to function.

- An *encryption key management* system is specifically geared toward secrets that are encryption keys, and will also allow you to perform functions like generating keys securely and performing wrap/unwrap functions with keys.

- A *certificate management* system is specifically geared toward X.509 certificates; it may allow you to generate and sign them and notify you when they're about to expire.

Putting It All Together in the Sample Application

Remember our simple web application from Chapter 1? Let's add identity and access management information to the diagram, which now looks like Figure 4-3. I've removed the whole application trust boundary to simplify the diagram. A description of the steps, many of which have multiple parts, follows.

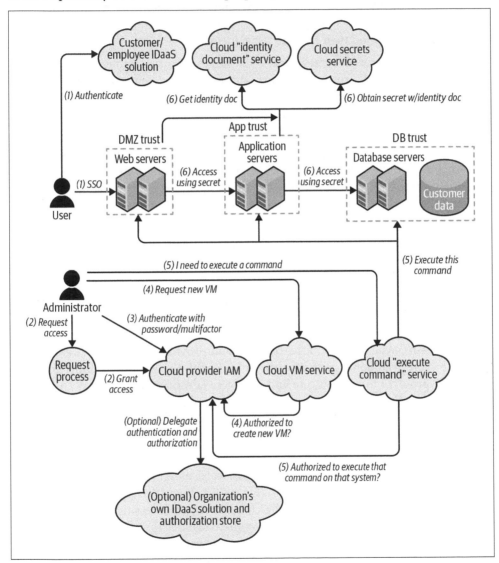

Figure 4-3. Sample application diagram with IAM

Unfortunately, that complicated the diagram quite a bit! Let's look at some of the new interactions in detail:

1. The end user attempts to access the application and is automatically approved for access by virtue of having a valid identity and optionally passing some anti-fraud tests. The user logs in with SSO, so the application identity is federated with the user's external identity provider, and the application doesn't have to validate passwords. From the user's perspective, they're using the same identity as they do at their company or on their favorite social media site.

2. The administrator requests access to administer the application, which is approved. The administrator is then authorized in a centralized authorization system. The authorization may take place within the cloud's IAM system, or the cloud's IAM system may be configured to ask the organization's own internal authorization system to perform the authorization.

3. The administrator authenticates with the cloud IAM service using a strong password and multi-factor authentication and gets an access token to give to any other services. Again, optionally, the cloud IAM service may be configured to send the user to the organization's internal authentication system.

4. The administrator makes requests to cloud provider services, such as to create a new virtual machine or container. (Behind the scenes, the cloud VM service asks the cloud IAM service whether the administrator is authorized.)

5. The administrator uses a cloud provider service to execute commands on the virtual machines or containers as needed. (Behind the scenes, the cloud "execute command" service asks the cloud's IAM service whether the administrator is authorized to execute that command on that virtual machine or container.) If this feature isn't available from a particular cloud provider, the administrator might use a more traditional method, such as SSH, with the virtual machine using the LDAP protocol to authenticate and authorize administrators against an identity store. Note that in a container environment, executing commands may not even be needed for normal maintenance and upgrades, because the administrator can deploy a new container and delete the old one rather than making changes to the existing container.

6. A secrets service is used to hold the password or API key for the application server to access the database system. Figure 4-3 shows the application server getting an identity document from the cloud provider, accessing the secrets server directly to get the secret, and accessing the database. If the database will accept the identity document directly, you may not even need the secrets server! The same process could happen for the authentication between the web server and the application server, but only one secrets service interaction is shown for

simplicity. The secrets service may be run by the organization, or may be an as-a-service offering from a cloud provider.

Note that every time one of our application's trust boundaries is crossed, the entity crossing the trust boundary must be authenticated and authorized in order to perform an action. There are other trust boundaries outside the application that are not pictured, such as the trust boundaries around the cloud and organization systems.

Conclusion

Many organizations have historically been somewhat lax about identity and access management in on-premises environments, and have relied too much upon other controls (such as physical security and network controls). However, IAM is supremely important in cloud environments. Although the concepts are similar in both cloud and on-premises deployments, there are new technologies and cloud services that improve security and make the job easier.

In the whole identity and access life cycle, it is easy to forget about the request, approval, and revalidation steps. Although they can be performed manually, many as-a-service offerings that initially handled only the authentication and authorization steps now provide workflows for the approval step as well, and this trend is accelerating.

Centralized authentication systems give administrators and end users a single identity to be used across many different applications and services. While these have been around in different forms for a long time, they are even more necessary in cloud environments, where they are available by default. Given the proliferation of cloud systems and services, managing identities individually for each system and service can quickly become a nightmare in all but the smallest deployments. Old, forgotten identities may be used by their former owners or by attackers looking for an easy way in. Even with centralized authentication, you must still use good passwords and multifactor authentication. Cloud administrators and end users often authenticate via different systems.

As with the authentication systems, centralized authorization systems allow you to see and modify everything an entity is authorized to do in one place. This can make granting and revalidating access easier, and make separation of duties conflicts more obvious. Make sure you follow the principles of least privilege and separation of duties when authorizing both people and automation for tasks, and avoid having super-powered identities and credentials for daily use.

Secrets management is a quickly maturing field, where secrets used for system-to-system access are maintained separately from other configuration data and handled according to strict principles of confidentiality and auditing. In some cases, system-to-system authentication can be performed using identity documents, which can reduce the need to have separately maintained secrets. Secrets management capabilities are available in existing configuration management products, standalone secrets server products, and as-a-service cloud offerings.

Now that you understand how to avoid one of the biggest causes of breaches—insufficient identity and access management—let's look at one of the other biggest causes, insufficient vulnerability management.

Exercises

1. What steps are commonly used in an access management life cycle? Select all that apply.

   a. Request access

   b. Approve access

   c. Use access

   d. Revalidate access

2. Which of the following statements about authentication is true?

   a. Authentication is about proving that you are who you say you are.

   b. Authentication is all you need to access an application.

   c. API keys can be used for multi-factor authentication.

   d. Authentication is not required for internal communications.

3. Which of the following statements about authorization are true? Select all that apply.

   a. Authorization is about being allowed to access a particular application or take a particular action.

   b. Unless everyone is authorized for a particular action, authorization is only useful when combined with authentication.

   c. Authorization can be effective when either centralized or decentralized.

4. Which of the following are true statements about cloud identity services? Select all that apply.

   a. A cloud identity service usually provides a central service that can authenticate users.

   b. A cloud identity service usually provides a central service that can authorize users.

   c. A cloud identity service usually provides a central service for storing secrets.

   d. Cloud identity services come in multiple forms, such as business-to-consumer and business-to-employee.

5. Which of the following statements about federation and single sign-on are true? Select all that apply.

    a. Federation and single sign-on are different technologies that accomplish similar goals.

    b. Federated identity is the concept of linking identities together on two different systems.

    c. Single sign-on is a way to use federated identities.

    d. Single sign-on is easier for users, but often comes with a trade-off of lower security.

CHAPTER 5

Vulnerability Management

In Greek mythology, Achilles was killed by an arrow to his only weak spot—his heel. Achilles clearly needed a better vulnerability management plan![1] Unlike Achilles, who had only one vulnerable area, your cloud environments will have many different areas where vulnerabilities can appear. After locking down access control, setting up a continuous process for managing potential vulnerabilities is usually the best investment in focus, time, and money that you can make to improve security.

There is considerable overlap between vulnerability management and patch management. For many organizations, the most important reason to install patches is to fix vulnerabilities rather than to fix functional bugs or add features. There is also considerable overlap between vulnerability management and configuration management, since incorrect configurations can often lead to vulnerabilities, even if you've dutifully installed all security patches. There are sometimes different tools and processes for managing vulnerabilities, configuration, and patches, but in the interests of practicality, we'll cover them all together in this chapter.

Unfortunately, vulnerability management is rarely as easy as turning on automatic patching and walking away. In cloud environments, vulnerabilities may be found in many different layers, including the physical facilities, the compute hardware, the operating system, code you've written, and libraries you've included. The cloud shared responsibility model described in Chapter 1 can help you understand where your cloud provider is responsible for vulnerabilities, and the contents of this chapter will help you manage your responsibilities. In most cases, you'll need several different tools and processes to deal with different types of vulnerabilities.

---

1 Perhaps one that included wearing boots.

> ## Vulnerability Versus Patch Management
>
> The terms "vulnerability management" and "patch management" are often used inter-changeably, but they are different. Software patches often fix functional issues in addition to security vulnerabilities, and not all vulnerabilities are fixed by applying patches. For example, your vulnerability management process might identify insecure configurations that are fixed without patching, or it might mitigate a vulnerability by turning off a feature rather than applying a patch.

Differences from Traditional IT

The rate of change is often much higher in cloud environments compared to on-premises, and these constant changes can leave traditional vulnerability management processes in the dust. As discussed in Chapter 3, you must use inventory from cloud APIs to feed each system into your vulnerability management tools as it is created, to avoid missing new systems as they come online.

In addition to the rate of change, popular contemporary hosting models such as containers and serverless hosts change the way that you do vulnerability management, because existing tools either aren't applicable or aren't efficient. If you have a lot of containers, you cannot put a heavyweight vulnerability management tool that uses a few percent of your CPU in every container, like you would in virtual machines. You'd likely end up running hundreds of copies of the agent on the system and have no CPU time left for the real work!

Plus, even though continuous integration (CI), continuous delivery (CD), and micro-service architectures are separate from cloud computing, they often happen along with cloud adoption. Adoption of these techniques can also radically change vulnerability management.

For example, a traditional vulnerability management process might look something like this:

1. *Discover* that security updates or configuration changes are available.
2. *Prioritize* which updates need to be implemented based on the risk of security incidents.
3. *Test* that the updates work, in a test environment.
4. *Schedule* the updates for a production environment.
5. *Deploy* the updates to production.
6. *Verify* that production still works.

This type of process is reasonably designed to balance the risk of a security incident against the risk of an availability incident in production environments. As I often like to tell people, security is easy—just turn everything off and bury it in concrete. Securing environments while keeping them running and usable is much more difficult.

However, in our brave new world of cloud computing, infrastructure as code, CI/CD, and microservice architectures, we have options for reducing the risk of an availability incident and changing the balance:

- Cloud offerings and infrastructure as code allow the definition of the environment to be part of the code.[2] This allows a new environment and new code to be tested together, rather than combining the environment and the code at the end when you install on an existing machine. In addition, because you can create a new production environment for each deployment and switch back to (or recreate) the old one easily if needed, you can reduce the risk of getting into a state where you cannot roll back quickly. This is similar to "blue/green" deployments in traditional environments,[3] but with the cloud you don't need to pay for the "green" environment all the time, so infrastructure as code can be used even for smaller, lower-budget applications.

- Continuous integration and continuous delivery allow smaller changes to be deployed to production on each iteration. Smaller changes reduce the risk of catastrophic failures and make troubleshooting easier for problems that do arise.

- Microservice architectures can decouple services, so that changes in one microservice are less likely to have undesired side effects in other microservices. This is especially true in container-based microservice environments, because each container is isolated from the others.

- Microservice architectures also tend to scale horizontally, where the application is deployed across more machines and containers as needed to handle the load. This also means that changes can be rolled out in phases across the environment, and bugs that got missed in testing or potentially disruptive scans[4] will take down only some of the capacity of the application.

---

2 For example, all major cloud providers can be used with HashiCorp Terraform, and AWS also has its proprietary CloudFormation.

3 A blue/green deployment is where you have old (blue) and new (green) versions of an application running at the same time. You move traffic a little at a time from the blue version to the green version, so that any issues with the new version don't impact all of your customers at once and you can quickly move everyone back to blue if something is wrong with the new version.

4 One of the barriers to vulnerability scanning is that if you actually find a vulnerability, sometimes the scan will crash the affected component. Sure, you found a problem, but at the cost of incurring downtime! The risk of an outage is much lower if the scan can only crash one of the instances of the application at a time.

Each of these items swings the balance toward higher availability, which means that security updates can be more proactive while still raising the overall availability of the system. This in turn reduces your overall risk. The new vulnerability management process looks like this:

1. *Automatically pull* available security updates as part of normal development efforts. For example, this might include updated code libraries or updated operating system components. Note that if you're doing this regularly, the changes will tend to be smaller and easier to digest.

2. *Test* the updates along with other application changes as part of the normal application test flow for a deployment. Only if you find a problem at this stage do you need to step back to evaluate whether the updates need to be included.

3. *Deploy* the new version, which automatically creates a new production environment that includes code changes, security updates, and potentially updates to the configuration. In many cases, this new deployment will only get a small subset of the production traffic initially, so that if there is an issue it will only affect a small subset of the users before being rolled back.

4. *Discover* and address any additional vulnerabilities in test or production environments that aren't covered as part of the normal delivery process, add them as bugs to the development backlog, and address them in the next iteration (or as a special release if really urgent).

You still have some manual vulnerability management work to do in step 4, but far less than in the standard process. As you'll see in this chapter, there are many types of vulnerabilities, but this high-level process will work for most.

Vulnerable Areas

What types of vulnerabilities do you have to worry about? Imagine that your application is part of a stack of components, with the application on top and physical computers and facilities at the bottom. We'll start at the top of the stack and work downward. There are many different ways to categorize the items in the stack, but we'll use the shared responsibility model diagram from Chapter 1 (see Figure 5-1).

Let's look at each layer of this diagram in more detail from the perspective of vulnerability management, starting at the top. Your responsibilities will differ depending on the delivery model (IaaS, PaaS, or SaaS).

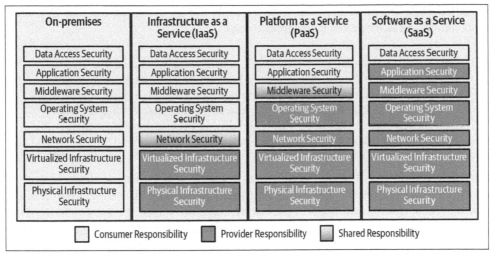

On-premises	Infrastructure as a Service (IaaS)	Platform as a Service (PaaS)	Software as a Service (SaaS)
Data Access Security	Data Access Security	Data Access Security	Data Access Security
Application Security	Application Security	Application Security	Application Security
Middleware Security	Middleware Security	Middleware Security	Middleware Security
Operating System Security	Operating System Security	Operating System Security	Operating System Security
Network Security	Network Security	Network Security	Network Security
Virtualized Infrastructure Security	Virtualized Infrastructure Security	Virtualized Infrastructure Security	Virtualized Infrastructure Security
Physical Infrastructure Security	Physical Infrastructure Security	Physical Infrastructure Security	Physical Infrastructure Security

☐ Consumer Responsibility   ■ Provider Responsibility   ☐ Shared Responsibility

Figure 5-1. Cloud shared responsibility model

Data Access

Consumer responsibility for IaaS, PaaS, and SaaS

Deciding how to grant access to the data in the application or service is almost always the customer's responsibility in a cloud environment. Vulnerabilities at the data access layer almost always boil down to access management problems, such as leaving resources open to the public, leaving access intact for individuals who no longer need it, or using poor credentials. These issues were discussed in detail in Chapter 4.

Application

Consumer responsibility for IaaS and PaaS

If you're using SaaS, the security of the application code will be your provider's responsibility, but there may be security-relevant configuration items that you're responsible for as a customer. For example, if you're using a web email system, it will be up to you to determine and set reasonable configurations such as two-factor authentication or malware scanning. You also need to track and correct these configurations if they drift from your requirements.

If you're not using SaaS, you are probably writing some sort of application code, whether it's hosted on virtual machines, an aPaaS, or a serverless offering. No matter how good your team is, your code is almost certainly going to have some bugs, and at least some of those bugs are likely to impact security. In addition to your own code, you're often going to be using frameworks, libraries, and other code provided by third parties that may contain vulnerabilities. Vulnerabilities or malware in this inherited code are often more likely to be exploited by attackers, because the same basic attack will work across many applications.

 Vulnerabilities in popular open source components, such as Log4j, Apache Struts, and OpenSSL, have led to vulnerabilities in many applications that use those components. Exploiting these vulnerabilities is much easier for attackers than researching specific application code, so they tend to be an even higher risk than vulnerabilities in code you've written!

The classic example of an application vulnerability is a buffer overflow. However, many applications are now written in languages that make buffer overflows difficult, so while these attacks still happen, they don't make the top of the list any more. Following are a few examples of application vulnerabilities from the OWASP Top 10 list for 2021. In each of these examples, access controls, firewalls, and other security measures are largely ineffective in protecting the system if these vulnerabilities are present in the application code:

Broken access control

Whereas the Data Access section deals with errors in granting access, this deals with errors in the application code that actually enforces that access. A very common error for web applications is trusting something the browser is telling you, such as "I have verified that the parameter in this field is safe," when the browser is completely under the attacker's control and can't be trusted. Cross-site scripting is one example of this class of errors.

Injection attacks

This is when your application gets a piece of untrusted data from a malicious user and sends it to some sort of interpreter. A classic example is SQL injection, where the attacker sends information that causes the query to return everything in the table instead of what was intended.

Vulnerable and outdated components

If you're using a component in your application and the component has a vulnerability, your application is also likely to be vulnerable. Log4j is the one of the best-known examples of this, where a vulnerability in a seemingly harmless logging package allowed anyone to take over an application if they could get the application to put a particular string into the application logs.

Secure Software Standards and Frameworks

It can be difficult to know if the components and applications that you're using contain accidental vulnerabilities, or even malware that's been purposefully injected. There are several industry efforts aimed at helping with this problem.

Standards such as the NIST Secure Software Development Framework (SSDF) (*https://oreil.ly/HFyDp*) are similar to food safety standards, but for software; they provide requirements for producing secure software. These standards typically tell you what you need to accomplish, but not how to accomplish it.

A Software Bill of Materials (SBOM) is like an ingredients label for software, and can tell you what went into an application or component. This can make automated scanning for vulnerabilities in your dependencies much more accurate. Several tools can now generate and consume SBOMs, and at the time of this writing, there are two popular SBOM formats, CycloneDX (*https://cyclonedx.org*) and SPDX (*https://spdx.dev*). SBOMs are required by some standards, including the NIST SSDF, and are likely to be contractually required by organizations purchasing software in the future.

Security frameworks such as Supply-chain Levels for Software Artifacts (SLSA) (*https://slsa.dev*) provide a set of guidelines on how to secure your development and build environments and digitally sign applications and components. These can tell you how to meet some of the requirements in the standards, and if you're consuming components, the SLSA level can give you an idea of how mature the process for producing each component is.

Note that application-level attacks are possible regardless of how your application is deployed—on a virtual machine, on an aPaaS, or on a serverless platform. Some tools discussed in Chapter 6, such as web application firewalls, may be able to act as a safety net if there is a vulnerability in application code. However, make no mistake—quickly detecting and fixing vulnerable code and dependencies is your first and most important line of defense.

Although web application frameworks such as React can be a source of vulnerabilities you have to manage, they can also help you avoid vulnerabilities in your own code. Many frameworks have built-in protections against cross-site scripting (XSS), cross-site request forgery (CSRF), SQL injection (SQLi), clickjacking, and other types of attacks. Understanding the protections offered by your framework and using them can easily enable you to avoid some of these issues.

Middleware

Consumer responsibility for IaaS and some PaaS

In many cases, your application code uses middleware or platform components, such as databases, application servers, or message queues. Just as with dependent frameworks or libraries, vulnerabilities here can cause you big problems because they're attractive to attackers—the attacker can exploit that same vulnerability across many different applications, often without having to understand the applications at all.

If you're running these components yourself, you'll need to watch for updates, test them, and apply them. These components might be running directly on your virtual machines, or they might be inside containers you've deployed. Note that tools that work for inventorying what's installed on virtual machines will usually not find items installed in containers.

If the components are provided as a service by your cloud provider, your provider will usually have the responsibility for patching. However, there's a catch! In some cases, the updates won't be pushed to you automatically, because they could cause an outage. In those cases, you may still be responsible for testing and then pushing the button to deploy the updates at a convenient time.

In addition to applying patches, you also need to worry about how middleware is configured, even in a PaaS environment. Here are some real-world examples of middleware/platform configuration issues that can lead to a security incident or breach:

- A web server is accidentally configured to allow viewing of the password file.
- A database is not configured for the correct type of authentication, allowing anyone to act as a database manager.
- A Java application server is configured to provide debug output, which reveals a password when a bug is encountered.

For each component you use, you need to examine the configuration settings available and make a list of security-relevant settings and what the correct values are. These should be enforced when the component is initially brought into service and then checked regularly afterward to make sure they're all still set correctly and prevent "configuration drift." This kind of manual monitoring is often called *benchmarking*, *health checking*, or simply *configuration management*.

While you can certainly write benchmarks or configuration specifications from scratch, I recommend starting with a common set of best practices, such as the Center for Internet Security's CIS Benchmarks (*https://oreil.ly/BNjmr*). You can tailor these for your organization and deployments, and even contribute a change if you find a problem or want to suggest an enhancement. Because the benchmarks are a community-based effort, you're more likely to benefit from up-to-date configuration checks that take into account new threats and new versions of platform products and operating systems. Several popular products can perform the CIS Benchmarks checks out of the box.

Operating System

Consumer responsibility for IaaS

Operating system patches are what many people think of when they think of vulnerability management. It's Patch Tuesday,[5] time to test the patches and roll them out! But while operating system patches are an important part of vulnerability management, they're not the only consideration.

Just as with the middleware/platform layer of the stack, you must make sure the configuration is correct in addition to patching. You can do this by having benchmarks for the OS configurations that are set when deploying the operating system instance and then checked regularly afterward.

In addition, operating systems tend to ship with a lot of different components that are not needed in your environment. Leaving these components in a running instance can be a big source of vulnerabilities, either from bugs or misconfiguration, so it's important to turn off anything that's not required. This is often referred to as *hardening*. One advantage with containers is that you often start with a minimal container image and only install what you need for the application to run in the container, a process that hardens the container by default.

Many cloud providers have a catalog of virtual machine images that are automatically kept up to date, so that you should get a reasonably up-to-date system when deploying. However, if the cloud provider doesn't automatically apply patches upon deployment, you should do so as part of your deployment process.

---

5 In 2003, Microsoft decided to collect all of the patches from the previous month and release them on the second Tuesday of the month, and many other companies followed suit. The rumor is that Tuesdays were chosen because they give plenty of time to avoid ruining the weekend, and Mondays are already bad enough.

An operating system typically consists of a *kernel*, which runs all other programs, along with many different userspace programs. Many containers also contain the userspace portions of the operating system, and so operating system vulnerability management and configuration management also factor into container security.

In most cases, the cloud provider is responsible for the hypervisors. However, if you're responsible for any hypervisors, they're also included in this category because they're essentially special-purpose operating systems designed to hold other operating systems. Hypervisors are typically already hardened, but they do still require regular patching and have configuration settings that need to be benchmarked and set correctly for your environment.

Network

Consumer responsibility for IaaS

Vulnerability management at the network layer involves two main tasks: managing the network components themselves and managing which network communications are allowed.

The network components themselves, such as routers, firewalls, and switches, typically require patch management and security configuration management similar to operating systems, but often through different tools.

Managing the security of the network flows going through those devices is discussed in detail in Chapter 6.

Virtualized Infrastructure

Provider responsibility

In an Infrastructure-as-a-Service environment, the virtualized infrastructure (virtual network, virtual machines, storage) will be the responsibility of your cloud provider. However, in a container-based environment, you may have security responsibility for the virtualized infrastructure or platform on top of the one offered by the cloud provider. For example, vulnerabilities may be caused by misconfiguration or missing patches of the container runtime, such as Docker, or the orchestration layer, such as Kubernetes.

Physical Infrastructure

Provider responsibility

In most cases, physical infrastructure will be the responsibility of your cloud provider. There are a few cases where you may be responsible for configuration or vulnerability management at the physical level, however. If you are running a private cloud, or if you get bare-metal systems provisioned as a service, you may have some physical infrastructure responsibilities. For example, vulnerabilities can be caused by missing BIOS/microcode updates or poor security configuration of the baseboard management controller that allows remote management of the physical system.

Finding and Fixing Vulnerabilities

Now that you're armed with an understanding of all of the places vulnerabilities might be hiding, you need to identify which types of vulnerabilities are most likely to be a problem in your environment. As I've repeated several times in this book, go for the biggest bang for the buck first—pick the most important area for your organization, and get value from it before moving on to other areas. A common pitfall is having four or five different sets of tools and processes in place just so you can check off some boxes on a list of best practices somewhere, none of which are actually providing a lot of value in finding and fixing vulnerabilities.

If you recall the asset management pipeline discussed in Chapter 3, this is the part where we put our fancy tools into the pipeline (Figure 5-2) to make sure we know about and deal appropriately with our risks.

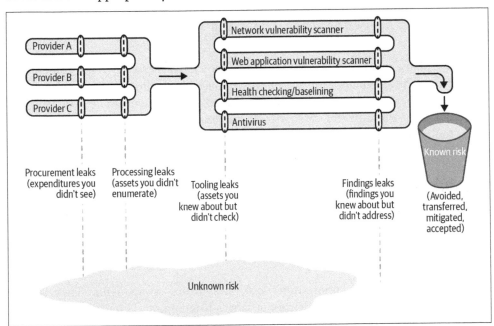

Figure 5-2. Sample asset management pipeline

In Chapter 3, we were concerned with the left half of the diagram—watching procurement to find out about shadow IT and making sure we inventoried the assets from all the different cloud providers. Here, the goal is to plug the leaks shown on the right half of the diagram. For example, this is where we can minimize our "tooling" leaks (which result from not protecting known assets) as well as our "findings" leaks (which result from not properly dealing with known findings).

First, look at the tooling leaks area of the figure. Imagine the sizes of the pipes in your environment as being determined by a combination of how many problems you might find in these areas, as well as how critical to the business those problems might be. I've found that when I imagine this, I sometimes realize that there is a lot of water gushing out in a particular area, either because there's no tool in that area or because the tool doesn't have visibility to a lot of assets. This can lead to a lot of unknown risk!

For example, if your environment contains a lot of Windows systems with critical data, fixing leaks in your antivirus pipeline might be near the top of your list. On the other hand, if you have mostly web applications running on Linux, an aPaaS, or a serverless platform, you probably want to focus on making sure you find and remediate web application vulnerabilities first before worrying too much about a small number of Windows systems that have less-critical data.

Next, look at the findings leaks area of the figure. This time, imagine that the sizes of the pipes are determined by the number of findings coming out of each tool and how critical those findings might be. You may realize that you have tools from which you're ignoring a lot of important output, and you're therefore creating a lot of unknown risk.

There are many, many different types of tools, which overlap a lot in the vulnerabilities they search for. Some of the tools have been used in traditional environments for years, and others are newly introduced by cloud environments. The following are explanations of the different categories of vulnerability and configuration management tools, but note that many products will address more than one of these categories.

Network Vulnerability Scanners

Alongside operating system patches, *network vulnerability scans* are the other best-known piece of vulnerability management. This is for a good reason—they're very good at finding some types of vulnerabilities—but it's important to understand their limitations.

Network vulnerability scanners don't look at software components. They simply make network requests, try to figure out what's listening, and check for vulnerable versions of server applications or vulnerable configurations. As an example, a network vulnerability scanner could determine that one of the services on a system is allowing insecure connections, which would make the system vulnerable to a POODLE attack (*https://oreil.ly/DDsB4*), based on the information in an SSL/TLS handshake. The scanner can't know, however, about the different web applications or

REST APIs served up on that network address, nor can it see components such as library versions inside the system.

Obviously, network vulnerability scanners cannot scan the entire internet, or your entire cloud provider, and magically know which systems are your responsibility. You have to provide these tools with lists of network addresses to scan, and if you've missed any addresses, you're going to have vulnerabilities you don't know about. This is where the automated inventory management discussed in Chapter 3 is vital. Because many cloud components are open to the internet, and because attackers can exploit vulnerabilities that they discover in common components very quickly, your cycle time for inventorying internet-facing components, scanning them, and fixing any findings needs to be as fast as possible.

In addition, don't make the mistake of thinking network vulnerability scans are unnecessary just because you have isolated components, which will be described in Chapter 6. There is often a debate between network teams and vulnerability scanning teams on whether to poke holes in the firewall to allow the vulnerability scanner into a restricted area. I maintain that the risk of having an unknown vulnerability is much higher than the risk that an attacker will leverage those specific firewall rules to get into the restricted area, so vulnerability scanners should be allowed to scan every component, even if it means weakening the perimeter network controls very slightly. I have seen many incidents where an attacker got behind the perimeter and exploited a vulnerable system there. In contrast, although it has probably happened some-where, I have not personally seen or heard of any incidents where the attacker took over the scanner and used its network access to attack systems.

Network vulnerabilities found on a segment of a protected virtual private cloud net-work have a lower priority than vulnerabilities on a component directly exposed to the internet, but you should still discover them and fix them. Attackers have a very inconvenient habit of ending up in parts of the network where they're not supposed to be.

Depending on how your deployment pipeline works, you should incorporate a net-work vulnerability scan of the test environment into the deployment process where possible. Any findings in the test environment should feed into a bug tracker, and if not marked as a false positives, they should ideally block the deployment.

There are several cloud-based network vulnerability scanners that you can purchase and run as a service, without purchasing any infrastructure. However, you may need to create relay systems or containers inside your network for scanning areas that are not open to the internet.

Network-based tools can find vulnerabilities without knowing what processes they're talking to; they just see what process answers on different TCP/UDP ports on a given IP address. They're very useful because they see the same things an external attacker will see. However, this can also generate false positives, because the tool will often use the reported version of a component, which may not be correct or may not indicate that security patches have been installed. You must have a well-documented, effective process for masking false positives, or you run the risk of teams ignoring all of the scan results because some of them are incorrect.

Agentless Scanners and Configuration Management Systems

If network vulnerability scanners bang on the doors and windows of the house, agentless scanners and configuration management systems come inside the house and poke around. Agentless scanners also connect over the network, but use credentials to get into the systems being tested. The term "agentless" distinguishes these scanners from the ones described in the next section, which require an "agent" to run on each target system. In some cases, one tool may perform both network scans and agentless/agent scans.

When using agentless scanners, remember the least privilege principle and give the scanner credentials with the minimum permissions needed to perform the scan. Unfortunately, many scanners need full administrative privileges to function, but this is beginning to change, and some scanners have a "least privilege" option.

Agentless scanners can find vulnerabilities that network vulnerability scanners can't. For example, if you have a local privilege escalation vulnerability that allows a normal user to take over the entire system, a network vulnerability scanner won't have the "normal user" privileges needed to see it, but an agentless scanner does.

Agentless scanners often perform both missing patch detection and security configuration management, as the following examples show:

- The agentless scanner may run package manager commands to check that installed software is up to date and has important security fixes. For instance, some versions of the Linux kernel or C libraries have problems that allow someone without *root* privileges to become *root*; these problems can be detected by up-to-date scanners.

- The agentless scanner may check that security configurations are correct and meet policy requirements. For example, the system may be configured to allow Telnet connections (which could allow someone snooping on the network to see passwords, and therefore should be prohibited by policy); the scanner should detect that Telnet is enabled and flag an alert.

In some cases, these tools can actually fix misconfigurations or vulnerable packages in addition to just detecting the problems. But as mentioned earlier, such automated fixes can disrupt availability if they introduce new problems or don't match your environment's requirements. Where possible, it's preferable to roll out an entirely new system that doesn't have the vulnerability rather than trying to fix it in place.

With all of this capability, why would you need both an agentless scanner and a network vulnerability scanner? Although there's a lot of overlap, agentless scanners fundamentally have to understand the system they're looking at, which means that they don't function well on operating system versions, software, or other items they don't recognize. The fact that network vulnerability scanners are "dumber" and only bang on network addresses is actually a strength in some cases, because they can find issues with anything on the network—even devices that allow no logins, such as network appliances, IoT devices, or containers.

Agent-Based Scanners and Configuration Management Systems

Agent-based scanners and configuration management systems generally perform the same types of checks as agentless scanners. However, rather than having a central "pull" model, where a controller system reaches out to each system to be scanned and pulls the results in, agent-based scanners install a small component on each system—the agent—that "pushes" results to the controller.

There are both benefits and drawbacks to this approach, described in the following subsections.

Credentials

Agent-based scanners eliminate one source of risk inherent to agentless scanners by making it the problem of whoever or whatever is deploying the agents in the first place.

As mentioned in the previous section, agentless scanners must have credentials for all the systems they scan—and usually privileged credentials—in order to perform their scans. Although the risk of granting those credentials is generally much less than the risk of unknown vulnerabilities in your environment, it does make the agentless scanner a really attractive target for attackers. In contrast, agent-based scanners require privileges to deploy initially, but the scanner console just receives reports from the agents and has only whatever privileges the agent permits the console to use (which may still be full privileged access).

Deployment

Agents have to be deployed and kept up to date, and a vulnerability in the agent can put your entire infrastructure at risk. However, a well-designed agent in a "read-only" mode may be able to mitigate much of the impact of an attacker taking over the scanner console; the attacker will still get a wealth of vulnerability information but may not get privileged access on all systems.

Agentless scanners don't require you to deploy any code, but you often have to configure the target systems in order to provide access to the scanner. For example, you may need to create a user ID and provide that user ID with a certain level of *sudo* privileged access.

Network

Agentless scanners must have inbound network access in order to work. As previously mentioned, allowing this network access can increase the risk to your environment. Most tools also have the option of deploying a relay system inside your network that makes an outbound connection and allows control via that connection, but the relay system is another system that requires management.

Agent-based systems can make only outbound connections, without allowing any inbound connections. Outbound connections still have some risk, but it's often lower than the risk associated with inbound connections.

Least privilege

With both agentless and agent-based scanners, you can follow the principle of least privilege by allowing only the necessary privileges to the user ID that is used by the scanner or agent. However, some operating systems offer additional ways to limit what running processes are able to do, such as SELinux or AppArmor on Linux systems. These can be difficult to apply effectively, but tend to work better to limit what agents can do rather than individual scanner users.

Choosing an agent-based or agentless scanner

Some tools can perform checks using either an agent model or an agentless model. Which is best? Ultimately, there's no right answer for all deployments, but it's important to understand the benefits and drawbacks of each when making a decision. I typically favor an agent-based model, but there are good arguments for both sides, and the most important thing is that you address configuration and vulnerability management.

 Several cloud providers offer agent-based scanners in their support for your cloud environment. These can be simpler to automatically deploy, and you won't have to manually pull a list of assets from your cloud provider and feed them into the scanner.

Cloud Workload Protection Platforms

Tools in the cloud workload protection platform category are offered by both cloud providers and third parties. They usually gather configuration and vulnerability management information via agents or agentless methods, via the deployment pipeline, or from a third-party tool. They're typically marketed by the providers as a "one-stop dashboard" for multiple security functions, including access management, configuration management, and vulnerability management throughout the development and deployment phases.

These tools may also offer the ability to manage infrastructure or applications not hosted by the cloud provider—either on-premises or hosted by a different cloud provider—as an incentive to use them for your entire infrastructure. They're sometimes also called cloud native application protection platforms (CNAPPs).

Container Scanners

Traditional agentless and agent-based scanners work well for virtual machines, but often don't work well in container environments. Containers are intended to be very lightweight processes, and deploying an agent designed for a virtual machine environment in each container can lead to crippling performance and scalability issues. Also, if used correctly containers usually don't allow a traditional network login, meaning that agentless scanners designed for virtual machines will fail.

Two approaches are popular as of this writing. The first approach is to use scanners that pull apart the container images and look through them for vulnerabilities. If an image is rated as vulnerable, you know to avoid deploying new containers based on it and to replace any existing containers deployed from it. This has the benefit of not requiring any access to the production systems, but the drawback is that once you identify a vulnerable image, you must have good enough inventory information about all of your running containers to ensure you replace all of the vulnerable ones.

In addition, if your containers are mutable (change over time), additional vulnerabilities may have been introduced that scanning the source image won't reveal. For this reason and others, I recommend the use of immutable containers that are replaced by a new container whenever any change is needed. Regularly replacing containers can also help keep threat actors from persisting in your network, because even if they compromise a container, it will be wiped out in a week or so—and the new container will hopefully have a fix for the issue that led to the compromise.

The second approach is to concentrate on the running containers, using an agent on each container host that scans the containers on that system and reports which containers are vulnerable so that they may be fixed (or preferably, replaced). The benefit is that, if the agent is deployed everywhere, you cannot end up with "forgotten" containers that are still running a vulnerable image after you have created a new image with the fix. The primary downside, of course, is that you must have an agent on each host. This can potentially be a performance concern, and may not be supported by your provider if you're using a Container-as-a-Service offering.

These approaches are not mutually exclusive, and some tools use both. If you're using containers, or planning to use containers soon, make sure you have a way to scan for vulnerabilities in the images and/or running containers and feed the results into an issue tracking system.

Dynamic Application Scanners (DAST)

Network vulnerability scanners run against network addresses, but dynamic web application vulnerability scanners run against specific URLs of running web applications or REST APIs. *Dynamic application security testing* (DAST) tools can find issues such as cross-site scripting or SQL injection vulnerabilities by using the application or API like a user would. These scanners often require application credentials.

Some of the vulnerabilities found by dynamic scanners can also be blocked by web application firewalls (WAFs), as discussed in Chapter 6. That may allow you to put a lower priority on fixing the issues, but you should fix them fairly quickly anyway to offer security in depth. If the application systems aren't configured properly, an attacker might bypass the WAF and attack the application directly.

Dynamic scanners can generally be invoked automatically on a schedule, so that they can flag new known vulnerabilities that have been discovered. They can also be incorporated into a continuous deployment pipeline to run when changes are made to the application. DAST tools should feed their results into an issue tracking system rather than depending on someone to remember to check the report.

Static Application Scanners (SAST)

Whereas dynamic application scanners look at the running application, *static application security testing* (SAST) tools look directly at the code you've written. For this reason, they're a very good candidate for running as part of the deployment pipeline as soon as new code is committed, to provide immediate feedback. These tools can spot security-relevant errors such as memory leaks or off-by-one errors that can be very difficult for humans to see. Because they're analyzing the source code, you must use a scanner designed for the language that you're using. Luckily, scanners have been developed for a wide range of popular languages, and can be run as a service. The OWASP Source Code Analysis Tools page (*https://oreil.ly/w4vIb*) is a good resource for finding a tool that will work for your application.

The biggest problem with static scanners is that they tend to have a high false positive rate, which can lead to "security fatigue" in developers. If you deploy static code scanning as part of your deployment pipeline, make sure that it will work with the languages you're using and that developers can quickly and easily mask false positives so that they aren't overwhelmed with a lot of useless findings on every scan.

Software Composition Analysis Tools (SCA)

Arguably an extension of static code scanners, *software composition analysis* (SCA) tools look primarily at the open source dependencies that you use rather than the code you've written. Most applications today make heavy use of open source components such as frameworks and libraries, and vulnerabilities in those can cause big problems. SCA tools automatically identify the open source components and versions you are using, then cross-reference against known vulnerabilities for those versions. They can help you discover high-risk vulnerabilities in your dependencies, such as vulnerabilities in Log4j, Apache Struts, or the Spring Framework. Some tools can automatically propose code changes that use newer versions.

In addition to vulnerability management, some products can look at the licenses the open source components are using to ensure that you don't use components with unfavorable licensing. Some of these tools can also generate a Software Bill of Materials for your application, similar to an ingredients label for food. Some organizations, including the US federal government, now require an SBOM for any products that they purchase. The US government's guidance is laid out in the Software Supply Chain Security Guidance (*https://oreil.ly/jjqfF*) document, and it's likely that other governments and large organizations will adopt similar guidance in the future.

Interactive Application Scanners (IAST)

Interactive application security testing (IAST) tools do a little bit of both static scanning and dynamic scanning. They see what the code looks like and watch it from the inside while it runs. This is done by loading the IAST code alongside the application code to watch while the application is exercised by functional tests, a dynamic scanner, or real users. IAST solutions can often be more effective at finding problems and eliminating false positives than either SAST or DAST solutions.

Just like with static code scanners, the specific language and runtime you're using must be supported by the tool. Because this is running along with the application, it can decrease performance in production environments. With modern application infrastructure and deployments, that concern can usually be mitigated either by horizontal scaling or by having the deployment pipeline run the IAST tool in a test environment that mimics a production workload closely.

Runtime Application Self-Protection Scanners (RASP)

Runtime application self-protection (RASP) tools may sound similar to the scanners described previously, but this is not a scanning technology. RASP solutions, like IAST solutions, involve an agent deployed alongside your application code, but RASP tools are designed to block attacks rather than just detect vulnerabilities. (Several products do both—detect vulnerabilities and block attacks—making them both RASP and IAST solutions.) Like IAST tools, RASP tools can degrade performance in some cases because more code is running in the production environment.

RASP solutions offer some of the same protection as a distributed WAF, because both block attacks in production environments. For this reason, RASP and WAF solutions are discussed in Chapter 6.

Manual Code Reviews

Manual code reviews can be expensive and time-consuming, but they can be better than application testing tools for finding many types of vulnerabilities. In addition, having another person explain why a particular piece of code has a vulnerability can be a more effective way to learn than trying to understand the results from automated tools.

Code reviews are standard practice in many high-security environments. In many other environments, they may be used only for sections of code with special significance to security, such as sections implementing encryption or access control.

Penetration Tests

A *penetration test* (pentest) is performed by someone you've engaged to try to get unauthorized access to your systems and tell you where the vulnerabilities are. It's important to note that automated scans of the types discussed earlier are *not* penetration tests, although a pentester may use those scans as a starting point. Larger organizations may have pentesters on staff, but many organizations contract with an external supplier.

 Penetration tests by an independent third party are required by PCI DSS (*https://oreil.ly/r0EtT*) and FedRAMP moderate/high (*https://oreil.ly/o6sL7*) standards, and they may be required for other attestations or certifications.

In pentesting, I recommend that you provide the pentester with information about the design of the system, but not any secret information such as passwords or API keys. In some cases, you may also choose to provide more initial access than an outside attacker would start with, either for testing the system's strength against a malicious insider or for seeing what would happen if an attacker found vulnerabilities in the outer defenses.

You can also choose to point the pentester at the application without any additional information or to provide only limited information. But providing as much information as possible about the application (other than credentials) is usually more effective and a better use of time because the pentesters spend less time on reconnaissance and more time on finding actual vulnerabilities. Remember that real attackers will usually have more time to try to break into your system than your pentesters do!

It's important to note that a pentester will typically find one or two ways into the system, but not *all* the ways. A pentest with negative or minimal findings gives you some confidence in the security of your environment. However, if you have a major finding and you fix that particular vulnerability, you need to keep retesting until you get acceptable results. Pentesting is typically an expensive way to find vulnerabilities, so if the pentesters are coming back with results that an automated scan could have found, you're probably wasting money and time. Pentesting is often done near the end of the release cycle, which also means that problems found during pentesting are more likely to make a release late.

Automated testing often finds potential vulnerabilities, but pentesting (when done correctly) shows actual, successful exploitation of vulnerabilities in the system. Because of this, you should prioritize fixing high-severity pentest results above all other findings other than user reports.

 Most cloud service providers require you to get approval prior to conducting penetration tests of applications hosted on their infrastructure or platform. Failure to get approval can be a violation of the provider's terms of service and may cause an outage, depending on the provider's response to the intrusion.

Penetration Testing and Red/Blue Teaming

A penetration test is typically scoped to a specific target, such as a new application or service, and is scheduled to occur at a specific time, such as prior to production deployment. A pentester will often start by using various scanning tools to find potential vulnerabilities and then will attempt to exploit those vulnerabilities.

A *red team* will often use many of the same tools as a pentester but is more loosely engaged to roam around the entire network or organization looking for vulnerabilities. A *blue team* is a defensive team and will attempt to detect the red team (as well as real attackers!). Some organizations also form *purple teams*, where the red and blue teams collaborate on fixing issues after they're found and on creating more effective defenses.

User Reports

In a perfect world, all bugs and vulnerabilities would be discovered and fixed before users see them. After you've stopped laughing, you need to deal with reports of security vulnerabilities that you receive from your users or bug bounty programs.

This means you need to have a well-defined, fast process to verify whether each reported vulnerability is real or not, and if so roll out a fix and communicate to the users. In the case of a bug bounty program, you may have a limited amount of time before the vulnerability is made public, after which the risk of a malicious attack increases sharply.

User reports overlap somewhat with incident management processes. In some cases, external user reports straddle the line between being a helpful report and an extortion attempt! If your security leaders are not comfortable dealing with end users, public relations, or legal issues, you may also need to have someone in the process who specializes in communications and/or a lawyer to assist the security team in avoiding a public relations or legal nightmare. There are often multiple concerns at odds with one another: there's a desire to say as little as possible to avoid legal liability, and a desire to communicate transparently to avoid a public relations nightmare, and a desire to keep things quiet to avoid a breach while the vulnerability is being fixed. There have been several notable cases where a poor response to a reported vulnerability or breach was much more damaging to an organization than the initial issue![6]

Example Tools for Vulnerability and Configuration Management

Most of the tools listed in the previous sections can be integrated into cloud environments, and most cloud providers have partnerships with vendors or their own proprietary vulnerability management tools.

Because so many tools address more than one area, it doesn't make sense to categorize them into the areas listed earlier. I've put together a list of some representative solutions in the cloud vulnerability and configuration management space, with a very brief explanation of each. Some of these tools also provide features for incident detection and response (Chapter 7), access management (Chapter 4), inventory and asset management (Chapter 3), or data asset management (Chapter 2).

I'm not endorsing any of these tools by including them, or snubbing other tools by excluding them; these are just some examples so that when you get past the initial marketing blitz by the vendor of whatever solution you're considering you'll be able to recognize, "Oh, this tool claims to cover areas x, y, and z." I've included some tools

---

6 Some examples of poor breach handling: Uber (*https://oreil.ly/J8gw3*) has paid over $148 million in a settlement agreement for attempting to cover up a breach, and LastPass (*https://oreil.ly/YJHGG*) harmed its reputation by attempting to downplay the severity of an August 2022 security incident.

that fit neatly into a single category, some tools that cover many different categories, and some tools that are specific to popular cloud providers. This is a quickly changing space, and different projects and vendors are constantly popping up or adding new capabilities.

Here's the list of tools, in alphabetical order:

- Amazon Inspector (*https://oreil.ly/2gMY8*) is an agent-based scanner that can scan for missing patches and poor configurations on Linux and Windows systems, as well as being a container and serverless scanner.

- Ansible (*https://www.ansible.com*) is an agentless automation engine that can be used for almost any task, including configuration management.

- AWS Config (*https://oreil.ly/9-Oav*) checks the configurations of your AWS resources in detail and keeps historical records of those configurations. For example, you can check that all of your security groups restrict SSH access, that all of your Electric Block Store (EBS) volumes are encrypted, and that all of your Relational Database Service (RDS) instances are encrypted.

- AWS Systems Manager (SSM) (*https://oreil.ly/InzKp*) is a security management tool that covers several areas, including inventory, configuration management, and patch management. The State Manager component can be used to enforce configurations, and the Patch Manager component can be used to install patches; both of these functions are executed by an SSM agent installed on your instances.

- AWS Trusted Advisor (*https://oreil.ly/O-3Z5*) performs checks in several areas, including cost, performance, fault tolerance, and security. It can perform some high-level checks in the area of configuration management for AWS resources, such as whether a proper IAM password policy is in place or CloudTrail logging is enabled.

- Azure Update Management (*https://oreil.ly/Nf9AX*) is agent-based and primarily aimed at managing operating system security patches, but it can also perform software inventory and configuration management functions.

- Burp Suite (*https://oreil.ly/c7_vr*) is a dynamic web application scanning suite.

- Chef (*https://docs.chef.io*) is an agent-based automation tool that can be used for configuration management, and the InSpec (*https://www.inspec.io*) project specifically targets configuration related to security and compliance.

- Contrast (*https://www.contrastsecurity.com*) provides IAST and RASP solutions.

- Google Cloud Security Command Center (*https://oreil.ly/LAV66*) is a security management tool that can pull in information from the Google Cloud Security Scanner and other third-party tools, and also provide inventory management and network anomaly detection functions.

- Google Cloud Web Security Scanner (*https://oreil.ly/JIGFs*) is a DAST tool for applications hosted on Google Cloud Platform.
- IBM Cloud Security and Compliance Center (*https://oreil.ly/N9Gyl*) is a security management tool that can pull in vulnerabilities from IBM Vulnerability Advisor as well as network anomaly information.
- IBM Vulnerability Advisor (*https://oreil.ly/KiA25*) scans container images.
- Mend.io (*https://www.mend.io*), formerly WhiteSource, has several products, including an SCA solution.
- Microsoft Defender for Cloud (*https://oreil.ly/VBgly*), formerly Azure Security Center, is a security management tool that can manage your cloud configuration and integrate with your code pipeline and system agents to pull in vulnerability information.
- Palo Alto's Prisma Cloud (*https://oreil.ly/fq2mQ*), formerly Twistlock, can perform configuration and vulnerability management on container images, running containers, and the hosts where the containers run.
- Puppet (*https://puppet.com*) is an agent-based automation tool that can be used for configuration management.
- Qualys (*https://www.qualys.com*) has products that cover many of the categories we've discussed, including network vulnerability scanning, dynamic web application scanning, and others.
- Tenable (*https://www.tenable.com*) has a range of products including the Nessus network scanner, agent-based and agentless Nessus patch and configuration management scanners, and a container scanner.

Statistically speaking, people are terrible at statistics. When you evaluate marketing claims, it's important to use tools that have reasonable false positive *and* false negative rates. As an extreme example, if a tool flags everything as a problem, it will catch every one of the real problems (100% true positive rate), but the false positive rate will be so high that it's useless. Similarly, if the tool flags nothing as a problem, its false positive rate is perfect (0%), but it has missed everything. Beware of marketing claims that focus on only one side of the equation!

Risk Management Processes

At this point in the process you should understand where the most vulnerable areas are in your environment and which tools and processes you can use to find and fix vulnerabilities. Now you need a system to prioritize any vulnerabilities that can't be fixed quickly, where "quickly" is usually defined in relation to time periods in your security policy.

This is where a risk management program comes in, near the end of the pipeline shown in Figure 5-2. Each vulnerability you find that can't be addressed within your accepted guidelines needs to be evaluated as a risk, so that you consciously understand the likelihood of something bad happening and the impact if it does. In many cases, you might accept the risk as a cost of doing business. However, the risk evaluation might lead to additional controls (to reduce the likelihood) or mitigations (to reduce the impact), such as putting in place some extra detection or prevention tools or processes. Risk evaluation might also lead to avoidance, such as turning off the system entirely in some cases.

A leak in the pipeline here means you found vulnerabilities but couldn't fix them right away, and you also failed to actually understand how bad they could be for your business. Using an existing framework for evaluating risk, such as NIST 800-30 or ISO 31000, can be much easier than starting from scratch.

You don't need a really complicated risk management program to get a lot of value; a simple risk register with an agreed-upon process for assigning severity to the risks goes a long way. However, you're not finished with vulnerability management until you've made a conscious decision about what to do with each unresolved vulnerability. These decisions need to be reevaluated periodically—say, quarterly—in case circumstances have changed.

Vulnerability Management Metrics

If you can't measure how you're doing with your vulnerability management program, you generally can't justify its usefulness or tell if you need to make changes. Metrics are useful but dangerous things; they help drive continuous improvement and reveal problems, but they can also lead to silly decisions. Make sure that part of your process of reviewing metrics and results includes a sanity check on whether there are reasonable extenuating factors to a metric going the wrong direction, or whether the metrics are being manipulated in some way.

There are many different metrics available for vulnerability management, and many tools can automatically calculate metrics for you. Metrics can generally be reported by separate teams or business units. Sometimes a little friendly competition helps motivate teams, but remember that some teams will naturally have a harder job to keep up with vulnerability management than others!

Every organization will be different, but here are some metrics that I've found useful in the past.

Tool Coverage

For each tool, what percentage of the in-scope systems is it able to cover? For example, for a dynamic application scanner, what percentage of your web applications does it test? For a network scanner, what percentage of your cloud IP addresses does it scan? These metrics can help you spot leaks in your asset and vulnerability management pipeline. These metrics should approach 100% over time if the system scope is defined properly for each tool.

If you have tools with a really low coverage rate on systems or applications that should be in scope for them, you're not getting much out of them. In many cases, you should either kick off a project to get the coverage percentage up, or retire the tool.

Mean Time to Remediate

It's often useful to break the mean time to remediate metric down by different severities and different environments. For instance, you may track by severity (where you want to see faster fixes for "critical" items than for "low-severity" items) and break those out by types of systems (internal or internet-facing). You can then decide whether these time frames represent an acceptable risk, given your threat model.

Remember that remediation doesn't always mean installing a patch; it could also be turning off a feature so that a vulnerability isn't exploitable. Mitigation through other means than patch installation should be counted correctly.

Note that this metric can be heavily influenced by external factors. For example, when the Spectre/Meltdown vulnerabilities hit, patch availability was delayed for many systems, which caused mean time to remediate (MTTR) metrics to go up. In that particular case, the delays didn't indicate a problem with the organization's vulnerability management program; it meant that the general computing environment had been hit by a severe vulnerability.

Systems/Applications with Open Vulnerabilities

The systems/applications with open vulnerabilities metric is usually expressed as a percentage, since the absolute number will tend to go up as additional items are tracked. This metric is often broken down by different system/application classifications, such as internal or internet-facing, as well as the severity of the vulnerability and whether it's due to a missing patch or an incorrect configuration.

Note that the patch management component of this metric will naturally be cyclical, because it will balloon as vulnerabilities are announced and shrink as they're addressed via normal patch management processes. Similarly, changes to the benchmark may cause the configuration management component of this metric to temporarily balloon until the systems have been configured to match the new benchmark.

Some organizations measure the absolute number of vulnerabilities, rather than systems or applications that have at least one vulnerability. In most cases, measuring the number of vulnerable systems or applications is more useful than measuring the absolute number of vulnerabilities. A system that has one critical vulnerability poses about the same risk as a system with five critical vulnerabilities—either can be compromised quickly. In addition, the absolute number of vulnerabilities often isn't much of an indication of the effort required to resolve all issues, which would be useful for prioritization. You might resolve hundreds of vulnerabilities in a few minutes on a Linux system with a command like `yum -y update; shutdown -r now`.

Variations of this metric can also be used to derive additional metrics around overall risk and effectiveness. For example, this metric may be subdivided into "systems/applications with open vulnerabilities that have been risk accepted" and "systems/applications with open vulnerabilities that exceed policy timeline and have not been risk accepted" to give you an indication of whether you're accepting too much risk or whether you're able to patch quickly enough.

Percentage of False Positives

The percentage of false positives metric can help you understand how well your tools are doing, and how much administrative burden is being placed on your teams due to issues with tooling. As mentioned earlier, with some types of tooling, false positives are a fact of life. However, a tool with too many false positives may not be useful.

Percentage of False Negatives

It may be useful to track how many vulnerabilities should have been detected by a given tool or process but were instead found by some other means. A tool or process with too many false negatives can lead to a false sense of security.

Vulnerability Recurrence Rate

If you're seeing vulnerabilities come back after they've been remediated, that can indicate a serious problem with tools or processes.

A Note on Vulnerability Scoring

The first question almost everyone asks about a given vulnerability is, "How bad is it?" The most commonly accepted standard for "badness" is the Common Vulnerability Scoring System (CVSS). CVSS has been around since 2005, and two major versions are in heavy use (v2 and v3). Both versions have their proponents and critics, but most security professionals agree that the base number you get from either CVSSv2 or CVSSv3 doesn't tell the whole story for your environment and your organization. It's important to have some method to adjust CVSS scores for the threat landscape and your specific environment, either by using CVSS temporal and environmental scores or some other method.

However, this can quickly turn into a game of changing the classification of items to avoid going overdue. While metrics are useful, it's important that you don't lose track of the real goal, which is to prevent security incidents.

In many cases, we don't need to think too hard about how bad the vulnerability is. *The default action in cloud environments should be to automatically apply security patches and run automated tests to see whether they have caused issues.* Only if a security patch or configuration change isn't available, causes problems, or can't be executed for other reasons should you go through the trouble of manually evaluating how big of a risk it is to your environment.

Change Management

Many organizations have some sort of *change management* function. In its simplest form, change management should ensure that changes are made only after they're approved, and that there has been some evaluation of the risk of making a change.

Change management can assist with vulnerability management by making sure that proposed changes don't introduce new security vulnerabilities into the system. If done poorly, change management can also hinder vulnerability management and increase overall risk by slowing down the changes needed to resolve vulnerabilities.

As discussed earlier in the chapter, some of the new technologies in cloud environments may reduce the risk of an overall outage, so that less manual change management is needed to achieve the same level of operational risk. Part of an overall cloud vulnerability management program may be modifying change management processes.

For example, pushing new code along with security fixes to production may be a business-as-usual activity that's automatically approved by a change control board, provided that there's a demonstrated process for quickly getting back to a good state. That might be accomplished by pushing another update, rolling back to a previous version, or turning off application traffic to the new version while the issue is being worked out. However, larger changes, such as changes to the design of the application, may still need to go through a manual change management process.

Ideally, there should be at least one security practitioner involved with the change control process, either as a change control board member or as an advisor.

 A documented change management process is required for several industry and regulatory certifications, including SOC 2, ISO 27001, and PCI DSS.

Putting It All Together in the Sample Application

Remember the really simple three-tier sample application from Chapter 1? It looked like Figure 5-3.

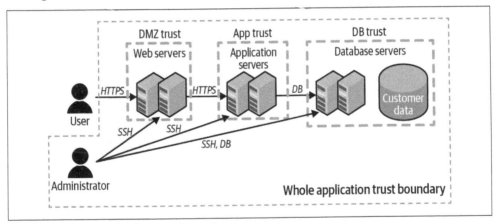

Figure 5-3. Diagram of a sample application

If you're in an orchestrated, container-based microservice environment, with test and production Kubernetes clusters, your sample application may look a bit different. However, you can still spot the same three main tiers in the middle of the diagram (Figure 5-4).

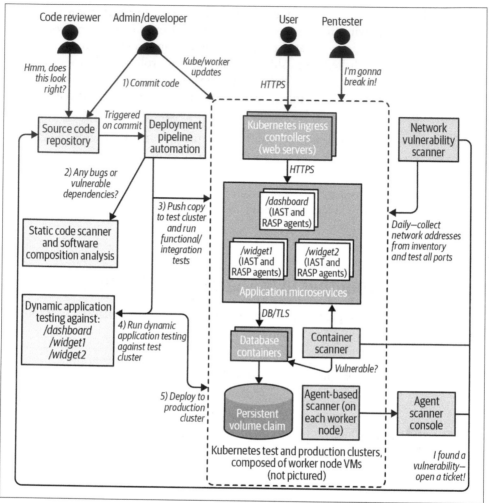

Figure 5-4. Diagram of a sample microservice application

For simplicity, the worker nodes that actually run the containers aren't shown in this diagram, and only one cluster is pictured rather than separate test and production clusters. Let's look at how we might design a vulnerability management process in this environment. First, consider the roles shown at the top:

1. Before deployment, a pentester tries to break into the system, just like a real attacker would. This test might be run by an external team that's contracted to test this specific system at a given time, an internal red team that roams around doing unannounced testing of systems, or both.

2. The user will use the application, just as in the previous examples. End users may report security vulnerabilities in addition to functional bugs.

3. The admin/developer is a role with both development and operations/adminis-tration responsibilities. In your organization, these responsibilities might lie with a single person or multiple teams, but whoever is filling this role must do the following:

   a. Ensure that the infrastructure and platform components, such as the Kuber-netes master and the worker nodes, are up to date.

   b. Make code updates. Note that in an infrastructure-as-code environment, these code updates might also represent changes to the infrastructure, such as new microservices or modifications to the "firewall" for each microservice to allow different connections.

   c. Push to production and/or switch traffic to the new version of the application. The process for and decision of when to do this will be organization-specific but for major deployments should usually include business stakeholders in addition to IT staff.

4. The code reviewer may be part of a separate team, but is often simply another developer in the organization. Not every organization uses manual code reviews, but they can be a good way to spot vulnerabilities in security-critical areas of code such as authentication or authorization routines.

Second, let's look at the pipeline to deploy, on the left side of the figure:

1. An admin/developer will commit a change to the codebase, which will trigger the deployment pipeline automation.

2. A static code scanner will flag problems in your proprietary code, such as accept-ing input without validation. A software composition analysis tool will also look at any open source dependencies to see if there are known vulnerabilities in them. Ideally, the developer will get almost immediate feedback if an issue is found, and issues that are severe enough will block deployment of the new code unless overridden.

3. The automation will start up a copy of the new code in a test environment and run test cases to verify that the code functions.

4. The automation will invoke a dynamic application tester to find any problems. Again, ideally the developer will be notified of any issues here, and severe issues will stop the process.

5. If all tests pass, the code will be deployed as a new instance to production, where the administrator can choose to direct some or all of the production traffic to the new instance. If everything works fine, all traffic can be sent to the new instance and the old instances can be deleted.

Third, let's look at the periodic scanning tools on the right side of the figure. These are needed because the world changes when new vulnerabilities are discovered, even if the code doesn't change! For each of these, if a problem is found, a ticket will automatically be entered as an issue in a tracking repository (shown here as part of the source code repository), and issues will go through the risk management process if they stay around for too long:

1. The network vulnerability scanner will test all of the TCP and UDP[7] ports on the IP addresses of the worker nodes that make up the cluster. In a well-configured cluster, the scanner may only see the HTTPS (tcp/443) ports open, but it may find problems with those (such as a vulnerable version of a web server or a configuration allowing weak TLS ciphers). It may also spot NodePorts opened accidentally that allow traffic in to some other service besides the frontend web server. For example, perhaps someone accidentally left the database open to the internet instead of only to the application microservices!

2. The container scanner will look for problems in each running container. Perhaps the operating system components used by the containers have known vulnerabilities, such as binary libraries that can't be detected by the SCA tools.

3. The agent installed on each worker node (virtual machine) in the cluster will watch to make sure that the operating system components are kept up to date and that the CIS Benchmarks for that operating system pass.

4. Finally, the IAST agent that's part of each microservice will open a ticket for issues found while the code was executing, and the RASP agent will attempt to block attacks.

There's a lot going on! Don't panic, though. This is for educational purposes, and many smaller environments won't need all the tools pictured here. Also, many products perform multiple functions: for example, a single tool might perform static scanning, dynamic scanning, and IAST/RASP. In a perfect world, all of the vulnerabilities would funnel into one place to be dealt with, like issues in a code repository, but here in the real world you may be stuck with multiple tool consoles to check. The important thing is to understand what the different types of tools do and select tools that address the biggest threats to your application.

Stated more bluntly, just buying a tool and installing it may look good on reports to management, but you need to actually do something with what the tool is telling you. Concentrate on finding real issues and creating a good feedback loop back to your developers and administrators, that you can measure with some useful metrics, before adding another tool into the mix.

---

7 UDP scanning, like any other UDP communications, is somewhat unreliable by design.

Conclusion

Vulnerability management, patch management, configuration management, and change management are separate disciplines in their own right, with separate tooling and processes. In this chapter, I've combined them to quickly cover the most important aspects of each, but there are entire books written on all of these subjects.

Vulnerability management in cloud environments is similar in many ways to on-premises vulnerability management. However, with cloud computing often comes a heightened business focus on rapid deployment of new features. This leads to a need for vulnerability management processes that can keep up with quickly changing infrastructure.

In addition, the philosophies of immutable infrastructure and continuous delivery are often adopted along with the cloud, and these can considerably reduce the risk of an outage due to a change. This alters the balance between operational and security risk. Because applying security fixes is a change, and you can make changes more safely, you can afford to roll out security fixes more quickly without risking bringing the system down. This means that you should usually adopt different vulnerability management, patch management, and change management processes in cloud environments. In addition, there are both cloud-aware and provider-specific tools that can make vulnerability management easier than it is on-premises.

After access management, vulnerability management is the most critical process to get right for cloud environments. Attackers can get unauthorized access to your systems through vulnerabilities at many different layers of your application stack. You need to spend some time understanding the different layers, what your vulnerability management responsibility is for each of those layers, and where the biggest risks to your environment are likely to be. You then need to understand the different types of vulnerability management tools available and which ones address the areas that are highest risk for you.

Every vendor will try to convince you that their tool will do everything for you. That's rarely the case; you'll usually need at least a few different tools to cover vulnerability management and configuration management across your cloud environment. Focus on getting value from each tool you use before throwing more into the mix. For each tool, you should be able to explain clearly what types of vulnerabilities it will find. You should also be able to sketch out a pipeline of how the tool gets valid inputs, how it finds and/or fixes vulnerabilities, how it communicates vulnerabilities back to the teams who are responsible for fixing them, and how you track the vulnerabilities that can't be fixed right away as risks.

In the next chapter, I'll finally talk about what most people think of first when they think about cybersecurity: firewalls and network controls.

Exercises

1. What are some common areas where the consumer is responsible for vulnerabilities in IaaS cloud environments? Select all that apply.

   a. Physical attack surface vulnerabilities, such as door locks

   b. Missing operating security patches

   c. Incorrect middleware configurations, such as database configurations

   d. Incorrect application configurations, such as granting access to the wrong person

2. Which of the following types of tools can discover missing operating system patches? Select all that apply.

   a. Network vulnerability scanners

   b. Agentless scanners and configuration management

   c. Dynamic application scanners

   d. Static application scanners

3. Which of the following types of tools can discover coding errors that you've made in code you maintain? Select all that apply.

   a. Agentless scanners and configuration management

   b. Container scanners

   c. Dynamic application scanners

   d. Static application scanners

4. True or false: You can be confident that your cloud environment is reasonably secure once you have fixed all vulnerabilities found in a network vulnerability scan.

5. True or false: You can be confident that your cloud environment is reasonably secure once you have fixed all vulnerabilities found in a penetration test.

6. True or false: You must fix every vulnerability found in order to have an acceptable level of risk for your cloud environment.

CHAPTER 6

Network Security

In both traditional and cloud environments, network controls are an important part of overall security, because they rule out entire hosts or networks as entry points. If you can't talk to a component at all, it's difficult to compromise it. Sometimes network controls are like the fences around a military base; they make it difficult for people to approach the base without being detected. At other times they're like a goalie that stops the ball after all other defenses have failed.

In this day and age, remaining disconnected from the internet is not an option for most companies. The network is so fundamental to modern applications that it's also almost impossible to tightly control every single communication. This means that network controls are in many cases secondary controls and are here to help mitigate the effects of some other problem. If everything else were configured *absolutely perfectly*—that is, if all of your systems were perfectly patched for vulnerabilities, and all unnecessary services were turned off, and all services authenticated and authorized any users or other services perfectly—you could safely have no network controls at all. However, we don't live in a perfect world, so it's really important to make use of the principle of defense in depth and add a layer of network controls to the controls we've already discussed.

Differences from Traditional IT

Despite cries of "the perimeter is dead!," for many years, administrators depended heavily upon the network perimeter for security. Network security was sometimes the only security that system administrators relied upon. That's never been a good model for any environment, traditional or cloud. Fortunately, the new focus on zero trust has helped bring awareness that firewalls can't always save you to a larger audience.

In an on-premises environment, the perimeters are often easy to define. In the simplest case, you draw one dotted line (trust zone) around your *demilitarized zone* (DMZ; also called the perimeter network) and another dotted line around your internal network, and you carefully limit what comes into the DMZ and what comes from the DMZ into your internal network (more on that in "DMZs" on page 129).

In the cloud, the decision of what's inside your perimeter, and the implementation of that perimeter, are often quite different from in an on-premises environment. Your trust boundaries aren't as obvious. If you're making use of a Database as a Service, is that inside or outside of your perimeter? If you have deployments around the world for disaster recovery and latency reasons, are those deployments all inside the same perimeters or different perimeters? In addition, creating these perimeters is no longer costly when you move to most cloud environments, so you can afford to have separate network segments for every application and use other services, such as web application firewalls, quickly and easily.

The most confusing thing about network controls in cloud environments is the large variety of delivery models you can use to build your application. What makes sense is different for each delivery model. You need to consider what a reasonable network security model looks like for the following models:

IaaS environments (e.g., bare-metal and virtual machines)
These are the closest to traditional environments, but they can often benefit from per-application segmentation, which is not feasible in most on-premises environments.

Orchestrated container-based environments (e.g., Docker and Kubernetes)
If applications are decomposed into microservices, more granular network controls are possible inside the individual applications.

Application PaaS environments (e.g., Cloud Foundry, Elastic Beanstalk, and Heroku)
These differ in the number of network controls available. Some may allow for per-component isolation, some may not provide configurable firewall functions at all, and some may allow the use of firewall functions from the IaaS down.

Platform PaaS environments (e.g., databases)
These are often open to the internet by default but may offer network ingress controls as an option.

Serverless or Function-as-a-Service environments (e.g., AWS Lambda, OpenWhisk, Azure Functions, and Google Cloud Functions)
These operate in a shared environment that may not offer network controls, or offer them only on the frontend.

SaaS environments
> While some SaaS offerings provide simple network controls (such as access only via VPN or from allowlisted IP addresses), many do not.

In addition, many applications use more than one of these service models as part of the overall solution. For example, you might use both containers and traditional IaaS in your application, or a mixture of your own code with SaaS. This may mean that some areas of your application can have better coverage for network controls than others, so it's important to keep your overall threat model and biggest risks in mind.

Concepts and Definitions

Although cloud networking brings some new ideas to the table, many traditional concepts and definitions are still relevant in cloud environments. However, as described in the following subsections, they may be used in slightly different ways.

Zero Trust Networking

As mentioned in Chapter 1, zero trust is a concept, and not a product or service. There are many different aspects of zero trust, ranging from verifying end-user devices to evaluating context such as user behavior in authorization decisions.

When securing a cloud environment network, the most important part of zero trust is that you secure communications between resources in your cloud environment—meaning authentication, authorization, and encryption—even if the communication takes place entirely inside your perimeter. An example of this is using TLS for all connections except for "localhost only" communications.

Securing connections is often combined with micro-segmentation, because it is usually easier and cheaper to create more network segments in a cloud environment than in on-premises environments. Micro-segmentation ensures that when you allow network access from one component to another, you do not allow access to more resources than necessary. An example of this would be the use of security groups and small VPC subsets, described later in this chapter, to prevent communications that aren't necessary for the application to function.

Allowlists and Denylists

An *allowlist* (also called a *whitelist*) is a list of things that are allowed, with everything else denied. An allowlist may be contrasted with a *denylist* (also called a *blacklist*), which is a specific list of things to deny, while allowing everything else. In general, we want to be as restrictive as possible without being silly, so we want to use allowlists if feasible.

IP allowlists are what many people think of as traditional firewall rules. They specify a source address, a destination address, and a destination port.[1] IP allowlists can be useful for allowing only specific systems even to try to get access to your application. But because IP addresses are so easy to spoof, they should not be used as the *only* method to authenticate systems. That bears repeating: it's almost *never* a good idea to authenticate a system or authorize access solely based on what part of the network the request comes from, although allowlists can help. Techniques such as API keys or TLS certificates should be used to authenticate other systems, with IP allowlists playing a supporting role.

IP allowlists also aren't good for controlling user access. This is because users have the irritating habit of moving around on the network. (To some extent, this is also true of infrastructure in cloud environments, but generally you can at least specify a list of valid subnets that the requests will come from.) In addition, IP addresses don't belong to users, but to the systems they're using, and network address translation (NAT) firewalls are still ubiquitous enough to make those IP addresses ambiguous. So, IP allowlists don't authenticate individuals; they provide weak authentication for systems or local networks in a relatively easy-to-fool way.

In many cloud environments, systems are created and destroyed regularly. For that reason, IP allowlist source or destination addresses may need a much broader reach than is customary in on-premises environments. They may even be specified as 0.0.0.0/0 with a specific port (representing any address), which firewall administrators have traditionally not allowed for most rules. Remember that we are depending on many other controls besides just IP allowlisting to protect us!

With the rise of content delivery networks and global server load balancers (GSLBs), IP allowlists are also becoming less useful for some types of filtering (such as controls on outbound connections) because the network addresses can change rapidly. If you stick to requiring specific IP addresses for all rules and the CDN's addresses change every week, you will end up with a lot of incorrectly blocked connections. That said, restricting outbound (egress) connections is still one of the best methods to prevent something malicious that manages to get into your network from "calling home," although you may need to use a proxy instead of an IP allowlist.

With those caveats in mind, IP allowlisting remains an important tool for cutting off network access where it isn't needed, as long as it isn't used as the primary defense or the only method to authenticate systems and users. Zero trust principles in network communications mean that you will authenticate even those connections coming from "trusted" areas, but you should still use allowlists where feasible to quickly filter out attacks that may come from outside of those trusted areas.

---

1 To be needlessly pedantic, they should really be named "TCP/UDP allowlists" rather than "IP allowlists" if they include port information.

DMZs

A DMZ is a concept from traditional network controls that carries over well to many cloud environments. It's simply an area at the front of your application into which you let the least-trusted traffic (such as visitor traffic). In most cases, you'll place simpler, less trusted components in the DMZ, such as your proxy, load balancer, or static content web server. Compromising one of these components should not provide a large advantage to the attacker.

Your internal components will generally not allow any connections other than from the DMZ, but will still need to authenticate the connections coming from the DMZ. A separate DMZ area may not make sense in some cloud environments, or it may already be provided as part of the service model (particularly in PaaS environments).

Proxies

Proxies are components that receive a request, send the request to some other component to be serviced, and then send the response back to the original requester. In both cloud and traditional environments, they are often used in one of two models:

Forward proxies
> The proxy receives requests from your components and makes outbound requests on their behalf.

Reverse proxies
> The proxy receives requests from your users and relays those requests to your backend servers.

Proxies can be useful for both functional requirements (to spread different requests out to different backend servers) and security. Forward proxies are most often used to put rules on what traffic is allowed out of the network (see "Egress Filtering" on page 152).

Reverse proxies can improve security if there's a vulnerability in a protocol or in a particular implementation of a protocol. In that case, the proxy may be compromised, but it will usually provide an attacker with less access to the network or critical resources than the actual backend server would.

Reverse proxies also provide a better user experience by giving the end user the appearance of dealing with a single host. Cloud environments often make even more use of reverse proxies than traditional environments, because the application functions may be spread out across multiple backend components. This is particularly true for microservice-friendly environments, such as Kubernetes, which includes several proxies as part of its core functionality.

Although you can have a proxy for almost any protocol, in practice the term usually refers to an HTTP/HTTPS proxy.[2]

Software-Defined Networking

Software-defined networking (SDN) is an often overused term that can apply to many different virtualized networking technologies. In this context, SDN may be used by your cloud provider to implement the virtual networks that you use. The networks you see may actually be encapsulated on top of another network, and the rules for processing their traffic may be managed centrally instead of at each physical switch or router.

From your perspective, you can treat the network as if you were using physical switches and routers, even though the implementation may be a centralized control plane coordinating many different data plane devices to get traffic from one place to another.

Network Functions Virtualization

Network functions virtualization (NFV), also called *virtual network functions* (VNFs), reflects the idea that you no longer need a dedicated hardware box to perform many network functions, such as firewalling, routing, or intrusion detection and prevention. You may use NFV appliances in your design explicitly, and NFV is also how many cloud providers provide network functions to you as a service. When possible, you should use the as-a-service functions rather than maintaining your own services.

Overlay Networks and Encapsulation

An *overlay network* is a virtual network that you create on top of your provider's network. Overlay networks are often used to allow your virtual systems to communicate with each other as if they were on the same network, regardless of the underlying provider network.

This is most often accomplished by *encapsulation*, wherein packets between your virtual systems are put inside packets sent across your provider network (Figure 6-1). Some common examples of encapsulation methods are Virtual Extensible LAN (VXLAN), Generic Routing Encapsulation (GRE), and IP in IP.

---

2 If the protocol being proxied is IP, it's called *network address translation* and "routing" instead of "proxying," but the concept is the same!

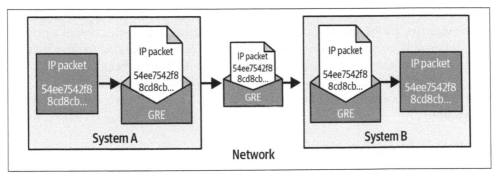

Figure 6-1. Encapsulating IP packets between systems

For example, if virtual machine A on host 1 wants to talk to virtual machine B on host 2, it will send out a packet. Host 1 will wrap that packet up in another packet and send it to host 2, which will unwrap it and hand the original packet to virtual machine B. From the perspective of the virtual machines, they're plugged into the same Ethernet switch and/or IP subnet, even though they may be physically located across the world from one another.

Virtual Private Clouds

In the older days of IaaS services, all provisioned systems were reachable on the internet, even if the systems did not require inbound access from the internet. Later, private clouds used the same delivery model as the public cloud, but for systems owned and operated by a single company instead of being shared among multiple companies. Private clouds could be located inside a company's perimeter, with no access from outside and no sharing of resources.

Although each cloud provider's definition may vary, a VPC hardly ever isolates virtual hosts to the same degree as a true private cloud. Shared resources in cloud IaaS often include storage, network, and compute resources. A VPC, despite the name, generally deals only with network isolation, by allowing you to create separate virtual networks to keep your applications separate from other customers or applications.

Marketing aside, VPCs are the best of both worlds for many companies. With VPCs, you get the cost and elasticity benefits of a highly shared environment and still have tight control over which components of your application you expose to the rest of the world. Cloud IaaS providers usually have other options for compute isolation (such as dedicated hosts) or storage isolation (such as per-customer encryption). Because providers implement VPCs using software-defined networking and overlay networks, you can stand up very complicated network topologies almost instantly, whereas it might take a traditional on-premises network team weeks or months to configure the same thing.

While it still makes sense in many cases for the front door of your application to be on the internet, a VPC allows you to keep the majority of your application in a private area designed to be unreachable by anyone but you. VPCs can also allow you to keep your entire application private, accessible only by a VPN or other private link. But even though VPCs allow you to configure the networking so that only you should have access, you should still follow zero trust principles and authenticate all incoming connections.

Network Address Translation

Network address translation was originally designed to combat the shortage of IP addresses by using the same IP addresses in multiple parts of the internet, and translating them to publicly routable addresses before sending them across the internet (Figure 6-2). *Source NAT* (SNAT, or *masquerading*) is changing the source addresses as packets leave your VPC area.[3] *Destination NAT* (DNAT) is changing the destination addresses of packets from the outside as they enter your VPC area so that they go to particular systems inside the VPC. If you don't perform DNAT to a system inside your VPC, then there's no way for an outside system to reach the inside system. Although IPv6 (discussed in the following section) will eventually save us from dealing with NAT, we're stuck with it for the foreseeable future.

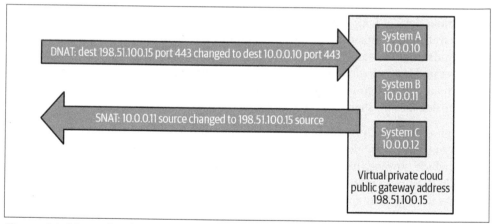

Figure 6-2. Network address translation in and out of a VPC

NAT is used heavily in cloud environments—particularly in VPC environments where you use private range addresses, defined in RFC 1918 (*https://oreil.ly/yo_7x*), for the systems inside the VPC. These addresses are easy to spot; they start with "10.," "192.168.," or "172.16." through "172.31.". The difference in cloud environments is

---

3 Technically, masquerading is a dynamic form of SNAT where the source address is set to the address of the interface it's leaving on, but most people use the terms interchangeably.

that you generally don't have to manually configure NAT rules in a firewall. In most cases, you can simply define the rules using the portal or API, and the NAT function will be performed automatically for you.

A commonly repeated phrase is that "NAT is not security." That is 100% true, but practically irrelevant. Performing NAT doesn't in itself provide any security; you're just making a few changes to the IP header as you route packets.

However, the presence of NAT implies the existence of a firewall capable of doing NAT, which is generally also allowlisting specific DNAT traffic and which is configured to drop all packets that don't match a DNAT rule. You can have exactly the same security without NAT by using IP allowlists for the traffic you want to forward, with an implied "drop everything else" rule at the bottom. Some people use NAT as shorthand for the translation plus the allowlisting, but it's the firewall providing the security, not NAT; using NAT in your solution doesn't mean you're relying only on the translation feature for security.

IPv6

Internet Protocol version 6 (IPv6) is a system of addressing machines that makes far more addresses available than the traditional IPv4. From a security perspective, IPv6 has several improvements, such as mandatory support for Internet Protocol Security (IPsec), transport security, cryptographically generated addresses, and a larger address space that makes scanning a range of addresses much more time-consuming.

IPv6 has the potential to make system administration tasks easier in the near future, because overlapping IPv4 ranges can make life difficult from the perspectives of asset management, event management, and firewall rules.[4] (Which host does that 10.1.2.3 refer to? The one over here, or the one over there?) Although the use of IPv4 on the internet will probably continue for decades, a move to IPv6 for internal administration purposes in larger enterprises is likely to happen sooner.

From a practical point of view, the most important thing with IPv6 is to ensure that you maintain IPv6 allowlists if your systems have IPv6 addresses. Even though many end users don't know about IPv6, attackers can use it to circumvent your IPv4 controls.

---

4 If you think about it, the problem of "we ran out of numbers" is a really silly reason to have to put up with these headaches.

Network Defense in Action in the Sample Application

Now that we've covered some of the key concepts, the remainder of this chapter will be based on our simple web application in the cloud, which is accessed from the internet and uses a backend database (Figure 6-3). In this example, we'll be protecting against a threat actor named Molly, whose primary motivation is stealing our customers' personal information from the database to sell on the dark web.

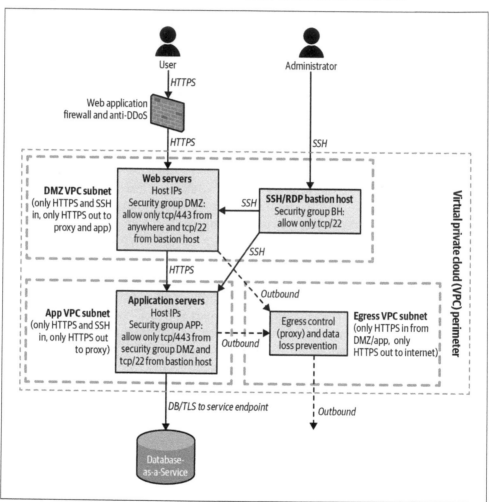

Figure 6-3. Sample application with network controls

Note that this is a somewhat intricate example intended for illustration purposes, so you may not need all of the controls pictured for your environment. I recommend that you prioritize network controls in the order listed in the following subsections. Don't spend a lot of time designing the later controls until you've put the earlier controls in place and have verified that they are effective; it's much better to have TLS and a simple firewall configured correctly and being monitored than to have five different network controls that are configured poorly and ignored.

To use an analogy, ensure your ground-floor doors are locked securely before putting bars on your second-floor windows!

Encryption in Motion

Transport Layer Security (TLS), formerly known as SSL, is the most common method for securing communication of data in motion (flowing between systems on the network). Some people may categorize this as an application-level control rather than a network-level control, because in a traditional environment it's often under the control of the application team rather than the network team. In cloud environments, those may not be separate groups, so it's included as a network control here. However you classify it, encryption in motion is a very important security control.

When implemented properly, TLS provides three controls for the price of one. With TLS, a server will generate a key pair (a public and private key), and then will get a certificate authority to sign the public key. The signed public key is called a *certificate*. A client system will look at that certificate, and who signed it, to decide if the server is who it says it is—in other words, the client will authenticate the server. In addition, once the server authentication step has happened, the two systems will agree on a symmetric encryption key used to encrypt that connection, which keeps attackers from breaching the confidentiality or integrity of the information as it flows through the connection.

Many components support TLS natively. In cloud environments, I recommend using TLS not just at the frontend, but for all communications that cross a physical or virtual network switch. This includes communications that may realistically cross such boundaries in the future as components are moved around. Communications between components that will always remain in the same network stack (or the same network namespace when using containers) do not gain any security benefit from using TLS. Examples of these communications are localhost connections within a virtual machine or between containers in a single Kubernetes pod.

There is debate in some circles as to whether it's a good idea to encrypt traffic going across networks you control, because you lose the ability to inspect the traffic as it passes through your network. The implicit assumption is that it's unlikely for an attacker to get through your perimeter to view the traffic that you want to inspect. As of this writing, one of the top causes of breaches (*https://oreil.ly/wQv6A*) is attacks on web applications, allowing an attacker into the application servers—which are behind the perimeter, it should be noted. There's no reason to think this trend will reverse. For this reason, I recommend encrypting all network traffic that contains information that would harm you if made public. This easy rule of thumb excludes network traffic, such as pings, that contains no useful information for an attacker. Rather than relying upon network inspection to detect an attacker, you should rely upon event information generated by your systems. Refer to Chapter 7 for more information.

Simply turning on TLS is not sufficient, however. TLS loses much of its effectiveness if you do not also perform the authentication step mentioned earlier, because it's not difficult for an attacker to hijack a connection and perform a man-in-the-middle attack. As an example, as Figure 6-4 shows, even in modern container environments it can be possible for a compromised container (M) to trick other containers (A and B) into sending traffic through it. Without certificate checking, A thinks it has an encrypted TLS connection to B, when in reality it has an encrypted connection to M. M decrypts the connection, reads the passwords or other sensitive data, and then makes an encrypted connection to B and passes through the data (possibly changing it at the same time). TLS encryption doesn't help at all in this situation without certificate checking!

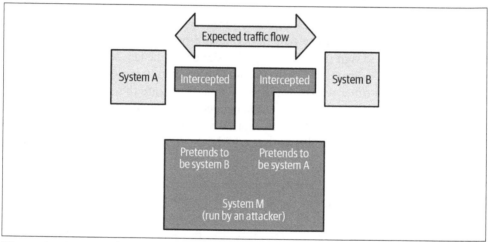

Figure 6-4. Man-in-the-middle attack

What this means is that you also have to perform *key management*—creating a separate key pair and getting a certificate signed for each one of your systems—which can be painful and difficult to automate.

Fortunately, in cloud environments this is becoming easier. One way to do this is via *identity documents*, which some cloud providers make available to systems when they're provisioned. The provisioned system can retrieve a cryptographically signed identity document that can be used to prove its identity to other components. When you combine an identity document with the ability to automatically issue TLS certificates, you can have a system automatically come online, authenticate itself with a public key infrastructure (PKI) provider, and get a key pair and certificate that are trusted by other components in your environment. In this fashion, you can be certain that you're talking to the system you intended to and not to a man-in-the-middle attacker. You do have to trust the cloud provider, but you already have to trust them because they create instances and manipulate existing instances.

Here are a couple of examples:

- You can automatically create certificates using tools such as AWS instance identity documents (*https://oreil.ly/mqi7y*) and HashiCorp Vault (*https://www.vault project.io*). When an AWS instance boots, it can retrieve its instance identity document and signature and send those to Vault, which will verify the signature and provide a token for reading additional secrets. The instance can then use this token to have Vault automatically generate a key pair and sign the TLS certificate.

- In Kubernetes environments with Istio (*https://istio.io*), Istio Auth can provide keys and certificates to Kubernetes containers. It does this by watching to see when new containers are created, automatically generating keys/certificates, and making them available to containers as secret mounts.

- Cloud certificate storage systems such as AWS Certificate Manager (*https://oreil.ly/iVRAj*), Azure Key Vault (*https://oreil.ly/Ai2qO*), and IBM Cloud Secrets Manager (*https://oreil.ly/VuYq-*) can easily provision certificates and safely store private keys.

The Heartbleed (*https://heartbleed.com*) vulnerability notwithstanding, TLS is still a very secure protocol if configured properly. At the time of this writing, TLS 1.3 is the current version of the protocol that should be used, and only specific ciphersuites[5] should be allowed. While there are definitive references for valid ciphersuites, such as NIST SP 800-52, for most users an online test such as one provided by SSL Labs (*https://www.ssllabs.com*) is the fastest way to verify whether a public-facing TLS interface is configured properly. Once you have verified your public interface, you can then copy a valid configuration to any non-public-facing TLS interfaces you have. Network vulnerability scanning tools such as Nessus can also highlight weak protocols or ciphersuites allowed by your systems.

You will need to include new ciphersuites as they become available and remove old ciphersuites from your configuration as vulnerabilities are discovered. You can review acceptable ciphersuites as part of your vulnerability management process, because network vulnerability scanners can spot out-of-date ciphersuites that are no longer

---

5 A *ciphersuite* is a set of encryption and signing algorithms that are used to protect the TLS connection. Although there are a lot of important details that are of interest to cryptographers, in general you just need to know which ones are currently considered safe and limit your connections to use those. In some cases, you may need to accept less-secure ciphersuites if you don't control the other end of the connection—for example, if you need to allow out-of-date browsers to connect.

secure. Fortunately, ciphersuites are compromised at a much lower rate than other tools in common use, where vulnerabilities are routinely discovered.

It's also important to generate new TLS private keys whenever you get a new certificate, or whenever the keys may have been compromised. Solutions such as Let's Encrypt (*https://letsencrypt.org*) generate new private keys and renew certificates automatically, which can limit the amount of time for which someone can impersonate your website if your private keys are stolen.

Our attacker, Molly, may be able to snoop on or manipulate the connections between users and web servers, or between the web servers and the application servers, or between the application servers and the database. But with a correct TLS implementation, she shouldn't be able to get any useful data (such as the credentials for accessing the database in order to steal the data).

Firewalls and Network Segmentation

Firewalls are a network control that is familiar to many people. Once you have a plan to secure all of your communications, you can begin dividing your network into separate segments (based on trust zones) and putting firewall controls in place. At their simplest, network firewalls implement IP allowlists between two networks (each of which may contain many hosts). Firewall appliances may also perform many other functions, such as that of a terminating VPN, IDS/IPS, or WAF; but for this section, we'll concentrate on the IP allowlist functionality.

Firewalls are usually used for two main purposes:

- Perimeter control, for separating your systems from the rest of the world
- Internal segmentation, to keep sets of systems separated from one another

You might use the same technologies to accomplish both purposes, but there's an important difference in what you should pay attention to. On the internet there's always someone trying to attack you, so alerts from the perimeter are very noisy. On internal segmentation firewalls, any denied connection attempts are either due to an attacker trying to move laterally or a misconfiguration. Either one should be investigated!

There are three main firewall implementations in the cloud:

Network access control lists
These are often called network ACLs, or NACLs. Instead of operating your own firewall appliances, you simply define rules for each network about what's allowed into and out of that network. Think of this like a "rough cut," or like a security guard allowing people into a building.

Security groups

Instead of operating your own host firewalls, you simply define security group rules and they're implemented as a service for your virtual hosts. Security groups apply at a per-host level rather than a per-network level. Some implementations may not have all the features that network ACLs provide, such as logging of accepted and denied connections. One nice thing about security groups is that you can use the members of a group as a source or destination. For example, if you have a set of database servers that all need to talk to each other on a certain port, then you can do that by referencing the server group for inbound and outbound rules, and you don't have to change the rules when adding new members to the group. Think of this like a "fine cut," or like a badge reader that only allows specific individuals into a particular room in the building.

Virtual firewall appliances

While still appropriate for some implementations, this is largely a lift-and-shift model from on-premises environments. Note that most virtual firewall appliances are next-generation appliances that combine allowlisting with additional functionality, such as a WAF or IDS/IPS. While you design and implement your network controls, treat these separate functions as if they were separate devices plugged in back to back, and don't worry about designing the higher-level controls until you have the perimeter and internal segmentation designed.

Table 6-1 shows, as of this writing, the IP allowlisting controls available on popular cloud services.

Table 6-1. IP allowlisting options offered by cloud providers

Provider	IP allowlisting features
Amazon Web Services IaaS	VPCs, network ACLs, security groups, and virtual appliances available in the marketplace
Microsoft Azure IaaS	Virtual networks, network security groups (NSGs), and network virtual appliances
Google Cloud Platform IaaS	VPCs, firewall rules, and target tags
IBM Cloud IaaS	VPCs with network ACLs, security groups, and gateway appliances
Kubernetes (overlay on an IaaS)	Network policies

Let's take a closer look at how to implement firewall controls in a cloud environment.

Perimeter control

The first firewall control you should design is a perimeter of some form. This may be implemented via a firewall appliance, but more often it will simply be a virtual private cloud with a network ACL. Most providers have the ability to create network ACLs. In that case, you don't need to worry about the underlying firewall at all; you simply provide rules between security zones, and everything below that is abstracted from you.

You may be tempted to share a perimeter among several different applications. In traditional environments, firewalls are often costly and time-consuming to use; they require a physical device, and in many organizations a separate team will configure the firewall. For those reasons, multiple applications that don't actually need to communicate with one another often share network segments. This can be a significant security risk, because a breach in a less important application can provide a foothold for an attacker to pivot to a more important application, often undetected.

In cloud environments, you should give each application its own separate perimeter controls. This may sound like a lot of trouble, but remember that in most cases you are just providing rules for the cloud provider's firewall to enforce. Defining the network perimeter rules separately for each application means you can manage the rules along with the configuration of the application, and each application can change its own perimeter rules without affecting other applications (unless the other applications are dependent on that application).

In our example, for perimeter control and internal segmentation, we'll put the entire application inside a VPC with private subnets for the backend web and application servers and network ACLs. Depending on the application, we might have also chosen to use only security groups without a VPC for all systems in the application, or to use virtual firewall appliances as the interface between the internet and the rest of the application.

On AWS, Google Cloud Platform, and IBM Cloud, we would create a VPC with one public subnet for the web servers (DMZ), and a private subnet for the application servers. On Azure, we would create virtual networks with subnets. We would then specify which communications should be allowed into our VPC from the internet.

Internal segmentation

Okay, now we have a perimeter behind which we can place our sample application (in the form of a VPC) so that we can allow only specific traffic in. The next step is to implement network controls inside our application. The application will likely have a few different trust boundaries, such as the web layer (the DMZ), the application layer, and the database layer.

In the traditional IT world, internal segmentation was often messy: you would need lots of different 802.1Q VLANs, which had to be requested via a ticket, or you would use a hosted firewall solution that you could centrally manage. In cloud environments, with a few clicks or invocations of the APIs, you can create as many subnets as you need, often without any additional charges.

Once we have created our three subnets (some of them may have been created automatically when we created a VPC), we're ready to apply network ACLs or security groups. In our simple example, we would allow only HTTPS traffic from the internet to the web subnet, HTTPS traffic from the web subnet into the application subnet, and SSH into both. This is very similar to traditional environments, except that we can create these subnets so quickly and easily that we can afford to have separate ones for each application, with no sharing.

Most cloud providers also allow you to use a command-line tool or a REST API to do everything you can on the portal. This is essential for automating deployments, although it does require you to do a little more manual plumbing work in some cases. In this case, we would create a VPC with one public subnet and two private subnets, attach an internet gateway, route traffic out the gateway, and allow only tcp/443 into the DMZ subnet. Rather than creating a script from scratch, I recommend that you use an infrastructure-as-code tool like HashiCorp Terraform or AWS CloudFormation. Tools such as these allow you to declare what you want your network infrastructure to look like and automatically issue the correct commands to create or modify your cloud infrastructure to match.

Cloud web consoles, command-line invocations, and APIs change over time, so the best reference is usually the cloud provider's online documentation. The important concept is that most cloud platforms allow you to create a virtual private cloud that contains one or more subnets that you can use for trust zones.

Security groups

At this point, we already have a perimeter and firewall rules, so why would we need more IP allowlists? The reason is that it's possible that our attacker has obtained a small foothold into one of our subnets (probably the DMZ), which gets her behind our existing subnet controls. We'd like to block or detect her attempts to move elsewhere within our application, such as by attacking our administrative ports. To do this, we'll use per-system firewalls.

Although you can certainly use local firewalls on your operating system, most cloud providers provide a method for the cloud infrastructure itself to filter traffic coming into your virtual system before your operating system sees it. This feature is often called *security groups*.[6]

 If you choose to use security groups to meet your internal network segmentation requirements, make sure that you can detect denied connections, because not all implementations permit feeding these denied attempts to a security information and event manager. Please refer to Chapter 7 for more information.

---

6 Some cloud providers distinguish between security groups, which apply to a single system, and network access control lists, which apply to the traffic entering and exiting the subnet. However, Microsoft Azure uses *network security groups* that can apply to both systems and subnets, and Google Cloud Platform uses firewall rules and target tags.

Just as in traditional environments, you should configure your security groups to allow traffic in only on the ports needed for that type of system. For example, on an application server, allow traffic in only on the application server port. In addition, restrict administrative access ports, such as SSH, to particular IP addresses that you know you'll perform administration functions from, such as your bastion host or corporate IP range. In most implementations, you not only can specify a specific IP source, but can also allow traffic from any instance that has another security group specified.

If you allow administrative access from your entire company's IP range, note that any compromised workstation, server, or mobile device in your environment can be used to access the administrative interface. This is better than leaving it open to the entire internet, but don't get complacent: these ports should still be protected as if they were open to the internet, because there are a lot of ways into a large corporate network! That means they should be scanned for vulnerabilities and all connections should be authenticated via complex passwords or keys and certificates.

In some smaller deployments, you might choose to put your entire application into a single subnet and use security groups for both perimeter control and internal segmentation. For example, the database server may have a security group in place that allows SSH access only from a subnet you trust, and allows database access only from your application servers. If there's a one-to-one correspondence between your security groups and your subnets (that is, everything on the same subnet also uses the same security group), defining subnets might create additional complexity without much benefit. While most implementations will benefit from both, security groups have a slight edge in that they offer better protection against a misconfigured service on one of your systems; with network ACLs, anything that gets into the subnet can exploit that misconfigured service.

Like many other network controls, internal segmentation is a redundant layer of security. It will help you if there's an issue somewhere else, such as because you've misconfigured your perimeter, an attacker has gotten in past your perimeter, or you've accidentally left a service running with default credentials.

Service endpoints

It's important to note that some layers of your application, like the database, might be shared as-a-service functions. This means that they're actually outside your perimeter, although they can be *virtually* behind your perimeter via proper access controls and service endpoints. To illustrate this, the version of the sample application in this chapter shows a Database as a Service in use.

Several cloud providers offer service endpoint functionality. An *endpoint* is just a place to go to reach the service, and a *service endpoint* makes your as-a-service instance directly reachable via an IP address on your virtual private cloud subnet.

This is convenient in that you don't have to specify outbound firewall rules to reach the instance, but the real beauty of this feature is that the service can be accessed *only* via that virtual IP address. For example, even if someone on the internet obtains the correct credentials for your database, they still cannot access the instance. They would need to get into your VPC and talk to the virtual IP address there using the credentials.

Even if service endpoint functionality is not available, the as-a-service function might allow you to allowlist which IP addresses can connect. If so, this is mostly equivalent to service endpoint functionality (although slightly more difficult) and can help guard against stolen or weak credentials for that service.

Container firewalling and network segmentation

What about isolating access in a container world? Although the implementation differs somewhat, the concepts are still essentially the same. At the time of this writing, Kubernetes is the most popular container orchestration solution, so I'll focus on it here.

For a perimeter, you will typically use existing IaaS network controls such as a VPC or security groups, but you may also use Kubernetes network policies to enact local firewalls on the worker nodes. In either case, the goal is to prevent any inbound traffic except to the NodePort, ingress controller, or whatever mechanism you're using to accept traffic from outside. This can be an extra safeguard to prevent a misconfigured backend service from accidentally being reachable from the internet.

For internal segmentation, you can use Kubernetes network policies to isolate pods. For example, the database pods can be configured to only allow access from the application server pods.

The equivalent functionality to security groups is already built in for many use cases. In container networking, you allow access only to specific ports on the container as part of the configuration. This performs much of the functionality of security groups at the container level. In addition, containers are usually running only the specific processes needed and no other unnecessary services. One of the primary benefits of security groups is that they act as a second layer of protection in case unnecessary services are running, to prevent access to them.

For a certain amount of virtual machine separation, you can also "taint" specific worker nodes so that only DMZ pods will be scheduled on those nodes. You might put those nodes into a separate subnet. Figure 6-5 shows an alternate version of the sample application using containers.

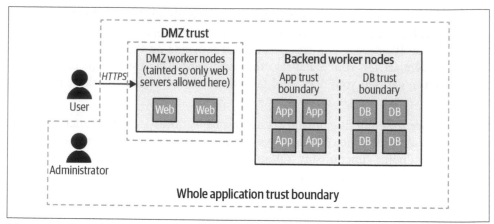

Figure 6-5. Sample container network controls

Note that this addresses only network isolation; compute isolation is still a concern in the container world, which is why Figure 6-5 showed the most vulnerable systems isolated to separate worker nodes. Containers all run on the same operating system, and an operating system provides a lot more functionality than the virtualized hardware of a VM, which means that there are more possibilities for an attacker who gets inside a container to break out and affect other containers.

Allowing Administrative Access

Now that you have set up some walls around your application and some internal trip-wires to catch anyone who's gotten inside, other systems or your administrators may need a way of getting past your perimeter to maintain your application.

One of the worst things our attacker, Molly, can do is get access to administrative interfaces—for example, direct access to our database administration interfaces—and pull all of our customer data out through the back door. Requiring that all administrative access take place via a VPN or a bastion host makes her have to go through considerable effort before even attempting to log in to our backend database. This section discusses when to use VPNs or bastion hosts.

 Your administrators might not need to get inside the perimeter if you have a method to run commands on servers (such as AWS Systems Manager Run Command, or kubectl exec), or if they can always diagnose problems via the logs coming out and replace any component that's acting up with a new version. It's ideal if you can run day-to-day operations without getting behind the perimeter, but many applications aren't designed for this.

Bastion hosts

Bastion hosts (also called *jump hosts*) are systems for administrative access that are accessible from a less trusted network (such as the internet). The network is set up so that all communication to the internal networks must flow through a bastion host.

A bastion host has the following useful security properties:

- Like a VPN, it reduces your attack surface, because it's a single-purpose hardened host that other machines hide behind.

- It can allow for session recording, which is very useful for advanced privileged user monitoring. Session recordings may be spot-checked to catch an insider attack, use of stolen credentials, or an attacker's use of a remote access trojan (RAT)[7] to control a legitimate administrator's workstation.

- In some cases (for example, incoming Remote Desktop Protocol connections where a user then uses a web browser for HTTPS connections), a bastion host performs a protocol shift. This can make things more difficult for attackers because they need to compromise both the bastion host and the destination application.

Many privileged access management tools, in addition to allowing administrators to check out credentials to use administrative identities when needed, can also operate in an "inline mode" where they have similar features to bastion hosts, such as session recording, session monitoring, session termination, or the ability to block certain commands from being issued.

I recommend using bastion hosts if the advanced capabilities of session recording or protocol shifts are useful in your environment, or if a client-to-site VPN is not suitable for some reason. Otherwise, I recommend using client-to-site VPNs provided as a service for administrative access, because it's one less thing for you to maintain.

Virtual private networks

Creating a VPN is like stretching a virtual cable from one location to another. In reality, the connectivity is actually performed by using an encrypted session across an untrusted network like the internet. There are two primary VPN functions, which are very different:

---

7 A *remote access trojan* is a type of malware used to control an unsuspecting user's system. For example, an administrator may browse to a malicious website, which silently installs a RAT. Late at night, when the administrator is asleep, an attacker may take control of the administrator's workstation and use open sessions or cached credentials to attack the system.

Site-to-site communications

Two separate sets of systems communicate with one another using an encrypted tunnel over an untrusted network such as the internet. This might be used for all users at a site to get through the perimeter to access the application, or for one application to talk to another application. It should not normally be used to protect administrative interfaces.

Client-to-site (or "road warrior") communications

An individual user with a workstation or mobile device virtually plugs in to a remote network. This might be used by an end user to access an application or by an administrator to work on the individual components of an application.

The following subsections describe these solutions and show their advantages and drawbacks.

Site-to-site VPNs

VPNs for site-to-site communications can provide additional security, but they can also lead to poor security practices. For this reason, I no longer recommend using a site-to-site VPN if all of the communication that flows between the sites uses TLS and if IP allowlisting is applied where feasible. Here are the reasons for this:

1. Setting up a site-to-site VPN is more work than using TLS. A VPN requires configuring two firewalls (or often four, as they're usually redundant pairs) with the proper parameters, credentials, and routing information.

2. Using a site-to-site VPN is arguably less secure if it leads to the use of insecure protocols. That's because VPNs leave the data in motion unprotected on either end before it enters the tunnel, so an attacker who manages to get inside the perimeter may be able to eavesdrop on that traffic.[8]

3. Site-to-site VPNs are too coarse-grained, in that they'll allow anyone on one network (often a large corporate network) to access another network (such as your administrative interfaces). It's better to perform access control at the administrative user level than the network level.

Of course, you can use both a VPN and TLS connections inside the VPN for additional security. However, your efforts are probably better spent elsewhere in most cases, and you should definitely prioritize end-to-end encryption with TLS first. There is some limited security benefit in hiding the details of your communications (such as destination ports) from an attacker. If you do choose to use both TLS and a VPN, you should use a different protocol for your VPN, such as IPsec, or the same

---

8 Internet users around the world became alerted to this potential through Edward Snowden's explosive revelations (*https://oreil.ly/VRAKX*).

vulnerability may allow an attacker to compromise both the VPN tunnel and the transport security inside it.

Client-to-site VPNs

I no longer recommend client-to-site VPNs for end-user access to most corporate applications unless they hold really sensitive information or have known weaknesses that are impractical to fix quickly.[9] VPNs are often inconvenient for end users and can be detrimental to battery life on mobile devices. Plus, once the user base is large enough, it's much more likely that an attacker can get access to the corporate network because there are so many individuals to attack. VPNs can be a good control in some cases, but they are second only to firewalls in terms of people assuming that they convey some sort of magical protection.

If you do decide to require VPN access for your internal application, I recommend using a completely different set of credentials for the VPN, such as a TLS certificate issued by a completely different administrative domain from the one issuing your normal user credentials. You should already have implemented the controls in Chapter 4, and you don't want your VPN layer to become a redundant implementation of the same access management controls your application is already using. Make sure that you do not relax any application controls based on the fact that users need a VPN to access the application.

Administrators are different from end users, however. Client-to-site VPNs can be a good way for your administrators to gain access to the internal workings of your cloud environment. (Another good way is a bastion host, or jump host, discussed previously). The reasons I suggest a VPN for administrators, and not for regular end users, are that the backend connections used by administrators are often higher risk (because there are more of them, so they're harder to secure), the cost to implement is lower (because there are fewer administrators than end users), and there should be few enough administrators that it's harder for an attacker to accidentally be granted access. So, in many cases, VPN access is worth it for administrators, but not for end users, though obviously this is highly dependent on your application and risk appetite.

VPNs have both the benefit and drawback of permitting more protocols than bastion hosts. Being able to use additional protocols can make life easier for administrators but can also make it easier for an attacker driving a compromised workstation to attack the production network. VPNs also don't support session recording, so for these reasons, higher-security environments will often use bastion hosts.

---

9 Google doesn't either (*https://oreil.ly/BGnmy*).

Client-to-site VPNs are usually easy to use but often require some sort of software to be installed on the administrator's workstation, which can be a concern in companies that restrict software installation, and sometimes different VPN products will conflict with one another. Most solutions support the use of complex credentials (such as a certificate or a key) and two-factor authentication to mitigate the risk of easily guessed credentials or stolen credentials.

Examples of client-to-site VPN access on different cloud platforms are listed in Table 6-2.

Table 6-2. VPN access in popular cloud providers

Provider	VPN features
Amazon Web Services	Amazon Client VPN
Microsoft Azure	VPN Gateway
Google Cloud Platform	Google Cloud VPN
IBM Cloud	IBM Cloud Client VPN for VPC

Some industry or regulatory certifications may require you log the creation of VPN connections. Make sure you can get connection logs out of your VPN solution!

Network Defense Tools

At this point you should have a perimeter, internal controls, and a way for your administrators to get through the perimeter as needed. Now, let's move on to some more advanced controls.

Web application firewalls

A web application firewall is a great way to provide an extra layer of protection against common programming errors in your application, as well as vulnerabilities in libraries or other dependencies that you use. A WAF is really just a smart proxy; it gets the request, checks the request for various bad behaviors such as SQL injection attacks, and then makes the request to the backend system if it's safe to do so. WAFs can protect against attacks that traditional firewalls can't, because the TCP/IP traffic is perfectly legitimate and the traditional firewalls don't look at the actual effects on the application layer.

WAFs can also help you respond quickly to a new vulnerability, because it's often faster to configure the WAF to block the exploit than to update all of your systems.

In traditional environments, WAFs can often be "blinky boxes"—they sit in a rack and blink lights reassuringly on the front panel, but are not actually effective at stopping anything. In both traditional and cloud environments, if you don't set up properly customized rules for your application, maintain those rules, and look at alerts, you probably aren't getting a lot of value from your WAF. Unfortunately, sometimes WAFs are just used to check a compliance box and are only in place because they offer an easier route to PCI compliance than code inspections.

In cloud environments, a WAF may be delivered as Software as a Service, as an appliance, or in a distributed (host-based) model. In the cases of a WAF service or appliance, you must be careful to ensure that all traffic actually passes through the WAF. This often requires the use of IP allowlists to block all traffic that's not coming from the WAF, which can lead to a minimal amount of additional maintenance because the list of IP addresses for requests coming from a cloud WAF offering will vary over time. It can also be difficult to route all traffic through your WAF appliance without creating a single point of failure. Some cloud providers offer services, such as AWS Firewall Manager, that help you ensure that your applications are always covered by a WAF.

A host-based model doesn't have these problems; all traffic will be processed by the distributed WAF regardless. You do need to have good inventory management and deployment processes to ensure that the WAF gets deployed to each system, but this is often an easier task than ensuring that all traffic flows through a SaaS or appliance.

RASP modules

A runtime application self-protection module is similar to a WAF in many ways. Like WAFs, RASP modules attempt to block exploits at the application layer, but the mechanism used is significantly different. A RASP works by running alongside your application code and watching how the application handles requests, instead of only seeing the requests. RASP modules must support the specific language and application environment, whereas WAFs can be used in front of almost any application. Some vendors have both WAF and RASP module offerings, and an application can be protected by both a RASP module and a WAF.

Our attacker, Molly, might attempt to come right in the front door as a normal user and find some problem with our application that allows her to steal all of our customer data. If we've accidentally left a way for her to fool our application into giving up the data, a WAF or RASP module might be able to block it.

Note that one of the most common methods of attacking web applications is the use of stolen or weak credentials. If Molly has a set of administrative credentials providing access to all data, a WAF or RASP module will not defend against this type of attack, which is why identity and access management is so important! However, I still recommend the use of SaaS or host-based WAFs and RASP modules for web applications in the cloud, and even APIs can get some limited benefits from parameter checking.

 A cloud WAF service will be able to see all of the content in your communications. This should not be an issue for most organizations, with the proper legal agreements in place and when dealing with a reputable WAF company, but may be a problem for some highly regulated organizations.

Anti-DDoS

Distributed denial-of-service (DDoS) attacks are a huge problem for many companies with internet-facing services. If you receive too many fake requests or too much useless traffic, you can't provide services to the legitimate requesters.

The other controls we've discussed are generally recommended; you should rarely accept the risk of doing without them. However, you need to check your threat model before investing too much in anti-DDoS measures. Put more bluntly, is anyone going to care enough to knock you off the internet, and how big of a problem is it for you if they do? Unlike a data breach, where you can never remove all copies of the stolen data, a DDoS attack will eventually end.

If you're running any sort of online retailing application, or a large corporation's web presence, or any other application such as a game service where downtime can obviously cost you money or cause embarrassment, you're potentially a target for extortionists who will demand money in return for stopping an attack. If you're hosting any content that's controversial, you're likewise an obvious target. Note that the bar to entry is very low; there are "testing" or "booter" services available cheaply that can easily generate too much traffic for your site to handle, so it only takes one individual with a few hundred dollars to ruin your day.

However, if you're running a back-office application where some downtime will not obviously limit your business or embarrass you, you may need very little in the way of anti-DDoS measures. If this is the case, make sure that you *clearly document that you're accepting the risk of DDoS attacks* and get agreement from all of your stakeholders! While foregoing (or having very limited) anti-DDoS protections may be the correct choice in some cases, it should not be the default choice, and it's not one to be made lightly.

Anti-DDoS measures can be blinky boxes or virtual appliances, but in most cases today, anti-DDoS protection is delivered in a SaaS model. This is largely due to economies of scale; anti-DDoS services often need a large internet pipe and lot of compute power to sort through all of the incoming requests and filter out the fake ones, but this capacity is needed only occasionally for each customer. An individual anti-DDoS appliance (or its network connection) can easily be overwhelmed by a large-scale volumetric attack.

If you choose to implement anti-DDoS measures, I recommend you use a cloud service. There are many providers in this space; two examples are Akamai and Cloudflare. You will need to route all of your traffic through the anti-DDoS service, tune your rules, and practice an attack scenario.

Some IaaS providers also provide anti-DDoS as a service. In addition, there are independent anti-DDoS cloud services, and some of these also include WAF functionality. Note that a cloud anti-DDoS service can function in some modes without decrypting your traffic, but a cloud WAF will need to be able to decrypt your traffic in order to function. For that reason, you need to ensure that any cloud WAF provider you engage can meet your security and compliance requirements.

Intrusion detection and prevention systems

In the traditional IT world, an *intrusion detection system* (IDS) is often a blinky box that generates alerts when the traffic that passes through it matches one of its rules. An *intrusion prevention system* (IPS) will block the traffic in addition to alerting. An IDS/IPS agent may also be deployed to each host, configured centrally, to detect and block malicious traffic coming to that host. IDS and IPS are almost always offered in the same product, and are generally treated as the same control. If you are more sure that a certain type of traffic is malicious, or if your risk tolerance is lower, you will configure a particular rule to block rather than just alert.

An IDS/IPS rule may be signature-based and trigger on the content of the communication—for example, upon seeing a particular stream of bytes included in a piece of malware. For this to work, the IDS/IPS needs to be able to see the clear-text communications, which it often does by having the keys to decrypt all of the communications. This is a valid model, but it makes the IDS/IPS a valuable target for attackers; not only can an attacker who compromises an IDS/IPS watch all traffic going through it, but if they obtain the signing certificates or private keys used by the IDS/IPS, they may be able to carry out attacks elsewhere on the network. In addition, newer ciphers with "forward secrecy" prevent this type of snooping. There are trade-offs, but for both functional and risk reasons, I do not normally recommend snooping on encrypted traffic on the network.

IDS/IPS rules may also be based on behavior, triggering only on the metadata of the network traffic. For example, a system that is initiating connections to a lot of network ports (port scanning) may be owned by an attacker, so you can have a rule that checks for that. Such rules can be useful even when traffic is encrypted end to end so that the IDS/IPS cannot look inside it.

For this control, there is not a lot of difference between traditional deployments and cloud deployments. In the blinky box model, the IDS/IPS will often be a virtual appliance instead of a physical box. However, all traffic must flow through that virtual appliance in order for it to detect or prevent attacks. This can sometimes lead to scalability concerns, because virtual appliances often cannot process as much traffic as a dedicated box with hardware optimizations. It can also be difficult to position an infrastructure IDS/IPS solution so that all traffic flows through it. If you succeed at this, you may still add latency and another potential point of failure as traffic takes extra hops to get to the IDS/IPS and then to the backend system, instead of going directly from the end user to the backend system.

Host-based IDS/IPS solutions in cloud environments also function similarly to their traditional counterparts, though they can often be baked into virtual machine images or container layers more easily than they can be rolled out to already installed operating systems. Incorporating them into images can be an easier model to use in cloud environments, because the systems being protected may be spread around the world.

Although there is some difference of opinion on the matter, an IDS/IPS might not add much value as part of a perimeter control if a WAF is used correctly. This is because the WAF prevents the IDS/IPS from seeing most attacks. However, an IDS/IPS can be very useful for detecting an attacker who has already gotten through the perimeter. If our attacker, Molly, attempts to perform reconnaissance via a port scan from one of our cloud instances, an internal IDS/IPS may be able to alert us to the threat.

If you have already correctly implemented and tested the other controls described in this chapter and want additional protection, I recommend baking a host-based IDS/IPS agent into each of your system images and having the agents report to a central logging server for analysis.

Egress Filtering

You've implemented all of the controls we've discussed, and you want to tighten down the environment even further. Great! You absolutely have to expect and block attacks from the outside. However, it's possible someone will take control of one of your components. For that reason, it is also a great idea to limit outbound, or *egress*, communications even from components that you should be able to trust. These are some reasons to perform egress filtering:

- Supply chain attacks are on the rise, with the SolarWinds hack being the best-known example as of this writing. While a big part of the solution to supply chain woes is better protections in the build and distribution processes, egress controls can also prevent damage by keeping a successful attacker from being able to call home for instructions.

- An attacker may want to steal a copy of your data by transferring it to some place outside your control. This is called *data exfiltration*. Egress filtering can help reduce or slow data exfiltration in the event of a successful attack. However, in addition to limiting normal connections, you must also take care to block other avenues of data exfiltration, such as DNS tunneling, Internet Control Message Protocol (ICMP) tunneling, and hijacking of existing allowed inbound connections. For example, if an attacker compromises a web or application server and puts the data on it, that system will happily serve up the data, bypassing any egress controls. This is primarily useful when you have a large volume of data to protect; smaller amounts of data could be written down or screenshotted.[10]

- Egress filtering can also help prevent *watering hole* attacks, although these are less common against servers than against end users. For example, your policy may require that all components be updated from an internal trusted source. However, due to human error, a service might be configured to make unauthorized calls out to an update server that could be compromised by an attacker to provide it with a malicious update. In this case, egress filtering would be a second line of defense against that attack, making it impossible for the misconfigured component to reach out to the update server.

 Egress filtering is required for some environments: for example, the NIST 800-53 Rev 5 controls list the requirement under SC-7(5) for moderate environments, and as an optional enhancement in SC-5(1) to prevent your own systems from participating in a denial-of-service attack against someone else. Egress filtering controls can include simple outbound port restrictions, outbound IP allowlists and port restrictions, or even an authenticating proxy that allows only the HTTPS traffic that a specific component requires.

Outbound port restrictions are the simplest way to limit traffic, but also the least effective. For example, you may decide that there's no good reason for any part of your cloud deployment to be talking to anything else other than over the default HTTPS port, tcp/443, but that you can allow tcp/443 traffic to any destination. While that may prevent a few types of malware from calling home, such a solution is not particularly effective and is often used to check a compliance box saying you have egress controls. In a cloud deployment, port-based egress filtering can be done via

---

10 Copying data via mobile device photos and videos, often called the "analog hole," is nearly impossible to block without very restrictive physical controls, such as searching individuals before allowing entrance to a secured area.

security groups or network ACLs, analogous to the way it's done for the ingress controls discussed earlier.

Outbound IP allowlisting can be effective when it works. However, like inbound IP allowlisting, outbound IP allowlisting is becoming less and less feasible with the rise of CDNs and GSLBs. While these are very important tools for making content and services available more quickly and reliably, they render IP-based controls ineffective because the content may reside at many different IP addresses around the world that change rapidly.

Proxies are the most effective way to implement egress controls. One variant is creating an *explicit proxy*. This is done by creating a proxy server and then only allowing components to talk to the proxy, not the outside world. The downside is that you must configure each component to ask the proxy to make connections on its behalf. Most operating systems have the ability to set an explicit proxy at the OS level; for example, on Linux, you can set the `http_proxy` and `https_proxy` environment variables, and on Windows you can change the proxy settings in the control panel. Many applications that run on the operating system will use this proxy if it's set, but not all. One nice feature is that in most cases, the proxy will set up the connection for you but will not be able to see the traffic.

Another option is using a *transparent proxy*. In this case, something on the network (such as an intelligent router) sends the traffic to the proxy instead of the requested destination. The proxy pretends to be the "real" destination, then evaluates the request (for example, to see whether it's going to an allowlisted URL) and makes the request on behalf of the backend system if it meets the validation requirements. The downsides with transparent proxies are that the proxy can see the information flowing through, and for a transparent proxy to work you must weaken protections in TLS that keep other systems from pretending to be the destination site!

Some newer technologies, such as Istio (*https://oreil.ly/xE7vy*), can transparently proxy only allowed traffic in a Kubernetes cluster. In the future, it's likely that more and more platforms will allow you to specify as part of the deployment which sites or URLs a component needs to reach, and the egress restrictions will be implemented automatically by the platform on a per-component basis.

While HTTP is certainly the most common protocol to proxy, there are proxies available for other protocols as well. Note that for HTTPS connections, the source should validate that the destination is the correct system by means of an X.509 certificate.[11] This validation will fail unless the transparent proxy has the ability to impersonate any site, which is risky.

---

11 Don't turn off certificate checking, except as a very temporary measure for troubleshooting connection errors. TLS provides no protection from man-in-the-middle attacks if certificate checking is turned off.

Like an IDS/IPS, a proxy itself becomes an attractive target for attackers. Anyone with access to the proxy can perform a man-in-the-middle attack and, depending on the proxy configuration, may be able to listen to or modify any data flowing through it. This can easily compromise the entire application. In addition, if the proxy has a signing certificate trusted by the components in your cloud deployment, an attacker who gets that signing certificate can impersonate any site until the certificate is removed from the trust stores of all components. If you choose to implement a transparent proxy for egress traffic, make sure that it is protected at least as well as the other components of the system.

With supply chain attacks becoming much more common, I now recommend the use of proxies for any higher-security environments. However, they can be painful to implement because you may not have a good list of all of the internet connections your different components are making. If you're willing to accept the risk that one of the products you're using may be compromised, then limited egress controls via network ACLs and security groups may suffice. In the example in Figure 6-3, I showed a combination egress proxy and data loss prevention system, but this may also be performed by an as-a-service offering.

Data Loss Prevention

Data loss prevention (DLP) watches for sensitive data that is either improperly stored in the environment or is being copied out of the environment. Cloud providers may offer DLP services as an add-on feature to other services, or you may choose to implement DLP controls yourself in your environment.

In an IaaS/PaaS cloud environment, DLP may be implemented as part of egress controls. For example, the web proxy for outbound communications may be configured with DLP technology to alert an administrator or block an outbound communication if it contains credit card information. DLP may also be integrated into an IDS/IPS device, or performed by a standalone virtual appliance through which traffic flows and is decrypted and inspected. The same trade-offs apply here as discussed with proxies: if the DLP appliance can read the information flowing through, then it has to be secured at least as well as the systems that hold the information, and technologies such as forward secrecy prevent both attackers and DLP devices from snooping on the traffic even if the key is known.

A SaaS environment may integrate DLP directly to prevent certain data types from being stored at all, or to automatically tag such information. This type of DLP, if available, can be considerably more effective than egress-based DLP controls, but it is highly specific to the SaaS.

If you have sensitive information, such as payment information or personal health data, you may need to incorporate DLP controls into your cloud environment. For the majority of cloud deployments, however, DLP may not be required. Unless you are willing to carefully configure the solution, follow up on alerts, and deal with false positives, DLP will only provide you with a false sense of security.

Conclusion

Do you know what our attacker, Molly, will actually do in a lot of cases? She will point scanning tools such as Nmap, Nessus, or Burp Suite at every system she can find. She'll find some viable command injection attack, or MySQL instance with default credentials, or vulnerable SMTP server, or some other silly thing that has been missed despite all of the vulnerability and asset management processes in place. She'll use default credentials, an unpatched vulnerability, or a similar problem to get in and compromise the rest of the system from there.

An attacker might gain entry for several reasons: maybe your asset management process has a leak, or items vulnerable to attack were turned on by accident, or your vulnerability management process missed a vulnerable component or configuration, or someone set a stupid password despite policies and controls to avoid it. The network controls may be either your first or last line of defense in those cases, but don't depend on them as your *only* line of defense.

As examples, the perimeter might be able to stop someone from getting in to exploit these failures in other processes, or at least give you a chance to notice an attack in progress and respond. TLS may prevent an attacker with a small foothold from sniffing credentials or data. The WAF may jump in front of an injection attack that would have tricked your application into giving out all of your data through the front door. An IPS/IDS may detect and block unauthorized scans inside your perimeter. Security groups may help protect you by saying, "Look, this is a virtual machine or container for component X. It needs to let in only specific traffic for component X, and also maybe some administrative stuff. Also, the administrative stuff should come only from over here, not from a kid in his parents' basement."

For those reasons, network controls are an important layer of protection for your cloud environment. While a lot of technically complicated controls are available, it's important to prioritize them to get the best protection for your efforts. I recommend that you go through the following steps in the order listed:

1. Draw a diagram of your application, with trust boundaries.

2. Make sure that your inbound connections use TLS, and that all component-to-component communications that may go across the wire use TLS with authentication.

3. Enforce a perimeter and internal segmentation, and provide a secure way for your administrators to manage the systems via a bastion host, a VPN, or another method offered by your cloud provider.

4. Set up a web application firewall, RASP, and/or IDS/IPS, if appropriate.

5. Set up DDoS protection if appropriate.

6. Set up at least limited egress (outbound) filtering, with more strict egress filtering for higher-security applications.

7. Check all of these configurations regularly to make sure they're still correct and useful. Some cloud providers provide services to check configurations, including network configurations. For example, you could have an automated check to make sure all of your systems' security groups are configured to only permit SSH access from specific IP addresses.

It should be somewhat obvious that none of the controls presented here are particularly effective in a "check-the-box" mode, where you deploy them and then do not take care to tune them, update them, and investigate what they're finding. It's very important not only to set up these controls, but also to continually review logs to detect intrusion attempts or attackers already in the network trying to move laterally. Investigating alerts from security tooling finds leads us into the subject of the next and final chapter: detecting, responding, and recovering from security incidents.

Exercises

1. Which of the following are likely to be useful in protecting your cloud environment from network-based attacks? Select all that apply.

   a. Security groups

   b. Network access control lists

   c. Virtual firewall appliances

   d. Physical firewall appliances

2. What features does a virtual private cloud (VPC) typically offer?

   a. Dedicated virtual network segments

   b. Dedicated storage

   c. Dedicated CPUs

   d. Dedicated encryption keys

3. What are some of the benefits of using Transport Layer Security (TLS)? Select all that apply.

   a. Server authentication

   b. Confidentiality of data transmitted

   c. Integrity of data transmitted

   d. Blocking network connections by attackers

4. True or false: There is no need for a perimeter in modern cloud environments.

5. Which of the following statements about internal network segmentation are true for cloud environments? Select all that apply.

   a. Internal network segmentation is typically easier to implement in cloud environments than traditional environments.

   b. Cloud providers usually do not charge additional fees for internal segmentation.

   c. Security groups allow you to create separate subnets for your different applications.

   d. Network access control lists allow you to prevent systems in one subnet from talking to another subnet.

6. True or false: Anti-DDoS appliances can effectively mitigate large scale volumetric DDoS attacks.

7. Which of the following statements about egress filtering are true? Select all that apply.

  a. Egress filtering can prevent malware from "calling home."

  b. Egress filtering can protect against exploitation of supply chain attacks.

  c. Egress filtering is most effective using IP-based controls.

  d. Egress filtering is most effective using proxies.

  e. Egress filtering is typically difficult in traditional environments, but easy to apply in cloud environments.

CHAPTER 7

Detecting, Responding to, and Recovering from Security Incidents

By now, you know what your cloud assets are, and you have put some reasonable protections in place for them. Everything's good, right?

When you're two-thirds of the way through a mystery novel and the mystery appears to be solved, you know the story isn't over. It's probably not a big surprise that you're not done with cloud security yet either, since there are still pages left in this book.

All of the previous chapters have dealt with identifying your assets and protecting them. Unfortunately, you won't always be successful. In fact, in some organizations and industries, minor security incidents are a routine part of life! At some point attackers will almost certainly attempt, sometimes successfully, to gain unauthorized access to your assets. At that point, the trick is to detect them as quickly as possible, kick them out, and do whatever damage control is needed. As part of this, it is helpful to understand what attackers often do and how attacks often proceed.

We've seen many high-profile breaches in the past few years. What often distinguishes a bad breach from a really bad breach—there are no good ones—is how long it took to detect what was going on and how effectively the victim responded. One recent study of more than 550 organizations (*https://oreil.ly/sQIQR*) showed that the mean time to identify a breach was 277 days, and that companies that identified a breach in fewer than 200 days saved more than $1 million compared to those that took more than 200 days. With that in mind, let's see what we can do to detect issues and respond to them before they become disasters.

Differences from Traditional IT

Take another look at the shared responsibility model diagram from Chapter 1 (Figure 1-8).

In a traditional environment, you had to worry about what was happening at every one of these levels. The good news about cloud environments is that intrusion detection and response are the provider's job, in the areas that are their responsibility. Rarely, you could be affected by a breach at your provider, in which case you should be notified and may need to perform response and recovery activities specific to the services you're using. However, in the vast majority of cases, all of your detection, response, and recovery activities will be in the areas marked "consumer responsibility."

For the most part, you don't get to see any logs from the levels that are the provider's responsibility, although you can sometimes see actions the provider has taken on your behalf, such as accessing your encryption keys. However, there's an important new source of privileged user logs in a cloud environment: you can track things your team did using the provider's portals, APIs, and command-line interfaces.

You won't be allowed to touch the physical hardware in a cloud environment. Many incident response teams use a "jump bag" with forensic laptops, hard drive duplicators, and similar technology. Although you may still need such tools for dealing with incidents involving non-cloud infrastructure (for example, malware infections on on-premises servers), you will need virtual, cloud-based equivalents of the jump bag tools for incident response in the cloud. This also means that the forensic parts of cloud incident response can be done from anywhere, although there may still be benefits to being physically colocated with other people involved in the response.

What to Watch

Any system of reasonable size offers so many different logs and metrics that it's easy to get buried in data that's not useful for security purposes. Picking what to watch is very important! Unfortunately, this will necessarily be specific to your environment and application, so you really need to think about your threat model—what assets you have and who is most likely to attack them—as well as what logs come out of the systems in your asset management pipeline, discussed in Chapter 3.

As an example, if you have many terabytes of data, watching metrics on the volume of your network traffic and the length of connections might be very useful to spot someone in the process of stealing it. However, network traffic metrics like that won't be as useful if you're distributing software that you think someone may try to compromise with a backdoor. In that case, the volume of data, destination, and session length won't change, but the content will be corrupted.

As another example, if you've paid for a specific tool such as antivirus software, and have done the work to ensure that all of your cloud VMs are running it, it's pretty silly to ignore it when it's screaming that it has found something. When you see alerts from that tool, it may have successfully protected you from the entire attack. However, it may also have blocked only part of the attack, or it may have detected something suspicious but not blocked it. You need to investigate to see how the malware got on the system and whether the attack was fully blocked or not.

Once you have a threat model in mind, and a good idea of what components make up your environment, the following sidebar covers some good general starting points for what to watch. We will look at more concrete examples when we consider the sample application at the end of the chapter.

Logs, Events, Alerts, and Metrics

A *log*, or *event*, is a record of a specific thing that happened. For example, your environment might generate a log record whenever someone authenticates, or makes a web request, or changes a configuration, or any number of other things that could happen in a complex environment.

An *alert* is a type of event where the system's rules indicate that it's worth notifying someone. The fact that antivirus software pulled updated definitions is an event. The fact that it actually found malware should be an alert!

Metrics are sets of numbers that give information about something. Metrics are usually time-based, so you might have a metric collected every minute for how many authentication requests have happened, how much free disk space is available, or the number of web requests made.

The primary advantage of logs is that they provide a lot more information about what has happened, but the cost of storing and searching logs can increase quickly as activity increases. If you have twice as many web requests, you have twice as many log records! On the other hand, while the numbers reported by metrics during each time period will get larger as activity increases, the cost of storing and processing the metrics doesn't increase (because it usually takes the same space to store the numbers 100 and 200). Both logs and metrics can be useful for detecting security incidents and generating alerts, and metrics can sometimes be a better choice for alerting when there are too many log entries to deal with.

For each of the following types of events, you need to make sure that the log entries contain enough data to be useful. At a minimum, this usually means *when*, *what*, and *who*: when the event happened, what happened, and who triggered the event. In some cases "who" might be a system or other automatic tool, such as when a system reports high CPU usage.

With one exception, you should never put passwords, API keys, sensitive personal information, protected health information, or any other sensitive data in logs. In most cases, not every individual who has access to the logs is authorized to see that information. In addition, having copies of sensitive information in more places than necessary increases the risk that it will be accidentally disclosed.

In fact, for privacy reasons, you should avoid directly logging personally identifiable data wherever feasible. If you need to be able to figure out who is referred to in logs, use non-personally identifiable unique IDs, such as GUIDs, and keep a table elsewhere that lets you correlate those GUIDs to the actual entities.

The exception to the rule about sensitive data in logs is session recording for privileged user monitoring, which may occasionally log API keys used on a command line or other sensitive information. In this case, access to the session records must be very tightly controlled, such as by sending them to a "deposit only" location so that only a small monitoring team is able to see them after they're generated. The risk reduction from being able to audit privileged user sessions will often outweigh the increased risk of occasional secrets in those records.

Privileged User Access

Almost everyone should be logging and at least spot-checking privileged user logins at all levels of their environments. Watching these can be a great way to trigger questions that lead to detecting malicious activity, such as "Why is that person logging in at all?" or "Didn't that person leave the company?" or "Does anyone recognize this account?"

Monitoring privileged user access doesn't mean you don't trust your administrators. In a perfect world, you wouldn't have to place 100% trust in any single individual. Every task that involves a risk would need to be approved by at least two people, requiring collusion in order to perform such tasks without being detected.[1] That level of diligence certainly isn't necessary for all tasks in all organizations, although you should consider it for high-value actions such as money transfers or access to secret data stores. What we're mostly focused on here is detecting an unauthorized person *pretending* to be an administrator. Given that one of the most prevalent causes of security incidents is lost or stolen credentials, watching what your administrators are doing is a great way to catch someone pretending to be an admin.

Cloud providers can keep good logs of when someone logged on as one of your administrators using the cloud administrative interfaces (the web portal, APIs, or command-line interfaces), and what they did—for example, you may see logs such as "created an instance," "created a database," or "created an administrative user." These logs may be collected by cloud services like AWS CloudTrail, Azure Activity Log, Google Cloud's operations suite, and IBM Cloud Activity Tracker; but in some cases you have to explicitly turn on the logging feature, specify where and how long to retain logs, and pay for the storage.

In addition to privileged user logs collected by the cloud provider, administrators often also have privileged access to the systems created in the cloud environment. For example, you may have administrative accounts on virtual machines, or on firewall appliances, or on databases. Access to these may be reported using a protocol like syslog. You may also have other systems used by administrators, such as a password vault to check out shared IDs. Generally speaking, any systems used by administrators to perform privileged actions should log those actions for later inspection.

Administrative activity logs should be divided into two types, which I'll label toxic logs and sanitized logs.

Toxic logs might contain sensitive information, such as passwords and API keys that could give an attacker direct access to the system. You may not have any toxic logs in your environment. In general, toxic logs should be accessed only during a suspected

---

1 This is sometimes also called the "four eyes principle," the "two-person rule," or the "two-man rule."

incident, or by a small, monitored team that regularly spot-checks administrative sessions. When toxic logs are accessed, that should also trigger some form of notification so that at least two people know the logs were accessed. Here are some examples of toxic logs:

- Secure shell session logs or other logs showing commands and options
- The exact commands executed by admins on virtual machines via a cloud provider feature such as Amazon EC2 Run Command, unless you have some way to keep secrets from being logged with those commands
- The exact commands executed by admins on containers, such as those beginning with kubectl exec, unless you have some way to keep secrets from being logged with those commands

Sanitized logs are specifically designed not to contain secrets. The vast majority of logs should fall into this category. Here are some examples of sanitized logs:

- Actions that the admin performs via a cloud API or the cloud provider console
- Actions that the admin performs on the Kubernetes console, such as deploying a new application or authorizing additional users
- Successful and failed authentication and authorization attempts for any of the components in the system (for instance, if an administrator successfully logs into the cloud console but is not allowed to create a resource there, both events should be logged)

Session Recording Tools

One of the functions usually included in privileged access management or privileged identity management systems is session management—the ability to record privileged sessions, as well as watch what a privileged user is doing in real time and disconnect sessions that are suspicious. This is particularly important in areas where the systems being managed have high confidentiality or integrity requirements, and there's a significant incentive for attackers to either access or change the data managed by these systems.

Session recording tools generally work in one of two models: either all sessions go through one central location for recording and control, or session recording happens using agents on the servers themselves. Having everything go through a central location has the downside of a single point of failure. Having everything logged by a local agent on the server has the downside that the privileged user often has the privileges to turn off the agent. In general, I recommend having centralized session recording, with a break-glass process to gain access if the session recording infrastructure is down.

The privileged users of most of the systems being managed and the privileged users who manage the session recording tool should generally be different groups. Again, you want to set up a system where no single individual (or attacker pretending to be that individual) can issue malicious commands and also disable the logging of those malicious commands.

As previously mentioned, session recording logs are "toxic," in that they may contain passwords or other secrets. I generally recommend that session recording tools be configured to deposit logs in a "drop box" fashion, where the recording tool can send logs to a centralized location but does not have a local copy and cannot see or modify the logs after sending them.

Logs from Defensive Tooling

If you have defensive tools like antivirus software, firewalls, web application firewalls, intrusion detection systems, or network monitoring tools, you need to be looking at the logs that these produce. You can't be certain that those tools will be 100% effective in preventing all attacks. In some cases, the tools may block the initial attack and let a subsequent attack through, or they may only log that something happened without blocking the attack. You need to collect and analyze the logs from these services, or you may be giving up a big early-warning advantage.

The problem is that some of these tools are necessarily noisy and have a high percentage of false positive alerts. Don't underestimate the risk of false positives! It's very easy to train yourself and your staff to ignore alerts that may actually be important. You need a feedback loop so that people seeing false positives have a way to try to either filter out specific logs from processing altogether or tune the system so that the tools don't produce false alerts as often. This is an art, of course, because you run the risk of filtering or tuning out true positives, but in most cases you should accept a small risk of tuning out a true positive to prevent your team from ignoring the alerts altogether. Just as you should have multiple layers of protection, you should also have multiple detection layers so that you're not dependent on only one tool to detect malicious activity.

The logging recommendations for most defensive tooling in cloud environments are very similar to in on-premises environments.

Anti-DDoS

Systems used to defend against denial-of-service attacks should be configured to alert on attacks. This should generally be a high-priority alert, such as paging someone, because DDoS attacks often escalate over time or are followed by an extortion attempt. In addition, a DDoS attack can be a distraction to cover up other breach activity, although there is disagreement as to how common this is.

Web application firewalls

Both distributed and centralized WAF solutions can alert on attacks that were blocked or on requests that look suspicious. These alerts can be useful to understand when an attack against your web applications has been attempted.

 WAFs are often used in lieu of manual code reviews for PCI DSS certification. As part of that, you'll also need to show that you're retaining and analyzing the logs from the WAF systems.

Firewalls and intrusion detection systems

Internet-facing firewalls and IDSs will need to be tuned fairly low for alerting, because systems exposed to the internet are under constant low-grade attack (such as port scans and password guessing). However, the historical data provided by these systems may be of use when an incident is suspected.

On the other hand, a firewall or IDS deployed inside your perimeter should be tuned to be fairly sensitive, because alerts here are probably indicative of misconfiguration or an actual attack. Aside from other defensive tools, which can be allowlisted so that they don't cause alerts, nothing else should really be scanning your internal network or causing failed connections.

In this same general category are *network traffic analysis* systems, which typically aggregate flow data from routers and switches to give an overall picture of how data is moving into, out of, and through your environment. These can also be configured to send alerts that might indicate something is wrong.

Antivirus

Ensure that you will get alerts if any in-scope systems in your asset management system aren't running antivirus software, and if any malware is found.

Note that when an attacker exploits a vulnerability to get into your system, their first step is usually to drop some malware on the system. If the attacker is smart, they'll make sure the malware they use is custom enough not to trip any antivirus software you have in place. Attackers can use services or may have labs to run their malware through every piece of antivirus software available to make sure it isn't detected. Fortunately, not all attackers are that smart, and these tools are still very helpful to catch the dumb ones. Don't reject tools just because they're not 100% effective!

In the infamous 2013 Target breach, one of the mistakes was not responding to the alerts from the antivirus software.

Detection and response tools

Whereas traditional anti-malware software focuses primarily on blocking malicious activity, *endpoint detection and response* (EDR) software is more focused on allowing teams to investigate and respond to threats that have gotten through the first line of defenses. If antivirus software is like the flame-retardant materials in a physical structure, the EDR software is like the smoke detector and sprinkler systems.

EDR is typically done by recording lots of information about the running systems, such as hash values of each executable or library that has run on the system, or a history of what network connections were attempted or made. While some of this information may be obtained via operating system or network logs, EDR software can accumulate it all in one place easily. There, it can be associated with threat intelligence feeds, such as newly discovered command-and-control servers or newly reported malware signatures, to detect both current and historical activity. Some EDR software can also be used to quarantine and investigate systems when an attack is identified.

While these capabilities are often used interactively by a response team, EDR solutions can also send alerts when threats are discovered in your environment, so they overlap somewhat with antivirus software.

All the DRs

The market is filled with many types of detection and response tools—as of this writing, EDR, NDR, and XDR are the most common categories. The definitions of these overlap somewhat and are not universally agreed upon, and many vendors will try to convince you that their tool can do everything. Let's take a quick look at each.

Endpoint detection and response (EDR) tools, as described earlier, offer three main benefits over traditional antivirus tools. The first is the use of many other signals besides signatures and process behaviors to alert on suspicious activity. The second is the ability to look back in history to see who or what is already infected, based on new information. The third is the ability to quickly quarantine an entire system that appears to have been compromised, rather than just quarantining a suspicious file.

Network detection and response (NDR) is similar, but for network flows. NDR tools often offer behavioral analysis in addition to signature checking, similar to network traffic analysis systems, as well as the ability to quickly lock down network flows in response to an active attack.

> Extended detection and response (XDR) is typically a combination of several different security products integrated together, although different vendors combine different functions and call it XDR.
>
> Regardless of the technologies you use, ensure that you're consuming the alerts from the tools and responding to them.

File integrity monitoring

Some files shouldn't change regularly, and if they are changed, that might be evidence of an attack. For example, if someone modifies the configuration of the logging system, that's suspicious. In fact, on a Linux system, most changes to the */etc* directory tree should be viewed with some suspicion.

File integrity monitoring (FIM) software can alert when specific files are changed, and some products also allow you to alert when certain Windows registry entries are changed. Some cloud providers offer FIM capability as part of the IaaS cloud management platform. There are also free and paid versions of FIM products that you can deploy to your systems.

 File integrity monitoring is explicitly required for PCI DSS certification, and some auditors may require it to cover not only flat files but also changes to the Windows registry.

Cloud provider monitoring tools

Cloud provider monitoring tools, such as AWS CloudTrail, Azure Monitor, and IBM Cloud Activity Tracker, can provide important insight into what the different entities inside your cloud account are doing. This is particularly important for privileged users or highly privileged service accounts.

These tools will typically have the ability to both collect logs and set alerts for actions that either should never happen or should be rare enough that they warrant notifying other users. Some examples of these types of actions may be assuming a privileged role inside the cloud account or changing security parameters of the cloud account or critical services in the account.

Cloud Service Logs and Metrics

In addition to logging administrator actions, most cloud providers also offer useful logs and metrics about their services. Browse through the logs and metrics available for the cloud services you're using, and think about which ones might go haywire in an attack and/or be useful for figuring out how bad things are after the fact. Here are some examples:

CPU usage metrics
> Spikes in CPU usage not explained by increased usage might indicate active ransomware encryption or cryptomining.

Network logs and metrics
> For example, if you are using virtual private cloud subnets, many cloud providers can provide metrics on the data passing into and out of these subnets, as well as flow logs showing accepted and denied traffic. Denied traffic when the source is your own component indicates either a misconfiguration or an attack, and should be investigated. Spikes in network traffic might indicate that a denial-of-service attack is beginning or that an attacker is actively stealing data.

Storage input/output (I/O) metrics
> A spike in I/O not explained by increased usage might indicate active ransomware, a denial-of-service attack, or an attacker in the process of stealing data.

Metrics on requests to platform components, such as databases or message queues
> If your database starts going crazy, that may be an indication of an attacker stealing large amounts of data. If your message queue starts going crazy, perhaps an attacker is in part of the system and is attempting to send messages to other components.

End-user logins and activity on SaaS offerings
> If a user starts pulling down huge amounts of data from a cloud storage service, that could be an indication that the account is compromised. If you're using a cloud access security broker (CASB) to mediate access to a cloud service, it may also generate more detailed events related to user activity that you can monitor.

Platform service logs and metrics
> Each platform service may have logs and metrics that are useful for detection and response in addition to operational monitoring. For example, if you're using an orchestration platform such as Kubernetes, you can turn on auditing. The Kubernetes documentation (*https://oreil.ly/Z6r_x*) explains how to turn on audit logging and how to direct those logs to a collection point. Similarly, object storage, databases, and other cloud services have service-specific logs and metrics.

Operating System Logs and Metrics

If you are running virtual machines or bare-metal machines in the cloud, the security of the operating system is generally your responsibility, and this includes collecting and analyzing logs. This is similar to on-premises infrastructure:

- The CIS Benchmarks (*https://oreil.ly/y91Sb*) list is a reasonable base set of events to log for many different operating systems, products, and services that you may have in your environment.

- If you're using Windows, Microsoft provides some good information about event IDs to monitor. For example, a fairly common type of attack is a pass-the-hash attack, and the documentation (*https://oreil.ly/p6JT8*) provides information about specific event IDs to monitor in order to spot such an attack.

- If you're using Linux, many Linux operating system vendors provide instructions on how to enable audit logging to meet different industry and regulatory requirements. Even if you don't have to comply with those requirements, the instructions can be a useful starting point for what to log and analyze in your environment.

- Metrics such as memory usage, CPU usage, and I/O can be very useful to security teams as well as operations teams.

Middleware Logs

If you're running your own database, queue manager, application server, or other middleware, you may need to turn on logging and metrics collection. In addition to any privileged user activities (see "Privileged User Access" on page 165), you may be able to set up alerts for all access to sensitive databases that originates from anywhere except a legitimate application ID or system, or for access to specific tables, or other alerts useful for tracking access to sensitive data.

Secrets Server

If you're running a secrets server, as discussed in Chapter 4, you should log all access to secrets. Here are some examples of unusual activity that you may wish to alert on and investigate:

- Authentication or authorization failures on the secrets server, which may indicate an attack

- An unusual amount of activity for secrets retrieval

- The use of administrative credentials

Your Application

If you've written a custom application or are running a third-party application, it may produce its own logs and metrics that could be useful to both operations teams and security teams. For example, a banking application may log all transfers, and transfers over a certain threshold might generate an alert.

Deception Techniques

In addition to other detection technologies, some technologies are designed to make life more difficult for an attacker without bothering your normal users and administrators. The most common example of this is a *honeypot*, which is a system that sits around pretending to be a functional part of the infrastructure, but whose sole purpose is to distract and slow down attackers and alert you when they're in the system.

In addition to honeypot systems, there are also honey tokens and honey IDs. *Honey tokens* can be embedded in useful-looking but fake files (such as *next-quarter-secret-plans.docx*) and alert you when and by whom those files are opened. They can also be normally unused items like API keys embedded in source code that alert you when used. *Honey IDs* are often unused, non-privileged IDs that look appealing to an attacker (like "superadmin") and which generate an immediate alert if someone tries to use them.

It's important to note that although "security through obscurity" is ineffective in general, secrecy is essential in the specific case of deception techniques. Do not document the presence of honeypots, honey tokens, or honey IDs in any location where anyone outside of your core security team can learn about them.

Deception technologies can be a useful way to leverage your "home court advantage" in defending your environment, because you can lay traps for attackers that only you know about. However, this is an advanced technique. Make sure you have your logging, monitoring, alerting, response, and recovery plans running effectively before investing much time and effort in deception.

Deception techniques can be used both on-premises and in the cloud. One cloud native example is Microsoft Sentinel Deception (*https://oreil.ly/Dh6fA*).

How to Watch

Now that we've covered what types of events and metrics might be good to watch for in your environment, let's look at how to effectively collect and use them to detect and respond to intrusions. Figure 7-1 shows the different steps in this process. These steps may all be done by a single product or service, such as a SIEM, or by multiple products and services acting together.

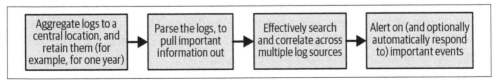

Figure 7-1. Logging and alerting chain

Make sure the time is synchronized on all of your systems, generally by using the Network Time Protocol (NTP). In addition, make sure either that all timestamps contain time zone information or that you use the same time zone (such as GMT) for all logs. This is usually very easy to configure, and it can avoid the nightmare of trying to correlate events between different log sources when the system clocks or time zones are off.

Aggregation and Retention

All of the logs described earlier need to be stored somewhere and kept for a minimum length of time. While allowing logs to collect on various different systems is far better than having no logs at all, it's far from ideal. Individual system disks may fill up, causing loss of logs and operational problems, and an attacker who gets into a system can erase the logs to cover their tracks. Plus, it can be very slow and inconvenient to get into dozens of different systems to search logs and pull together a picture of what's going on.

In the past, important logs would often be printed onto paper and shipped to a physically secure location. While that's a pretty safe way of securing them and making them unerasable by computer, paper has some pretty big drawbacks—it's not searchable by automation, it's heavy, it's expensive, and it's a fire hazard.

In the cloud, you can get many of the same benefits much more easily by locating your log aggregation service in a separate cloud account with different administrative credentials so that the logs can't be wiped out by someone with access to the primary systems. (This is also a good idea for backups, as discussed later.) Most cloud providers have services that can aggregate, retain, and search logs so you don't have to set up log aggregation from scratch.

You should retain most logs for at least one year. Longer retention periods can sometimes be helpful for investigating security incidents, but longer retention periods can sometimes conflict with privacy regulations. If you're subject to any industry or regulatory standards, look at the specific retention requirements for those logs, but as of this writing, one year is usually a safe choice.

Once you have all of your logs and alerts in a central, secure location with the proper retention period configured, you need to tackle the problems of looking through those logs to alert on suspicious behavior and of making sure the alerts get to the right people and are acknowledged and investigated.

Parsing Logs

If you have all your logs aggregated in a safe place, congratulations! A determined human can eventually go through all of those logs and get answers to important questions, although it may take a while. However, one of the primary motivations for inventing computers was to process data much faster than humans can.

Log parsers pull specific pieces of information (fields) out of the different types of events. Here are some examples of log parsers at work:

- For an operating system event, the parser will recognize the timestamp, the name of the system generating the event, and the event text. Further parsing may happen for some types of events; for example, for a failed login event, the parser can also recognize the IP address from which the login was attempted.

- For firewall logs, the parser will recognize the timestamp, source IP address, destination IP address, and accepted/denied result.

- For antivirus logs, the parser will recognize the timestamp, hostname, and event details such as a failed update or the discovery of malware.

Unfortunately, there are thousands of different log formats. There are a few common event log formats that make parsing a little easier, however. Many tools can parse logs in these formats into specific fields, although that doesn't always mean the fields are useful. Here are some examples:

- Syslog is a standard format for log messages, although "format" is a little generous.[2] There are actually a couple of popular syslog formats: RFC 3164 (*https:// oreil.ly/GfYSZ*) describes a collection of things seen in the wild, and RFC 5424 (*https://oreil.ly/meyxY*) is more prescriptive. Typically, a syslog record will contain a timestamp, the name of the system generating the message, the type of process sending the message, a severity level, and a mostly free-form message. It's often up to the parser to figure out what generated the free-form message and perform further parsing on it.

- The Common Log Format (CLF) and Extended Log Format (ELF) are primarily used by web servers to log requests.

- The Common Event Format (CEF) (*https://oreil.ly/QirhJ*) is an extension of the syslog format, primarily used by MicroFocus ArcSight, that provides additional structured fields.

---

2 The term "syslog" can be confusing because it is often used to refer to a program to accept syslog messages, a network protocol (usually running over udp/514 or tcp/514), and a format for lines in a log file.

- The Cloud Auditing Data Federation (CADF) (*https://oreil.ly/9x7WW*) standard is intended to allow switching between cloud providers without changing the log aggregation and parsing systems.

Searching and Correlation

Once the logs are aggregated and parsed, you can search based on the parsed fields and correlate events between different systems. For example, you can search for all login failures during a certain time period, all cases where a successful login happened without a VPN connection for the same user, or malware detection followed by a login.

The ability to perform quick searches across multiple different log sources and types of logs can be invaluable during incident response. Test the ability of the system to quickly handle multiple searches by many frantic people before you're in the middle of a security incident!

 Many systems have the idea of hot and cold storage. *Hot storage* can be queried instantly, whereas *cold storage* may need to be retrieved and reloaded before it can be searched.

Alerting and Automated Response

When an automated system sees something a human should look at, it raises an alert (occasionally called an "offense"), and in some cases may automatically respond by disabling access to or shutting down a component. Alerts may be based on certain events, on correlations of events happening, or on certain thresholds being reached.

This is really where the art lies in log analysis. If the system is tuned so sensitively that your security team is constantly getting false alerts, all of the alerts will quickly be ignored. On the other hand, if you're not getting at least some alerts regularly, you're probably not following up on some things that you should be. You need a feedback loop for each type of false alert to determine whether it makes sense to filter out those types of events, raise thresholds, or take other actions to reduce the false alerts. Consider running periodic tests that you know will generate alerts, to ensure that they're not ignored.

There are some alerts that you should almost always follow up on. Multiple login failures for privileged users, malware found on systems, and other alerts that may be precursors of a security incident should at least get a look, even if they're usually false alarms.

Don't forget that you also need to have alerts when logs stop flowing. That's a security issue too! In many cases, it just means something is malfunctioning, which might prevent you from seeing a future problem. In some cases, however, it might actually be an indicator of an attack in progress.

Automated response sounds great in principle, but it really has the potential to disrupt your business. In addition to outages caused by an incorrect response or an automated overreaction, automated response systems can be deliberately leveraged by attackers to cause outages. It's not fun to realize that you've spent a considerable amount of money to prevent denial-of-service attacks, only to unintentionally enable an attacker to conduct an easy denial-of-service attack using a simple port scanner or a few failed logins. Some environments have high enough security requirements that you're willing to suffer an outage rather than accept even a small risk of letting a possible attack continue until a human can investigate, but in most cases the operational and security risks have to be balanced carefully.

Alerting shouldn't be a fire-and-forget activity. You often need a way to rotate different individuals in and out, because nobody wants to be on call all the time, and you need some way to ensure that an alert is acknowledged within a certain amount of time or escalated to someone else to handle. There are cloud-based services for everything, and alerting is no exception. In most cases, the same system can be used for both operational response and security response activities.

Larger organizations will usually either build a system or contract with a managed security service provider (MSSP) for a 24×7 security operations center (SOC) to monitor and respond to alerts. A room with lots of screens displaying important-looking graphics is optional, but looks impressive to your C-suite management and customers and can help present important information quickly in an urgent situation. In many cases, organizations use a hybrid model where some of the lower-level monitoring and alerting is performed by an MSSP, and the more important alerts are escalated to in-house staff.

Modern systems can produce billions of log events. You can use even more automation to help deal with them—and this is where a SIEM can come in handy.

Security Information and Event Managers

A *security information and event manager* (SIEM) can perform some or all of the steps described in the previous sections. For example, you may have your SIEM aggregate logs, or you may instead have a separate system aggregate and filter logs and feed only a subset of them to the SIEM. Because many cloud providers have lower-cost, high-volume log aggregation services, and because logs are often used for operational troubleshooting in addition to security incident detection and response, many organizations have a cloud log aggregator feed security-relevant events into the SIEM.

SIEM rules can be used to detect potential bad behavior, sometimes by correlating events that happened in two different places or by comparing current and historical data. Here are some questions that might be raised by a security operator viewing alerts from a properly configured SIEM:

- "Database traffic is up 200% from the monthly average. Maybe the application is just really popular right now, but is someone systematically stealing our data?"

- "We just saw an outbound connection to an IP address that has been used by a known threat actor recently, according to this threat intelligence feed. Is that a compromised system talking to a command-and-control server?"

- "There were 150 failed login attempts on an account, followed by a success. Is that a successful brute-force attack?"

- "We saw a single failed login attempt on 300 different accounts, followed by a success on account #301. Is that a successful password spraying attack?"

- "A port scan was followed by a lot of traffic from a port that hasn't been used in months. Port scans happen all the time, but perhaps a vulnerable service was found and compromised?"

- "John doesn't normally log in at 3:00 AM EST, or from that country. Maybe that's not really John?"

- "Three different accounts logged in from the same system over the course of 30 minutes. It seems unlikely all of those people are actually using that system, so maybe the system and those accounts are compromised?"

- "A new administrative account was just created outside of normal business hours. Maybe someone's working late, but maybe there's an issue?"

- "Someone was just added to the administrator group. That's a rare event, so shouldn't we check on it?"

- "Why are there firewall denies with an internal system as the source? Either something is misconfigured or there's an unauthorized user trying to move around the network."

A SIEM can be run in-house, as a cloud service, or as part of a managed security services engagement. Many cloud infrastructure and platform providers have built-in services that provide at least some SIEM functions, and there are also many third-party solutions. Regardless of whether you choose to use a SIEM or not, make sure that you are meeting your requirements for aggregation and retention, parsing, searching and correlation, alerting, and automated response capabilities.

Threat Hunting

Only after you have the basics down—that is, you're collecting security-relevant logs and metrics, parsing them, and responding to alerts generated by your systems—should you move on to threat hunting.

Threat hunting is one of the few cases where it's okay to go "looking for trouble," rather than reacting to specific alerts. You start by creating a *hypothesis*, such as "Perhaps I'm being targeted by Advanced Persistent Threat 12345" or "Maybe someone is after the secret plans to my spaceship." You then query the data you have collected, and collect new data if needed, to gather evidence to either prove or disprove that hypothesis.

Preparing for an Incident

You have the logs, and you are doing useful things with them, such as getting alerts. Now you need to plan for what to do when one of those alerts is the real deal. Depending on the risk to your environment, your plans don't have to be exhaustive, because even a little bit of planning can help enormously.

The first decision that you need to make is this: at what point are you going to call for outside help? This will depend heavily upon the perceived risk to your organization, the severity of the incident, and the size of your security team. However, even large, well-prepared organizations may need outside help for more serious security incidents. A quick search will turn up many incident response firms, and it's a good idea to have vetted a couple of them ahead of time in case you need them.

In addition, you may want to consider cybersecurity insurance, particularly if you have a small team and little incident response can be done in-house. In some cases, this insurance may be included with general business protection policies, although many exclude cybersecurity incidents. As with any insurance, you need to carefully read the coverage and exclusions, as some policies exclude common types of attacks such as social engineering attacks, or deny coverage based on unclear security requirements for the insured. However, these policies can pay for most or all expenses associated with incident response.

The most important preparation work is the collection and retention of logs, described earlier, so that you can call up a reasonable amount of current and historical data to perform investigations. In addition to that, you need to put together a team, a plan, and some tools.

Team

The incident response team[3] has the stressful job of figuring out what's going on during an attack and containing the incident as much as possible. The first thing you need to do is identify primary and backup technical incident response leaders, because response activities cannot wait for someone to return from vacation. These people will be responsible for running any internal investigations and coordinating with any outside help.

You also need to identify primary and backup business leaders who can be available immediately to sign off on business decisions such as taking systems down or authorizing payments. In smaller organizations, the technical leaders and business leaders might be the same people, but you still need at least one primary and one backup person.

In addition to the team leadership, you will also need technical specialists in the different areas that are most likely to be attacked in your threat model. For example, if you are worried about someone taking data on your customers from your cloud web application, you might need to line up network specialists, web server specialists, database specialists, and specialists familiar with the inner design and workings of the application itself. You don't want to realize in the middle of an incident that you can't reach any of the people who understand a component where the problem is suspected.

Finally, you also need these primary and backup contacts:

- Your legal department (or someone from your legal firm), to help with questions about complying with contracts and regulations
- Your communications department, or someone authorized to speak with the media and to speak to law enforcement authorities should that be necessary

---

3 In many organizations, this is called the Computer Security Incident Response Team (CSIRT), to distinguish it from other incident response teams.

- Your HR department, or someone authorized to make hiring/firing decisions in case an insider threat is identified

All of these responsibilities may fall to different individuals, or these tasks may be performed by the leaders identified earlier in this section, provided that you have primary and backup coverage for each area.

Whether you have a full-time incident response team or not, you should also have the equivalent of a volunteer fire department. Identify knowledgeable people who can be trained in incident response, and get management preapproval to pull them off of what they're currently doing to deal with a high-priority incident.

A few other notes on creating and maintaining an incident response team follow:

- Nobody wants to be on call during a weekend or over a holiday. Unfortunately, attackers know this, so incidents are more likely to begin at these inconvenient times.

- If incident response is a regular activity in your organization, burnout is a serious concern. It is even more of a concern if you have a largely volunteer team that is attempting to deal with incident response on top of a normal workload. If possible, rotate people in and out so that they have a break from incident response activities.

- Determine general incident response roles for team members ahead of time and write them down so that during the incident, nobody is confused over who is responsible for what.

- Have the team meet at least quarterly to make sure everyone is still on board with the plans.

Once you have an incident response team, you need some plans for the team to follow.

Plans

Most of the team composition advice in the previous section is not cloud-specific, but your incident response plans will be. You need to come up with some likely scenarios in your cloud environment and have some plans to cover those scenarios.

As part of your planning, you need to understand what your cloud provider is committed to doing in the event of a security incident. Will they provide additional logs or take forensic images? Do they provide contact information for security incidents? You don't want to be in the middle of an incident trying to read the terms of service to figure out your provider's responsibility.

In many cases, the cloud provider will be responsible for responding to incidents involving breaches to its cloud services, but not to incidents that only involve your application. However, there are some exceptions, such as DDoS attacks, where the cloud provider may work with you to help mitigate the attack—or may turn off all outside network access to your application to prevent the attack from impacting its other customers! It's important to know what your provider can do for you ahead of time.

You also need at least a small, preapproved budget for dealing with security incidents. This doesn't mean the team has a blank check to purchase anything they want, but the allocation should be enough to cover reasonable items without going through a potentially lengthy procurement and approval process. For example, if part of the incident response plan is to contact an incident response firm, at least initial consulting charges should be preapproved. If part of the plan is to put people on planes right away, airfare should be preapproved. Try to budget for and preapprove items that are likely to be needed in the first few hours of an incident.

Prioritization is also an important part of incident response planning. You don't want to respond to an attempted attack in the same way that you respond to someone actively stealing your data. Create at least a few severity levels for security incidents, with some guidelines on what to do in each case. For example, you might list categories for "confirmed unsuccessful attack," "confirmed successful attack without data loss," and "confirmed successful attack with data loss." As incidents move up the scale, the response might change.

You should also have some organization-wide guidance for reporting suspected security incidents and not interfering with investigations. This can be as simple as an item in the employee handbook that says something like, "If you suspect that an unauthorized user is accessing our information systems, please call the following number to report a suspected security incident. You are permitted to shut down affected nonessential systems, but do not delete any systems or destroy any data, and do not attempt to retaliate."

If you haven't had a chance to test your incident response plans yet, consider performing a tabletop exercise. You can do this in-house, by inventing a plausible scenario and playing it out in a test environment. There are also firms that make this easier by providing scenarios, fake news bulletins, and other props, and that will critique how the plan was executed to help address weaknesses. For example, a likely scenario might be that there's an attack in progress and you need to go into lockdown mode. In a cloud environment, this might involve one or more of the following:

- A plan to disable all cloud portal and API access other than the minimum required during the incident. For example, you could decide that only four individuals need access in the short term and run scripts to disable all other users' access.

- A plan to disable all network access to your cloud environment, or some subset of it. This might disable the application completely, or temporarily disable some functionality.
- A plan to shut down the entire environment, lock the secrets server, and re-create a new environment.

 Part of your incident response plan should involve having backups that you can use to restore data and functionality. *Make sure your backups are in a separate cloud account, with separate administrative credentials from the production data.* There have been documented cases (*https://oreil.ly/_AXmF*) of attackers wiping not only the production data, but also all of the backups that were accessible from the production account.

It's important to understand how long restores will take, too. Sometimes you have a perfectly reasonable recovery strategy, except that it requires the entire world to stop turning for a week. You don't have to be able to function at 100% while recovery is taking place—delaying sending out bills or jotting down handwritten notes for entry into the IT systems later may be perfectly reasonable—but you do need to be able to carry out core business functions.

Tools

When developing your incident response plans, you'll realize that your team will need some tools to implement those plans. In a traditional environment, many incident response tools tend to be physical bags carrying laptops, cables, and similar materials (the "jump bags" mentioned earlier). A cloud environment offers virtual cloud equivalents of some of these items.

The tools needed will depend somewhat upon what your environment looks like and what your cloud provider offers, but at a minimum your team should probably have virtual images containing forensic analysis tools and a cloud account to create forensic infrastructure. Cloud accounts typically don't cost anything to own if nothing is provisioned in them, so you should keep a separate incident response cloud account active that can be connected to your production account. Some cloud providers also offer documentation on performing investigations and digital forensics in their environments that may point to specific tools.

Create detailed, *tested* procedures for the most common incident response tasks. For example, you may want a procedure for collecting memory and disk forensic information from a compromised Linux virtual machine in a cloud environment. Such a procedure should contain the exact commands to accomplish this, such as running LiME to capture a memory dump, generating a hash of the dump, verifying the dump with Volatility, performing a hard power-off of the compromised machine to prevent any malicious programs from cleaning up prior to reboot, and taking a snapshot of the disks.

Here are some other tools that may be helpful:

- Cloud-aware forensic analysis tools, such as Cloud Forensic Utils (*https://oreil.ly/PHIXx*), which can help you understand what happened in a cloud environment during a security incident.

- Up-to-date diagrams showing network configuration, data locations, and event logging locations.

- Tested communications systems. Will you be able to respond to a threat if your instant messaging platform, email, or telephone systems are down? In an emergency, perhaps you will permit people to use personal email and cell phones for work activities, even if that's normally disallowed. It's better to think about those decisions ahead of time.

- Contact lists, for both people internal to the organization and external contacts such as cloud providers, incident response firms, or other suppliers that may be involved in incident response.

- A war room. In cloud environments, you won't be physically touching the equipment in most cases, but you still need a physical or virtual war room where the team can meet, exchange information, and make decisions. If you may have remote attendees, make sure you have meaningful ways for them to participate, such as screen sharing and a reasonable audio system.

- Checklists. I'm not a fan of "checklist security" at all, where you tick off that you have a firewall, antivirus software, and similar items without actually verifying that they're being used effectively. However, incident response can be exhausting and very stressful. In these situations, checklists that help you implement plans are essential to ensure you haven't forgotten something really important. For example, one online checklist (*https://oreil.ly/aejnb*) suggests a useful set of logs to review during an incident.

- Forms for documenting incident response activities. For example, the SANS Institute offers some forms (*https://oreil.ly/krCsC*) that can be customized for your organization.

- Incident response software, which has components that can track incidents and built-in playbooks for incident response.

Responding to an Incident

Hopefully, you're not in the middle of an active security incident when you read this. If you are, and you have no incident response team, plan, tools, or checklists yet, your first priority should be containing the incident as much as possible without destroying evidence. Typically, you do this by some combination of shutting down or quarantining systems, changing passwords, revoking access, and blocking network connections. At the same time, you should probably call an incident response company for help, and take a few seconds here and there to jot down notes on what you need in order to be better prepared next time.

OK, so you've found something that looks like a real attack. Now what? Your response will largely be dependent upon what the attacker is doing and what your threat model looks like, but there are a few guidelines that will help.

First, mobilize at least part of your incident response team to do triage. You don't want to get 30 people out of bed for a malware infection that, after a few minutes' investigation, appears to be completely contained. It's easy to both overreact and underreact, so this is where having some predefined severity levels and response guidelines for each level can be helpful.

Then, start executing the plans you've implemented, trying to anticipate what the attacker's objectives are likely to be based on a kill chain or on an attack chain.

Cyber Kill Chains and MITRE ATT&CK

As mentioned in the sidebar at the beginning of this chapter, one of the most popular kill chains today is the Lockheed Martin Cyber Kill Chain. According to this model, threats pass through the following phases:

Reconnaissance
> The attacker does research to figure out what to get into and identify vulnerabilities that may help them. This might involve anything from Google searches to dumpster diving to social engineering to network port scans.

Weaponization
> The attacker comes up with some malware to exploit the vulnerabilities. More advanced attackers may write something custom, but less advanced attacks may use something already available.

Delivery
> The attacker gets the victim to execute that malware, either by a network attack, by emailing it, or by some other means.

Exploitation
> The malware runs and gains unauthorized access.

Installation

The malware gains persistence, or staying power, by installing itself in some way that the attacker hopes makes it difficult to find and remove. Often the first piece of malware downloads and installs a second piece for this part. In some cases this persistent malware is better supported and updated than your legitimate programs!

Command and control

The malware creates some sort of communication channel so that the attacker can remotely control it—a remote shell, an outbound web connection, or even reading commands from a legitimate cloud file storage service. At this point, access to your systems might be sold on the black market at a good price to someone who really wants it.

Actions on objective

An attacker (who may not even be the original attacker) does whatever they want—steals your data, defaces your website, attacks your customers, extorts money, etc.

Other popular resources, such as MITRE ATT&CK, view attacker actions as falling into distinct tactics used to accomplish their goals:

Initial access

The attacker gains initial access, often through stolen credentials or exploiting an unpatched vulnerability.

Execution

The attacker runs malicious code on your systems.

Persistence

The attacker installs code or similar functionality to allow access in the future.

Privilege escalation

The attacker uses existing access to get more access.

Defense evasion

The attacker hides from the defenders.

Credential access

The attacker uses techniques to gain passwords or API keys.

Discovery

The attacker pokes around, looking for vulnerabilities or paths to the objective.

Lateral movement

The attacker moves from one part of the environment to another.

Collection
> The attacker finds information in your environment.

Exfiltration
> The attacker steals data from your environment.

Impact
> The attacker does damage to your systems.

The MITRE ATT&CK tactics tend to be both less linear and more detailed than the Lockheed Martin Cyber Kill Chain phases, and the framework lists specific techniques that may be used to accomplish those tactical goals. Regardless of which you use, it's a good idea to be familiar with at least one of them so you have some idea of what the attacker might have already done and might do next.

The OODA Loop

You have your plans, and you may have some idea of the progress and objectives of your attacker. It's time to respond. A popular concept in incident response is the *OODA loop*—observe, orient, decide, and act:

1. In the *observe* phase, gather information from your systems, such as your cloud provider logs, firewalls, operating system logs, metrics, and other locations, to find odd behavior that may indicate an attacker is doing something.

2. In the *orient* phase, try to understand what is going on and what might happen next. This might involve both internal knowledge of where your most important assets are and external threat intelligence about who may be behind the attack and why. Not all threat intelligence costs money. For example, the US Cybersecurity and Infrastructure Security Agency (CISA) (*https://www.cisa.gov*) regularly releases alerts on malicious activities. If you're seeing suspicious behavior and CISA has released an alert indicating that your industry is being targeted by particular threat actors using particular tactics, techniques, and procedures, that may help you orient yourself.

3. In the *decide* phase, choose the next tactics you'll use for minimizing damage or enabling recovery. For example, you may decide to take certain systems offline, revoke access, quarantine systems, or build a new environment.

4. In the *act* phase, actually execute those tactics. This is where using cloud infrastructure can really be helpful, particularly if you have invested in repeatable methods to build your cloud environments rather than having them grow organically over time. Here are some examples:

- Most cloud environments have a stronger division between the compute infrastructure and storage than traditional environments. It's much harder—but not impossible—for attackers to persist (retain unauthorized access) just by modifying content in your data stores. Every instance of compute infrastructure contains thousands of executables and configuration entries, but these can typically be rebuilt much more easily than the data can. Given this division, you may be able to apply fixes to your images to close the vulnerability that allowed the attacker in, shut down all compute instances, replace them with fixed instances, and connect the new instances to your data stores with minimal downtime.

- You may also be able to easily quarantine systems, using scripts to invoke APIs that lock down security groups or network ACLs. In a traditional environment, you might have to manually log in to many different routers or firewalls, or start unplugging cables, to get the same effect.

After you act, the loop begins again—observe to see what the attacker is doing in response to what you've done, orient, decide, and act again. These loops should be relatively quick and should continue until your observations indicate that the incident is resolved.

You will almost never be prepared enough. Each incident will be messy in its own way, even if you're really well prepared. Take 15 seconds to jot down reminders of lessons learned while you're going along, because it can be difficult to remember afterward.

 Don't be afraid to call an incident response firm if things seem to be getting out of hand or if you can't make progress. Most attackers have a lot more experience attacking than defenders have defending!

Cloud Forensics

Cloud forensics might inspire images of the *CSI* television show, but unfortunately the reality is a little less exciting. Essentially, you just want to make a forensic copy of anything that might be important, and then use tools to analyze it.

It's important to make the copies in a documented, repeatable fashion so that you can always demonstrate that you have a good copy of the original data that hasn't been altered. This usually involves generating a verification string (cryptographic hash) that can be used to show that you have a copy of the uncorrupted data. A cryptographic hash, such as SHA-256, is designed to be fast to calculate but nearly impossible to use to create another piece of data that has the same hash. With a copy of the data and a cryptographic hash, anyone can quickly generate a hash and compare it against the original to ensure that their copy is the same as what the initial investigator collected. In addition, nobody can change the data (intentionally or accidentally) without the change being easily discoverable. You could also write the original copy to some read-only media and do a bit-for-bit comparison of the copies every time, but that would take a lot longer!

The sample procedure in "Tools" on page 183 showed one way to obtain forensic images for virtual machine memory and disk images, but you may need other forensic artifacts during an investigation. For example, you may want to take snapshots or backups of databases, to compare to see whether the attacker made any database changes. You may also want to look at network packet or flow captures to see what an attacker or malware was doing on the network.

Blocking Unauthorized Access

This may seem like a no-brainer, but it's often harder than it looks, particularly if an attacker has been in the system for a while and has gotten administrative access. Hopefully you've followed the instructions in Chapter 6 and have some internal segmentation so that the attack may be contained to a particular part of the network.

A common response here is to reset everyone's passwords and API keys (including automation), which can be disruptive to normal operations, as well as blocking inbound and outbound network access.

You should have pre-created tools and processes for blocking access quickly and all at once.

Stopping Data Exfiltration and Command and Control

If you didn't shut down network communications as part of blocking unauthorized access, you may still need to shut down outbound communications in order to stop connections attackers make to command-and-control servers, or to stop ongoing data loss.

Recovery

You've found the attack and you think you've stopped it, so now it's time to clean up and make sure that there are no leftover ways for the attackers to get back into your systems.

Redeploying IT Systems

By far, the simplest and most effective way to recover from an IT standpoint is to redeploy all affected systems. Again, this is a little easier in the cloud, because you don't have to purchase new physical hardware; your cloud provider will have capacity.

Any compromised cloud systems should be re-created, and the production traffic should be switched over to the new systems. Any affected workstations should be wiped and re-created from known good images. In the immortal words of Ellen Ripley in *Alien*, "Nuke the entire site from orbit. It's the only way to be sure."

If that's not possible, you need to have executive acknowledgment that you're accepting a substantial risk in continuing to operate systems that an attacker had control of for a time. You can run malware scanners, keep extra tabs on the network and processes for indicators of compromise, and enact some other security measures, but a single altered registry entry may be enough to let an attacker get back into your system, and a single piece of missed malware may be able to call out and provide an easy way back in.

Notifications

You may have regulatory or contractual obligations to notify your customers or report the breach to law enforcement authorities.

Even if you aren't required to notify the world, you may want to do so anyway to avoid a PR nightmare if word eventually gets out. For obvious reasons, we don't have good metrics on how many successful cover-ups there are, but there are some well-known examples of unsuccessful cover-ups by Yahoo!, Cathay Pacific, Uber, and others.

Lessons Learned

As soon as possible, after everyone's had a good night of sleep, you should look at lessons learned and make any updates to your team composition, plans, procedures, tools, and checklists that will help next time. Hopefully, during the incident you took the opportunity to jot down some quick notes and reminders that can be used.

Building an entire incident response team and process is a large topic. While I've covered the high points for cloud environments here, for further reading I recommend AT&T's Insider's Guide to Incident Response (*https://oreil.ly/w11VM*) and NIST SP 800-61 (*https://oreil.ly/GkXaN*).

Example Metrics

As with other business processes, if you can't provide some measurements on your detection, response, and recovery activities, it's difficult to know whether you're improving.

Here are a few example metrics that you may want to consider collecting:

Detection
> Number of events collected per month, number of alerts triggered per month, percentage of alerts that are confirmed incidents, percentage of alerts that are false positives

Response
> Time from when an alert was triggered to a review of the alert, time from a confirmed incident to closure of that incident

Recovery
> Time required to redeploy affected systems

Overall
> Estimated cost of each incident, including time, expenses, and damage to reputation

Example Tools for Detection, Response, and Recovery

The following is a listing of some representative solutions in the cloud detection, response, and recovery space. Just as in Chapter 5, I'm not endorsing any of these tools by including them, or snubbing other tools by excluding them. These are just examples of different tools that are popular as of this writing:

- Amazon GuardDuty can look for unusual or suspicious activity in your AWS account or systems.
- Amazon CloudWatch Logs, Azure Monitor, Google Cloud's operations suite logging, and IBM Log Analysis all allow you to store and search through your logs.
- Amazon CloudWatch, Azure Monitor, Google Cloud's operations suite, and IBM Cloud Monitoring provide performance metrics.
- AWS CloudTrail, Azure Monitor, and IBM Cloud Activity Tracker can monitor privileged user activity in cloud accounts.
- Azure Security Center can collect security data into a central location, as well as performing file integrity monitoring and other security functions.
- Cisco, McAfee, and Snort are popular network intrusion detection service providers that have cloud-based appliances available.
- Cloudflare, Akamai, and Signal Sciences provide cloud-based web application firewall solutions.
- OSSEC, Tripwire, AIDE, Netwrix Change Tracker, Fidelis CloudPassage Halo, Qualys, and many other products and services provide traditional or cloud-based file integrity monitoring solutions.

- CyberArk and Delinea are typically considered privileged identity management or privileged access management solutions, and can perform session recording and alert when privileged credentials are checked out.

- IBM QRadar, ArcSight Enterprise Security Manager, Splunk Enterprise Security, LogRhythm, and other SIEM providers collect log events, analyze them, and raise alerts.

- EnCase, FTK, Sleuth Kit and Autopsy, and Cloud Forensics Utils are forensic tools that have cloud capabilities.

Detection and Response in a Sample Application

Let's take one last look at our sample application, this time from the point of view of detection and response. Our threat model in this case involves large amounts of data about our customers in our database, and a likely attacker who will attempt to steal this data and sell it on the dark web. Note that our focus would be somewhat different if we were primarily concerned about our brand image, and we thought it was most likely that someone would try to deface our web pages to make us look bad.

Figure 7-2 shows sensitive systems that log security-related events, and how the security team handles them. The blue items (white text on a dark gray background if you're seeing this in black and white) run the functional parts of the application, the orange items (dashed borders) are cloud provider or orchestration systems used to create the application infrastructure, and the green items (black text on a light gray background) run our auditing framework. As a reminder, these are our detection and response security goals for the application:

1. Collect logs and metrics that will be useful both for operational troubleshooting and for detecting and responding to security incidents. The IDS/IPS, WAF, firewall, servers, database, and consoles/APIs are all configured to record security-relevant events and metrics.

2. Store those logs and metrics securely, where they can't be erased by an attacker. In practice, this means getting them off of the system quickly, to a system that's under separate administrative control. In this case, the logs are shown as going through log and metrics aggregator systems, which are under separate administrative control, but they might also go directly to a SIEM.

3. Analyze the collected data. This will let us see whether items require further investigation. In this case, the analysis is performed by a combination of the SIEM (using log parsing, correlation rules, machine learning, and other features mentioned in most SIEM marketing brochures) and the security operator's brain.

4. Automatically alert on items that require a human to investigate. In this example, the SIEM is configured to send alerts to people with the security operator role. These alerts might be false positives—there should be a separate feedback loop (not pictured in the diagram) for the security operators to tune out false positives where possible when they get a false alert, without masking any true positives.

5. Run through the incident response and recovery plans if an actual security incident is suspected.

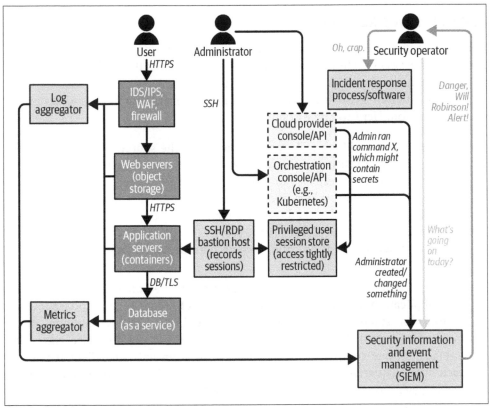

Figure 7-2. Sample application with detection capabilities

Monitoring the Protective Systems

First, let's look at the logs created by our protective systems during normal use of the system. In this picture, the IDS/IPS, WAF, and firewall systems generate logs, alerts, and metrics as the system is used or abused. Here are some examples:

- The IDS/IPS may log that someone appears to be port scanning or when it sees a known malicious signature.

- The WAF may log that someone is attempting a SQL injection attack or a deserialization attack.

- The firewall (or a component of the IaaS performing firewall duties) routinely logs accepted/denied connections, as well as tracking metrics indicating how much data is entering and leaving the network per minute.

Monitoring the Application

Next, let's look at the logs created by our application and infrastructure during normal use of the system. These logs will depend highly on what the application does and what components are used to create it. For illustrative purposes, I'll assume we've used many different technologies, although this may or may not be a good design for a real application. Here are some examples:

- The web servers will log each request, including the source IP address and the URL requested. In this case, the web servers are simply object storage instances presenting objects in response to web requests. We configure the object storage service to send its access logs (including when an object is modified) to the log aggregation service and to send metrics on how many requests are serviced to the metrics service. With an object storage service, we don't need to worry about any lower-level items such as operating system logs, because that's the cloud provider's job.

- The application servers in this example are pods hosted on a Kubernetes cluster. The application running in the pods logs each request to standard output (stdout) or standard error (stderr), with the URL of the component being invoked and what the response is. In this case, the application also allows file uploads, so one component of the application is an antivirus client that scans each upload, quarantines any uploads that contain malware, and sends an alert. A logging agent on the worker node will send the log information from each pod, as well as for the worker node itself, to the log aggregator. We'll also enable audit logging on the Kubernetes master itself so that it will tell us when someone authenticates to it or creates pods.

- The database is an as-a-service offering that will log any denied access attempts to the database or particular tables within the database, as well as any changes to the access settings for the database. It will also record metrics about how much data it's sending out at any given time. Given that we're most concerned about the theft of data from the database, we really need to pay attention to these items!

- The virtual private cloud networking infrastructure (not shown in Figure 7-2) is configured to send network metrics to the metrics aggregator, which can send an alert to the SIEM when network usage is high.

Monitoring the Administrators

We also need to monitor the administrators as they work. As I said before, this doesn't necessarily mean that we don't trust our system administrators! It means that we recognize that an attacker might have obtained valid administrative credentials via some nefarious means, and we have to detect and respond to any such attack.

For educational purposes, we'll assume the following:

- The admins are dealing with a combination of virtual machines and containers in this environment.
- The admins will use the cloud provider and container orchestration capabilities to run specific commands on VMs and containers where possible, but in emergencies may need to open an interactive session directly on the system.
- The admins go through a session recording service in order to reach the virtual machines.

In Figure 7-2, toxic session recording logs (which may contain secret information) and the normal sanitized logs are shown stored on separate systems. This is so that we can limit access to the toxic logs to as few administrators as possible. If you store both types of logs on the same system, ensure that all administrators of that system are authorized to see the toxic logs and that access to them is controlled carefully.

Understanding the Auditing Infrastructure

Now let's look at our auditing infrastructure. In this example application, the log aggregator, metrics aggregator, and SIEM are all shown as separate systems, but many products and services overlap in some or even all of these areas.

You may also have additional products or services sending alerts to the SIEM or directly to security personnel. For example, you may use a network traffic analysis system that watches for unusual network traffic patterns, or endpoint detection and response agents that collect information on what your servers or workstations are doing.

Let's take a closer look at these systems:

- The log aggregator may either be a cloud service (like Amazon CloudWatch Logs, Azure Monitor, Google Cloud's operations suite, IBM Log Analysis, or Splunk Cloud) or a separate installed product like Splunk or Logstash.

  The log aggregator should be under separate administrative control from the systems being monitored so that an attacker with access to one of the monitored systems can't also access the aggregator and erase the logs using the same credentials. I recommend putting the audit and logging components in a separate auditing cloud account for increased separation.

  The logs might contain both non-security-relevant information and security-relevant information, but in general only security-relevant logs should flow to the SIEM.

- The metrics aggregator may be a cloud service such as Amazon CloudWatch, Azure Monitor, Google Cloud's operations suite, or IBM Cloud Monitoring, or a separately installed tool.

- Both the log and metrics aggregators feed security-relevant items into the SIEM. For example, the log aggregator might feed in all authentication events, and the metric aggregator might push an event any time a metric such as the transfer rate exceeds a threshold for a specific amount of time.

- The SIEM has parsers to understand the different types of logs coming in, and it has rules to decide when something is worth telling a human about. In this case, the SIEM rules may alert when there are login failures for multiple accounts in quick succession (password spraying), or when the database and network metrics both show unusual activity, or when many other combinations of suspicious or alarming events happen.

In this sample application, we're now looking at anything our protective tools are flagging as an issue, monitoring for unusual traffic or activity in the application components, watching what our administrators (or attackers impersonating our administrators) are doing, and collecting evidence for forensic analysis and audits. With these tools and processes in place, we now have a good chance of detecting an attack.

Conclusion

Even after you have put reasonable protections in place, your security isn't complete until you have confidence that you can detect attacks, respond to them promptly and effectively, and recover.

Detection isn't just about logging; you can't just vacuum up every log source available and hope that it's useful for security. You need to figure out what is important to watch given your environment and your threat model. In almost all environments, you will have some privileged users, and it's almost always important to watch their activity. Ask yourself, "If some likely bad thing happened, would I see it?" If not, you may need to collect additional information, or make sure the information you're already collecting gets to the right place to be visible. One excellent indication that your detection abilities need to improve is if you perform a pentest and you don't detect the pentesters attacking your systems.

Once you have figured out what it's important to watch, make sure that you're effectively collecting those logs and metrics and looking through them. In larger environments, that often means using a SIEM to help go through the large amounts of data. Make sure you have synced your time across systems, and perform some simulated attacks to make sure that you would notice the real thing.

Finally, you need to be prepared to deal with a successful attack when it happens. That means putting together a team, some plans, and some tools ahead of time. When an attack happens, your team needs to understand how attacks often unfold and how to lock down the environment and clean up—and when it's time to call for additional help.

When you're performing recovery actions, it's very risky to attempt to clean your systems. Once someone has obtained administrative access, you really have no way of knowing you've gotten everything out, because there are so many places for malware to hide. The safest option by far is to wipe and restore each compromised system, or delete it and provision a new one. Fortunately, that's easy to do in the cloud! Don't underestimate the risk of trying to clean up in-place; a single access control permission, a single registry entry on Windows, or some other hard-to-find backdoor can allow an attacker to walk right back in easily.

Cloud computing is a wonderful, innovative model that has enabled lots of people with great ideas to get started quickly and scale up with very little capital investment. We started this book by exploring some security concepts, and from there worked through ways to protect data and assets in the cloud and how to implement controls such as good access management, vulnerability management, and network controls. Finally, we finished by examining ways to detect security issues and respond to them effectively.

This is an incredibly deep and fast-moving field. My goal was to provide enough useful information, in an accessible form, so that readers can get started and also know the right questions to ask to learn more. I hope you've enjoyed reading *Practical Cloud Security*, and that you'll find the information here both practical and useful for enhancing the security of your cloud environments. Good luck!

Exercises

1. Which of the following statements about logs, alerts, and metrics are true? Select all that apply.

   a. A log is a record of something that happened.

   b. An alert is when the system notifies someone that something has happened.

   c. Metrics refer to how many logs are generated per unit of time.

   d. Most logs contain sensitive information such as personally identifiable information.

2. Which of the following types of logs should you monitor? Select all that apply.

   a. Logs of privileged user activity

   b. Logs from detection and response tools

   c. Logs from cloud services

   d. Logs from operating systems

3. True or false: You must use the same tool for log aggregation and analysis.

4. What are some functions usually provided by a security information and event manager (SIEM)? Select all that apply.

   a. Parsing logs

   b. Correlating events between different systems

   c. Alerting humans when an event reaches a particular threshold

   d. Automatic cleanup of affected systems

5. According to the MITRE ATT&CK framework and the Lockheed Martin Cyber Kill Chain, what are some common attacker actions? Select all that apply.

   a. Installation of malware, or persistence

   b. Exploitation, or execution of code to make use of a vulnerability

   c. Actions on objectives, or impact to the affected organization

6. What are some steps you can take to recover from an attack after it's over? Select all that apply.

   a. Run antivirus software to clean up systems that have been controlled by attackers.

   b. Provide any notifications required by contractual obligations or regulations.

   c. Review lessons learned.

Exercise Solutions

Here are the answers for the exercises at the end of each chapter.

Chapter 1

1. A, C, and D. Requiring multi-factor authentication is also a good idea, but it's an example of the principle of defense in depth, not least privilege.

2. A and D. Strict firewall controls may help, but they don't demonstrate defense in depth unless paired with another control. Trust boundaries are also important, and may be used to define controls, but are not a defense in depth control.

3. A, B, C, and D. Threat actors may want to do all of these things, although historically making money is by far the largest motivator. In addition, some threat actors may be motivated simply by the challenge of breaking in or enhancing their reputations in hacking circles.

4. A. Depending on the service delivery model, network security and operating security may be the cloud provider's responsibility, or may not be. Data access security—choosing who gets access to the data—is almost always the consumer's responsibility.

5. A and B. Most risk assessment systems use some form of likelihood and impact assessment to determine the overall risk level. Transferring a risk doesn't determine the severity of the risk, but may be a way to deal with the risk. Your risk severity is also not directly affected by whether the attacker's actions are legal or not, although taking illegal actions may raise the attacker's risk of going to jail.

Chapter 2

1. A. While you may need more than 3 data classification levels, 30 is excessive for almost all organizations, and 300 is in there just to see if you read the question at all before answering.

2. A, B, C, and D. While the IP addresses themselves are public information, when linked to customer requests on your systems, they are considered personal information in many jurisdictions and need to be protected.

3. A, B, and C. While data can be cryptographically erased to make it unreadable, that doesn't involve encrypting the data at the time of deletion. Cryptographic erasure works by deleting the encryption keys, so that the already encrypted data can no longer be decrypted.

4. C. Hardware security modules have the benefit of being physically tamper-resistant and are required for some high-risk areas or compliance regimes, but you can perform proper key management without one. Storing encrypted (or "wrapped") encryption keys along with the data is a completely acceptable practice, as long as the key encryption key (KEK) is stored elsewhere, but storing unprotected encryption keys alongside the data is useless.

5. C. An attacker in the application or the database will request the data, and the disk controller will decrypt the data on disk and provide it. This is required for normal functioning of the system.

Chapter 3

1. A and B. Many organizations don't have a single team that's responsible for deploying cloud assets, but having such a team would not making tracking the assets more error-prone. Cloud APIs will allow you to use automation to export lists of cloud assets, so they make tracking of cloud assets easier, not harder.

2. A, B, and C. Encryption is used to protect data at rest, in motion, and in use, but is not a type of asset. A key management instance used to manage encryption keys for your data could be a cloud asset, however.

3. False. Containers do have a larger attack surface by default than virtual machines, and may not be a good choice for running untrusted code without additional protections, but they are not inherently insecure.

4. A, B, and C. Having only known risks, and an acceptable quantity and severity of them for the organization's risk appetite, is a good goal and not an issue.

5. A, B, C, and D. These are all reasonable tags you can apply to assets that can be helpful for tracking assets and creating security policies.

Chapter 4

1. A, B, C, and D. All of these are common access management life cycle activities.

2. A. Authentication followed by authorization is what allows you to access an application, although some applications allow access to all authenticated users. API keys are not multifactor authentication, but they are a stronger single factor authentication method than simple passwords, and are often used by automation that cannot perform multi-factor authentication. The final statement is also incorrect, because following zero trust principles, internal communications also require authentication and authorization.

3. A, B, and C. All of these are true about authorization; while centralized authorization has advantages and is becoming more popular, decentralized authorization can still be very effective.

4. A, B, and D. While Cloud IAM systems often have methods for authenticating and authorizing users and other entities, different cloud services such as secrets management services and encryption key management services are generally used for storing secrets and encryption keys.

5. B and C. A is not correct because federation is the concept, and single sign-on is a technology that allows users to use federated identities. D is not correct because single sign-on is generally more secure, because fewer applications see the user's password.

Chapter 5

1. B, C, and D. While physical security controls are very important, they are almost always the IaaS cloud provider's responsibility, and are not a significant factor in known breaches. Everything else is your responsibility when using IaaS services.

2. A and B. Dynamic and static application scanners are useful to find security issues with code that you maintain, but won't find missing operating system patches.

3. C and D. Agentless scanners and configuration management tools are generally focused on the operating system and middleware layers, and not the application layer. Container scanners will typically find vulnerable configurations and missing patches in container images or running containers, but will not typically find application-level issues unless combined with another tool type.

4. False. A network vulnerability scan will generally only find operating system or middleware issues, and will not find application vulnerabilities unless the tool also includes dynamic application scanner capabilities and you have specifically configured it to test the web application.

5. False. Penetration testers will generally only find one or a few ways in, not all possible ways into a vulnerable system. If your penetration test scope is the complete application and environment and it shows only minor issues, you can be fairly confident. If the penetration test scope leaves out important parts of the environment, or if major issues are found, you need to retest with a complete scope after fixing those issues.

6. False. After looking at the likelihood and impact of someone exploiting a vulnerability, you may decide to accept the risk, either as is or after applying additional controls or mitigations. It's important not to accept too much risk in aggregate (if you have 100 things, each with a 1% chance of happening, one of them is likely to happen) but you must usually accept a certain amount of risk to function.

Chapter 6

1. A, B, and C. While a few cloud providers allow you to rent physical network appliances, for the most part you will rely upon security groups and network access control lists, and occasionally on virtual firewall appliances.

2. A. In most cases, VPC offerings don't provide dedicated storage, although you are typically provided with isolation by encryption. VPCs also typically don't provide dedicated CPUs or bare-metal systems, although that is a separately orderable option in many cases. Use of VPCs doesn't affect encryption keys.

3. A, B, and C. A firewall will block network connections, but TLS will not.

4. False. Although a perimeter may not always be possible, and may require more access than some traditional environments, many applications can still benefit from having a perimeter as long as it's not the only line of defense.

5. A, B, and D. Security groups are also useful, but they are like "host firewalls" and operate independently from subnet creation.

6. False. While anti-DDoS appliances can mitigate denial-of-service attacks that depend on sending traffic that's difficult to service, a single appliance (or its network connection) will generally be overwhelmed by a large-scale volumetric attack.

7. A, B, and D. Egress filtering is not typically very effective using IP-based controls, because you will typically need to open up the same ports, such as tcp/443, that attackers and malware use. Also, egress filtering is not an easy control to implement in either cloud or traditional environments, because you often don't have a good inventory of all of the outbound calls that your application and its dependencies need to make.

Chapter 7

1. A and B. Metrics refer to any sort of count of activity over time, such as web requests. In addition, most logs do not need to contain sensitive information or personally identifiable information, although it may be unavoidable in a few limited cases.

2. A, B, C, and D. All of these are good sources of security-relevant logs and metrics.

3. False. You may use a combined tool to aggregate logs and analyze them, or you may choose to use one tool to aggregate the logs and then feed security-relevant logs to another tool for analysis. Both functions are very important, but do not have to be performed by the same tool.

4. A, B, and C. As of this writing, there's no reliable way to automatically clean up an affected system other than rebuilding it.

5. A, B, and C. Attackers are very inconsiderate and will often try to do all of these things.

6. B and C. Antivirus software and other tools generally cannot remove all persistent malware from a system with a high level of confidence, so rebuilding the systems controlled by attackers is by far the safest route.

Index

A

access management, defined, 57
access policies
    allowing administrative access, 144-148
    deny by default, 2
ACLs (network access control lists), 138
administrative access, 144-148
    bastion hosts, 145
    VPNs, 145-148
administrative activity logs, 165
agent-based scanners, 105-106
    choosing, 106
    deployment, 105
agentless scanners, 104-105
    choosing, 106
    deployment, 105
alerts, 163, 176-177
allowlists, 127-128, 154
Amazon Inspector, 113
Amazon Macie, 19
Amazon Simple Storage Service (Amazon S3),
    11
analog hole, 153
Ansible, 113
antivirus (AV) software, alerts from, 168
API keys, 69
application architectures, diagramming, 4-7
application code security, 95-97
Application Platform-as-a-Service (aPaaS), 42
application-level encryption, 30
asset management, 17
asset management pipeline, 49-52
    (see also cloud asset management and pro-
        tection; data asset management and pro-
        tection)

findings leaks, 52
processing leaks, 51
procurement leaks, 50
tooling leaks, 52
attacks
    on containers, 40
    injection attacks, 96
    man-in-the-middle attacks, 136
    on middleware, 98-99
    pass-the-hash attack, 172
    POODLE attacks, 102
    supply chain attacks, 152
    on virtual machines (VMs), 37
    watering hole attacks, 153
authentication (authn), 63-79
    authorization versus, 57-58
    business-to-consumer and business-to-
        employee, 64-65
    cloud IAM identity services, 63
    defined, 57
    federated identity, 71
    instance metadata and identity documents,
        73-75
    multi-factor authentication, 65-68
    overview of, 63
    passwords, passphrases, API keys, 68-70
    SAML and OIDC, 72-73
    secrets management, 75-79, 172
    shared IDs, 70
    single sign-on (SSO), 71-73
authorization (authz), 79-82
    authentication versus, 57-58
    centralized authorization, 80
    defined, 58
    overview, 79

roles, 81-82
automated alert responses, 176-177
automated revalidation, 82
AV (antivirus) software, alerts from, 168
AWS Config, 113
AWS Instance Identity Documents, 137
AWS Systems Manager (AWS SSM), 113
AWS Trusted Advisor, 113
Azure Update Management, 113

B

backup and restore, 183
bare-metal systems, 39
bastion hosts, 145
benchmarking, 98
biometric authentication, 67
bits of entropy, 69
blacklists (see denylists)
block storage, 44
Burp Suite, 113

C

CADF (Cloud Audit Data Federation), 176
CASB (cloud access security broker), 171
CD (continuous delivery), 92
CDNs (content delivery networks), 48, 154
CEF (Common Event Format), 175
Center for Internet Security CIS Benchmarks,
    99
centralized authorization, 80
certificate management system, 84
certificate storage, 47
change management, 118
Chef, 113
CI (continuous integration), 92
CIA triad security model, 18
ciphersuites, 137
CIS Benchmarks list, 171
CLF (Common Log Format), 175
client-side encryption, 28
client-to-site VPNs, 147-148
cloud access security broker (CASB), 171
cloud asset management and protection, 35-55
    asset management pipeline, 49-52
    compute assets, 37-43
    network assets, 48-49
    overview of, 54
    storage assets, 43-48

tagging cloud assets, 52-54
traditional IT versus, 35
types of cloud assets, 36-49
cloud assets, 17
Cloud Audit Data Federation (CADF), 176
cloud databases, 46
cloud native application protection platforms
    (CNAPPs), 107
cloud provider monitoring tools, 170
cloud service delivery models, 8
cloud service logs, 170-171
cloud shared responsibility model, 8-12
cloud workload protection platforms, 107
code reviews, 110
cold storage, 176
command-and-control servers, blocking access
    to, 189
Common Event Format (CEF), 175
Common Log Format (CLF), 175
Common Vulnerability Scoring System (CVSS),
    118
compliance, 19
compute assets, 37-43
    Application Platform-as-a-Service (aPaaS),
        42
    containers, 40-42
    serverless functions, 43
    virtual machines (VMs), 37-39
confidential computing, 24
configuration management, 98
configuration management systems
    agent-based scanners and, 105-106
    agentless scanners and, 104-105
    storing secrets with, 77
configuration storage, 46
container management systems, 22
containers
    attacks on, 40
    container firewalling/network segmenta-
        tion, 143-144
    container scanners, 107
    Mini-VM container model, 41
    native container model, 40
    orchestration systems, 42
content delivery networks (CDNs), 48, 154
continuous delivery (CD), 92
continuous integration (CI), 92
Contrast, 113

CPU usage metrics, 171
credential vault, 84
credentials, agent-based scanners and, 105
credit card information, 19, 20
criminals, 4
cryptographic erasure, 28
cryptography, quantum-safe, 31
cryptomining, 171
customer notifications, 190
CVSS (Common Vulnerability Scoring System), 118
cyber kill chains, 185
cybersecurity insurance, 179

D

DAST (dynamic application security testing), 108
data asset management and protection
    data identification and classification, 17-20
    locating and inventorying data in the cloud, 21-22
    protecting data in the cloud, 23-32
    strategic planning, 31
    tagging cloud resources, 22-23
data assets, defined, 17
data encryption keys (DEK), 27
data exfiltration, 153, 189
data identification and classification
    CIA triad security model, 18
    example data classification levels, 18-19
    industry and regulatory requirements, 19-20
data loss prevention (DLP), 155
data restoration, 183
database-level encryption, 30
DDoS attacks (see distributed denial-of-service (DDoS) attacks)
deception technologies, 173
defense in depth, 2
defensive tooling logs, 167-170
    anti-DDoS, 167
    antivirus software, 168
    cloud provider monitoring tools, 170
    detection and response tools, 169
    file integrity monitoring, 170
    firewalls and IDSs, 168
    web application firewalls, 168
demilitarized zone (DMZ), 126, 129

deny by default, 2
denylists, 127-128
deployment pipelines, 47
destination NAT (DNAT), 132
diagrams, 4-7
Diceware passwords, 69
directory service, 84
disk-level encryption, 29
distributed denial-of-service (DDoS) attacks
    alerting, 167
    anti-DDoS measures, 150-151
DLP (data loss prevention), 155
DMZ (demilitarized zone), 126, 129
DNAT (destination NAT), 132
DNS spoofing, 48
Domain Name System (DNS) records, 48
dynamic application security testing (DAST), 108

E

EDR (endpoint detection and response), 169
egress filtering, 152-155
ELF (Extended Log Format), 175
encapsulation, 130
encryption, 24-31
    application-level, 30
    confidential computing, 24
    cryptographic erasure, 28
    of data at rest, 25-28
    of data in motion, 135-138
    disk-level, 29
    key management, 26-27
    platform-level, 30
    protection offered from various attacks, 29-31
    quantum-safe cryptography, 31
    server-side versus client-side, 27-28
    strategic planning, 31
    zero-knowledge encryption, 58
encryption key management system, 84
encryption key storage, 47
endpoint detection and response (EDR), 169
events, defined, 163
example applications, diagramming, 4-7
explicit proxies, 154
Extended Log Format (ELF), 175

F

face readers, 67
Federal Information Security Management Act (FISMA), 20
Federal Risk and Authorization Management Program (FedRAMP), 20
federated identity, 71
FIDO Universal 2nd Factor (U2F) standard, 67
file integrity monitoring (FIM), 170
file storage, 44
findings leaks, 52, 102
fingerprint readers, 67
firewalls, 138-144, 168
    container firewalling/network segmentation, 143-144
    internal segmentation, 140
    perimeter control, 139
    security groups, 141-142
    service endpoints, 142
FISMA (Federal Information Security Management Act), 20
forensic analysis tools, 188
forward proxies, 129

G

General Data Protection Regulation (GDPR), 20
global server load balancers (GSLBs), 154
Google Cloud Data Loss Prevention API, 19
Google Cloud Security Command Center, 113
Google Cloud Security Scanner, 114
groups, roles versus, 82

H

hacktivists, 4
hardening, 99
hardware security modules (HSMs), 25
hash-based one-time passcodes (HOTPs), 67
HashiCorp Vault, 137
health checking, 98
Health Insurance Portability and Accountability Act (HIPAA), 20
honeypots, 173
hot storage, 176
HOTPs (hash-based one-time passcodes), 67
HSMs (hardware security modules), 25
hypervisor breakout, 37

I

IaaS (Infrastructure as a Service), 8, 9, 100
IAST (interactive application security testing), 109
IBM Cloud Security and Compliance Center, 114
IBM Vulnerability Advisor, 114
identity access management system, 84
identity and access management (IAM)
    authentication (authn), 63-79
    authentication versus authorization, 57-58
    authorization (authz), 79-82
    cloud-based versus traditional, 59-60
    create, delete, grant, or revoke, 63
    IAM approvals, 62
    IAM requests, 62
    life cycle for identity and access, 60-63
    overview of, 87
    revalidation, 82-83
    sample application, 85-87
identity documents, 73-75, 136
identity governance system, 84
identity provider (IdP), 71, 84
identity, defined, 57
Identity-as-a-Service (IDaaS), 64
IDS (intrusion detection system), 151-152, 168
images, 41, 45
in-memory encryption, 24
incident recovery
    lessons learned, 190
    notifications, 190
    redeploying IT systems, 189
incident response
    blocking unauthorized access, 189
    cloud forensics, 188
    cyber kill chains and MITRE ATT&CK, 185
    OODA loop, 187-188
    stopping data exfiltration and command and control, 189
incident response firms, 179
incident response plans, 181-183
incident response teams, 180
incident response tools, 183-184
Infrastructure as a Service (IaaS), 8, 9, 100
injection attacks, 96
inside attackers, 4
InSpec, 113
instance metadata, 74

instances, 45
interactive application security testing (IAST), 109
internal segmentation, 140
International Traffic in Arms regulations (ITAR), 20
Internet Protocol version 6 (IPv6), 133
internet-facing firewalls, 168
intrusion detection system (IDS), 151-152, 168
intrusion prevention system (IPS), 151-152
IP allowlists, 128, 154
Istio Auth, 137, 154
ITAR (International Traffic in Arms regulations), 20

J

JSON Web Tokens (JWTs), 73
judgment-based revalidation, 83
jump bags, 162
jump hosts, 145

K

key encryption key (KEK), 27
key management, 26-27
    encryption key storage, 47
    key management services (KMSs), 25
    using identity documents, 136
key management services (KMSs), 25
kill chains, 162, 185
Kubernetes, 22, 42, 171

L

law enforcement notifications, 190
least privilege, 2, 80, 106
lessons learned (incident recovery phase), 190
Lockheed Martin Cyber Kill Chain, 162, 185
logs
    aggregation and retention of, 174
    alerts and automated responses, 176-177
    application logs, 172
    cloud service logs, 170-171
    cloud service logs/metrics, 170-171
    defensive tooling logs, 167-170
    defined, 163
    items to monitor, 163-173
    middleware logs, 172
    operating system logs and metrics, 171

parsing, 175
privileged user access, 165-167
searching and correlating log events, 176
secrets server, 172
security information and event manager (SIEM), 177-179

M

malware, 168
man-in-the-middle attacks, 136
managed security service provider (MSSP), 177
manual code reviews, 110
masquerading (source NAT), 132
mean time to remediate (MTTR), 116
Meltdown vulnerability, 10
Mend, 114
message queues, 46
metrics
    defined, 164
    for security incidents, 190
    for vulnerability management, 115-118
microservice architectures, 92
Microsoft Defender for Cloud, 114
middleware, 11, 98-99, 172
Mini-VM container model, 41
MITRE ATT&CK framework, 162, 185
monitoring process
    aggregation and retention of logs, 174
    alerting and automated responses, 176-177
    parsing logs, 175
    searching and correlating events, 176
    security information and event manager (SIEM), 177-179
    synchronizing timestamps, 174
    threat hunting, 179
MSSP (managed security service provider), 177
MTTR (mean time to remediate), 116
multi-factor authentication, 65-68

N

native container model, 40
NDR (network detection and response), 169
negative confirmation, 83
network access control lists (ACLs), 138
network address translation (NAT), 132-133
network assets, 48-49
    content delivery networks, 48
    DNS records, 48

TLS certificates, 49
virtual private clouds (VPCs), 48
network defense tools, 148-152
    anti-DDoS measures, 150-151
    intrusion detection/prevention systems,
        151-152
    RASP modules, 149
    web application firewalls, 148-149
network detection and response (NDR), 169
network functions virtualization (NFV), 130
network logs and metrics, 171
network security, 11, 125-157
    agent-based versus agentless scanners, 106
    allowing administrative access, 144-148
    allowlists and denylists, 127-128
    cloud-based versus traditional, 125-127
    concepts and definitions, 127-133
    data loss prevention, 155
    demilitarized zones, 129
    egress filtering, 152-155
    encryption in motion, 135-138
    firewalls and network segmentation,
        138-144
    IPv6, 133
    network address translation, 132-133
    network defense tools, 148-152
    network functions virtualization, 130
    overlay networks and encapsulation, 130
    overview of, 156-157
    proxies, 129
    sample application, 134-156
    software-defined networking, 130
    virtual private clouds, 131
    zero trust networking, 127
network segmentation, 138-144, 143-144
Network Time Protocol (NTP), 174
network vulnerability management, 100
network vulnerability scanners, 102-104
NFV (network functions virtualization), 130

O

OAuth 2.0, 73
object storage, 44
OIDC (OpenID Connect), 73
    Authorization Code Flows, 73
    Implicit Flows, 73
one-way hash, 69
OODA loop, 187-188

operating system security, 11, 99, 171
organized crime, 4
outbound IP allowlisting, 154
overlay networks, 130
OWASP Top 10 list, 96

P

PaaS (Platform as a Service), 8, 9
Palo Alto Prisma Cloud, 114
PAP (Policy Administration Point), 81
pass-the-hash attack, 172
password spraying, 70
password wallet, 84
passwords, 66, 68-70
patch management, 92
Payment Card Industry Data Security Standard
    (PCI DSS), 19, 20, 168
PDP (Policy Decision Point), 81
penetration tests (pentests), 110-111, 120
PEP (Policy Enforcement Point), 80
percentage of false positives/false negatives
    metric, 117
perimeter control, 139
perimeter network, 126
PHI (protected health information), 20
physical infrastructure, 100
PINs, 66
Pizza-as-a-Service analogy, 8
PKI (public key infrastructure), 136
Platform as a Service (PaaS), 8, 9
platform-level encryption, 30
Policy Administration Point (PAP), 81
Policy Decision Point (PDP), 81
Policy Enforcement Point (PEP), 80
POODLE attacks, 102
positive confirmation, 82-83
preparing for security incidents, 179-184
    backup and restore plans, 183
    incident response planning, 181-183
    incident response teams, 180
    incident response tools, 183-184
principle of least privilege, 2, 80, 106
principles and concepts
    cloud service delivery models, 8
    cloud shared responsibility model, 8-12
    defense in depth, 2
    least privilege, 2
    risk management, 12-13

threat actors, diagrams, and trust boundaries, 4-7
privileged access management system, 84
privileged identity management system, 84
privileged user access, 165-167
processing leaks, 51
procurement leaks, 50
production data, 183
protected health information (PHI), 20
proxies, 129
public key infrastructure (PKI), 136
publisher/subscriber models, 46
Puppet, 114
push notifications (to mobile device), 67

Q

Qualys, 114
quantum-safe cryptography, 31

R

ransomware, 18, 171
RASP (runtime application self-protection),
109, 149
RAT (remote access trojan), 145
red/blue teaming, 120
redeployment, 189
regulatory requirements, 19-20
customer and law enforcement notification,
190
Global PCI DSS, 168
remote access trojan (RAT), 145
retina readers, 67
revalidation step of IAM, 82-83
reverse proxies, 129
risk management, 12-13, 115
role-based access, 81
roles (trusted profiles), 79-82
runtime application self-protection (RASP),
109, 149

S

SaaS (Software as a Service), 8, 10
SAML (Security Assertion Markup Language),
72-73
sanitized logs, 166
SAST (static application security testing), 108
SBOM (Software Bill of Materials), 97

SCA (software composition analysis), 109
SDN (software-defined networking), 130
secrets configuration storage, 47
secrets management, 47, 75-79, 84, 172
secure erase feature, 26
Security Assertion Markup Language (SAML),
72-73
security fatigue, 108
security groups, 139, 141-142
security incidents, 161-197
cloud-based versus traditional, 162
importance of prompt identification, 161
items to monitor, 163-173
metrics for, 190
MITRE ATT&CK and kill chains, 162
monitoring process and tools, 173-179
overview of, 196-197
preparing for, 179-184
recovering from, 189-190
responding to, 185-189
root cause of many, 11
sample application, 192-196
tools for detection, response, and recovery,
191
security information and event manager
(SIEM), 177-179
security operations center (SOC), 177
separation of duties, 80
server-side encryption, 27-28
serverless assets, 43
service endpoints, 142
shared IDs, 70
shared responsibility model, 8-12
SIEM (security information and event manager), 177-179
single sign-on (SSO), 71-73
legacy applications and, 71-73
SAML and OIDC, 72-73
site-to-site VPNS, 146
SLSA (Supply-chain Levels for Software Artifacts), 97
SMS text messages, as authentication device, 66
SNAT (source NAT), 132
SOC (security operations center), 177
Software as a Service (SaaS), 8, 10
Software Bill of Materials (SBOM), 97
software composition analysis (SCA), 109
software-defined networking (SDN), 130

solid state drives (SSDs), 26
source code repositories, 47, 76
source NAT (SNAT), 132
Spectre vulnerability, 10
SPIFFE, 74
SSDs (solid state drives), 26
SSL certificates, 49
SSL Labs, 137
SSO (see single sign-on)
state actors, 4
static application security testing (SAST), 108
storage assets, 43-48
    block storage, 44
    certificate storage, 47
    cloud databases, 46
    configuration storage, 46
    encryption key storage, 47
    file storage, 44
    images, 45
    message queues, 46
    object storage, 44
    secrets configuration storage, 47
    source code repositories and deployment
      pipelines, 47
supply chain attacks, 152
Supply-chain Levels for Software Artifacts
    (SLSA), 97
syslog format, 175
systems/applications with open vulnerabilities
    metric, 117

T
tag, defined, 22
tagging cloud assets/resources, 22-23, 52-54
Target breach (2013), 169
Tenable, 114
text messages, as authentication device, 66
threat actors, 4
threat hunting, 179
time zone information, 174
time-based one-time passcodes (TOTPs), 67
tokenization, 23
tool coverage metric, 116
tooling leaks, 52, 102
toxic logs, 165
transparent proxies, 154
Transport Layer Security (TLS), 48, 135
triage, 185

trust boundaries, 6-7
trusted profiles (roles), 79-82
two factor access (2FA), 65

U
Uber data breach, 112
user reports, 112

V
virtual firewall appliances, 139
virtual machines (VMs), 37-39
virtual network functions (VNFs), 130
virtual private clouds (VPCs), 48, 131
virtual private networks (VPNs), 145-148
    client-to-site, 147-148
    site-to-site, 146
virtualized infrastructure, 100
VM escape, 37
VMs (virtual machines), 37-39
vulnerability management, 91-123
    agent-based scanners and configuration
      management systems, 105-106
    agentless scanners and configuration man-
      agement systems, 104-105
    change management, 118
    cloud workload protection platforms, 107
    cloud-based versus traditional, 92-94
    container scanners, 107
    data access, 95
    dynamic application scanners, 108
    finding and fixing vulnerabilities, 101-115
    interactive application scanners, 109
    manual code reviews, 110
    mean time to remediate metric, 116
    metrics for, 115-118
    middleware, 98-99
    network management, 100
    network vulnerability scans, 102-104
    operating system security, 99
    overview of, 123
    patch management versus, 92
    penetration tests, 110-111
    percentage of false positives/false negatives
      metric, 117
    physical infrastructure, 100
    risk management processes, 115
    runtime application self-protection scan-
      ners, 109

sample application, 119-122
secure software standards/frameworks, 97
security of application code, 95-97
software composition analysis, 109
static application scanners, 108
systems/applications with open vulnerabilities metric, 117
tool coverage metric, 116
tools for, 112-114
user reports, 112
virtualized infrastructure, 100
vulnerability recurrence rate metric, 118
vulnerable areas, 94-101
vulnerability recurrence rate metric, 118

W
watering hole attacks, 153
web application firewalls (WAFs), 148-149, 168
whitelists (see allowlists)

X
X.509 certificates, 49, 154

Z
zero trust networking, 127
zero trust principles, 3
zero-knowledge encryption, 58

About the Author

Chris Dotson is an IBM Distinguished Engineer and an executive security architect in the IBM CIO organization. He has 11 professional certifications, including the Open Group Distinguished IT Architect certification, and over 25 years of experience in the IT industry. Chris has been featured as a cloud innovator on the IBM home page several times; his focus areas include cloud infrastructure and security, identity and access management, networking infrastructure and security, servers, storage, and bad puns.

Colophon

The image on the cover of *Practical Cloud Security* is the red kite (*Milvus milvus*). Related to eagles, buzzards, and harriers, this bird of prey inhabits Western Europe and parts of Scandinavia. It is seen as far east as the Ural mountains and migrates as far south as Israel and Egypt.

Its plumage is orange-red (rufous) on much of the body and the upper layers of the wing feathers (coverts). It averages 24 to 28 inches long (60 to 70 centimeters) with a wingspan of 68 to 70 inches (175 to 179 centimeters). Thanks to its large wingspan and light weight (about as much as a mallard duck), it soars gracefully in search of prey. The red kite can be identified in flight by its forked tail. Like an eagle, it has a hooked beak ideal for tearing meat. It feeds on small animals such as mice, voles, shrews, and rabbits as well as carrion.

Red kites are monogamous birds, and the male and female work together to build their nest and feed their chicks. They may return to the same nest year after year, and the next generation tends to nest within a few miles of where it was hatched.

During the middle ages, the red kite was valued for keeping villages free from rotting food and vermin. In the UK, it was later considered a pest and was hunted almost into extinction by the early 20th century. It was reintroduced in the late 20th and early 21st centuries and is now on the UK's green list, regarded as among the least threatened species.

Many of the animals on O'Reilly covers are endangered; all of them are important to the world. To learn more about how you can help, go to *animals.oreilly.com*.

The cover illustration is by Karen Montgomery, based on a black-and-white engraving from Richard Lydekker's *The Royal Natural History*. The cover fonts are Gilroy Semibold and Guardian Sans. The text font is Adobe Minion Pro; the heading font is Adobe Myriad Condensed; and the code font is Dalton Maag's Ubuntu Mono.

Milton Keynes UK
Ingram Content Group UK Ltd.
UKHW052100081223
434044UK00006B/14